MYTHOLOGIES

TRANSLATED FROM THE FRENCH BY RICHARD HOWARD / ANNETTE LAVERS

HILL AND WANG

A DIVISION OF FARRAR, STRAUS AND GIROUX

NEW YORK

MYTHO LOGIES

ROLAND BARTHES

Hill and Wang
A division of Farrar, Straus and Giroux
18 West 18th Street, New York 10011

Annette Lavers's translation of Part II: Myth Today originally appeared
in a selected version of Roland Barthes's *Mythologies* published in 1972
by Jonathan Cape Ltd., Great Britain, and Hill and Wang, New York.

The Library of Congress has cataloged the hardcover edition as follows:
Barthes, Roland.
    [Mythologies. English]
    Mythologies / Roland Barthes ; translated from the French by
Richard Howard [and] Annette Lavers.
    p. cm.
    Originally published: France: Éditions du Seuil, 1957.
    ISBN 978-0-374-53234-5 (hardback)
    1. France—Social life and customs. 2. Judgment (Logic)
3. Semantics. I. Title.

    AC25 .B3132 2012
    844'.912—dc23

                           2011041658

Paperback ISBN: 978-0-8090-7194-4

Designed by Jonathan D. Lippincott

www.fsgbooks.com

CONTENTS

TRANSLATOR'S NOTE

This is an unabridged English translation of *Mythologies*, Roland Barthes's third book, of which the fifty-three essays composing the first part of the book may be said to illustrate and exemplify the title, comprising as they do a number of reflections on certain myths of everyday French life. These were written (and published in several monthly magazines) from 1954 over a two-year period, and then, for their publication *en volume*, the author wrote a long, intricate study ("no denunciation without its proper instrument of close analysis") to explain, to justify, and in any case to accompany the intended miscellany (which was quite unlike anything he had undertaken in his first two studies), the two "determinations," as Barthes used to call them, that were published by Seuil in 1957. It is worth insisting a little on the difference between the two parts of the book—between the actual *Mythologies*, which its author modestly referred to as "Figures of rhetoric," and its ensuing companion, which he quite as modestly called "Myth Today"—because the author realized almost immediately upon finishing the second part that the first part, the figures which he had assumed were To Be Continued ("there may well be others: some may become worn out, others may come into being"), could be utterly transformed only if the existing work was to be continued as such ("no denunciation without its proper instrument of close analysis, no semiology which cannot ultimately be acknowledged as a *semioclasm*").

Fifteen years later, when Jonathan Cape published a book titled *Mythologies* in London, it consisted of a selection from the book still called *Mythologies*, leaving out twenty-five of those very Mythologies, in a translation by Annette Lavers. It included the fifty-page study which we now realize crucially accounted for the author's initial undertaking and which Lavers translated with great care and explanatory energy. I had always assumed that Lavers or her publisher regarded the excluded Mythologies to be insufficiently tempting to British tastes at the time (after all, "at the time" the word *semiology* had not yet appeared in any English-language dictionary); and I also suspect that Ms. Lavers, who remarks of her task, with a certain reserve, that "the characteristics of Barthes's style, an effort to account for the phenomena of mass culture by resorting to new models, have been kept in the hope of retaining some of the flavor of the original," has not avoided a patronizing tone in this reference to Barthes's vocabulary and usage—though I am amazed and delighted by her sympathetic and richly rewarding performance in translating *Myth Today*. I supposed I detected an echo of good British common sense in the face of a bit too much Gallic flummery, but I may be unduly sensitive to all those exclusions and elucidations; *Mythologies* is Barthes's first book to reveal his discovery that he was a great imaginative writer, a gift evident in all his subsequent texts (even the Collège de France lectures the year of his death, re-created from the author's "mere" notes). Annette Lavers's lucid and responsive version of *Myth Today* has all the breathless abstract brilliance of Roland Barthes's early work, and it is our happy obligation to bring the two strangely complementary texts together—this new version of *all* the Mythologies and Annette Lavers's minutely exact *Myth Today*—in an English-language realization of Barthes's first great literary text as he intended its complex figuration in 1957.

Richard Howard, July 2011

PREFACE TO THE 1970 EDITION

This book has two determinants: on the one hand, an ideological critique of the language of so-called mass culture; on the other, an initial semiological dismantling of that language: I had just read Saussure and emerged with the conviction that by treating "collective representations" as sign systems one might hope to transcend pious denunciation and instead account *in detail* for the mystification which transforms petit bourgeois culture into a universal nature.

It is evident that the two gestures at the source of this book could today no longer be performed in the same way (which is why I have made no attempt to correct the original text); not because their reasons for existing have vanished; but because, first of all, *ideological criticism*, precisely when the need for it was brutally obvious (May 1968), has become or at least ought to have become more sophisticated, and, secondly, *semiological analysis*, initiated, at least as far as I'm concerned, in the closing text of *Mythologies*, has developed, ever more precise, more complex, more differentiated: it has become, in our time and in the West, the theoretical locus in which a certain liberation of the signifier can be enacted. In other words, I could not, today, write new mythologies in their previous form (presented here).

However, what remains, besides the capital enemy (the bourgeois Norm), is the necessary conjunction of these two gestures: no denunciation without its proper instrument of close analysis, no semiology which cannot ultimately be acknowledged as a *semioclasm*.

R.B., February 1970

PREFACE TO THE 1957 EDITION

The following texts were written one a month for about two years, from 1954 to 1956, in the light (or darkness) of current events. My effort at the time was to reflect regularly on some myths of French daily life. The material prompting such reflections could be quite various (a newspaper article, a photograph in a magazine, a film, a theatrical performance, a gallery exhibit), and their subject quite arbitrary, depending of course on my own interests at the time.

The starting point of these reflections was usually a feeling of impatience with the "naturalness" which common sense, the press, and the arts continually invoke to dress up a reality which, though the one we live in, is nonetheless quite historical: in a word, I resented seeing Nature and History repeatedly confused in the description of our reality, and I wanted to expose in the decorative display of what-goes-without-saying the ideological abuse I believed was hidden there.

Right off, the notion of *myth* seemed to me to account for these phony instances of the obvious: at that time I was using the word in its traditional sense. But I was already operating on one conviction from which I would try to draw all the consequences: myth is a language. Therefore, though concerned with phenomena apparently quite remote from literature (a wrestling match, an elaborately cooked dish, an exhibition of plastics), I had no intention of abandoning that general semiology of our bourgeois world, whose literary aspects I had approached in previous essays. Yet it was only after having explored a certain number of current nonliterary subjects that I attempted to define contemporary myth in any methodical way: that text of course I put at the end of this book, since it merely systematizes previous materials.

Written month after month, these essays made no claim to constitute an organic development: what links them together is a matter of insistence, of repetition. Actually I don't know whether I agree with the proverb that repeated things give pleasure, but I do know that at least they signify. And what I've sought in everything here are indeed significations. Are they *my* significations? In other words, is there a mythology of the mythologist? Doubtless there is, and the reader will soon see for himself where I stand. But to tell the truth, I don't think that's the right way to frame the question. "Demystification," to keep using a word that's showing signs of wear, is not an Olympian operation. What I mean is, I don't share the traditional belief that there's a divorce in nature between the objectivity of the scientist and the subjectivity of the writer, as if the former were endowed with a "freedom" and the latter with a "vocation," both of them likely to spirit away or sublimate the true limits of their situation: my claim is to live to the full the contradiction of my time, which can make sarcasm the condition of truth.

R.B., 1957

I

MYTHOLOGIES

TRANSLATED BY RICHARD HOWARD

IN THE RING

... The emphatic truth of gesture in life's grander circumstances.
—Baudelaire

The virtue of wrestling is to be a spectacle of excess. Here we find an emphasis which must have been that of the ancient theaters. Moreover, wrestling is an open-air spectacle, for the essence of the circus or the arena is not the sky (a romantic value best suited to fashionable celebrations) but the dense vertical character of the flood of light: even in the depths of the dingiest Parisian halls, wrestling partakes of the nature of the great solar spectacles, bullfights and Greek theater: in all these places a light without shadow elaborates an emotion without secrets.

Some people consider that wrestling is an ignoble sport. Wrestling is not a sport, it is a spectacle, and it is no more ignoble to watch a wrestled performance of Suffering than the sorrows of Arnolphe or Andromaque. Of course there is such a thing as a fake wrestling which goes to great lengths to produce the useless appearances of a fair fight; this is of no interest. True wrestling, incorrectly called amateur wrestling, takes place in second-rate halls, where the public spontaneously adjusts itself to the spectacular nature of the combat, as does the public of B films. These same audiences are subsequently outraged that wrestling matches are fixed (which, moreover, should mitigate their ignominy). The public couldn't care less that the fight is or isn't fixed, and rightly so; the public confines itself to spectacle's primary virtue, which is to abolish all motives and all consequences: what matters to this public is not what it believes but what it sees.

It is a public which is quite aware of the distinction between wrestling and boxing; it knows that boxing is a Jansenist sport, based on a demonstration of excellence; one can bet on the outcome of a boxing match; in wrestling, that would make no sense. The boxing match is a story constructed under the spectator's eyes; in wrestling, just the contrary, it is each moment which is intelligible, not their sum. The spectator is not interested in the development of a prowess, he is awaiting the momentary image of certain passions. Wrestling therefore requires an immediate reading of juxtaposed meanings, without its being necessary to connect them. The rational future of the combat does not interest the fan of wrestling, whereas on the contrary a boxing match always implies a science of the future. In other words, wrestling is a sum of spectacles, none of which is a function: each moment imposes the total knowledge of a passion which suddenly rises straight up on its own, without ever extending toward the consummation of an outcome.

Hence the wrestler's function is not to win but to perform exactly the gestures expected of him. It is said that judo contains a hidden symbolic dimension; even at its most efficient, judo's gestures are measured, precise but brief, carefully drawn but by a stroke having no volume. Wrestling, on the contrary, proposes excessive gestures, exploited to the paroxysm of their signification. In judo, a man who is down is hardly down at all, he rolls over, he withdraws, he evades defeat, or if defeat is obvious, he immediately leaves the match; in wrestling, a man down is exaggeratedly so, filling the spectators' entire field of vision with the intolerable spectacle of his powerlessness.

This emphatic function is quite the same as the one in the

ancient theater, whose resources, language and its accessories (masks and cothurns), concurred in the exaggeratedly visible explanation of a Necessity. The gesture of the vanquished wrestler signifying to the world a defeat which, far from concealing, he accentuates and *holds* like a pedal point, corresponds to the mask in antiquity intended to signify the tragic tone of the spectacle. In wrestling, as on the stage in antiquity, one is not ashamed of one's suffering, one knows how to cry, one has a taste for tears.

Each sign in wrestling is thus endowed with an utter clarity since everything must always be understood on the spot. Once the adversaries are in the Ring, the public is entrusted with the obviousness of the roles. As in the theater, each physical type expresses to excess the role assigned to the combatant. Thauvin, an obese and sagging fifty-year-old, whose type of sexless hideousness is always assigned feminine nicknames, displays in his flesh the characteristics of vileness, for it is his role to represent what in the classic concept of the *salaud* (bastard), a key concept in wrestling, is seen as organically repugnant. The nausea deliberately inspired by Thauvin thus operates very deeply in the order of signs: not only is ugliness utilized here to signify vileness, but furthermore, this ugliness is scrupulously projected into a particularly repulsive quality of matter: the sickly flabbiness of dead flesh (the public calls Thauvin *la barbaque*), so that the crowd's passionate condemnation no longer rises to the level of its judgment but reaches deeper into the zone of its humors. The crowd frenetically smears itself with a subsequent image of Thauvin entirely appropriate to this physical origin: his actions will perfectly correspond to the essential viscosity of his personage.

Thus it is the wrestler's body which is the first key to the combat. I know from the start that all of Thauvin's actions, his treacheries, his cruelties, his pusillanimities will not contradict the original image he presents of infamous behavior: I can count on him to perform intelligently and to the last detail every gesture of a certain sort of amorphous vileness and thereby to fulfill the image of the worst sort of bastard: the octopus-bastard. In other words, wrestlers possess a physique quite as peremptory as the characters of Commedia dell'Arte who display in advance, in their costumes and their postures, the future contents of their role: just as Pantaloon can never be anything but a ridiculous cuckold, Harlequin a cunning valet, and the Doctor a stupid pedant, so Thauvin will never be anything but a vile deceiver, Reinières (a tall blond fellow with a limp body and wild hair) the disturbing image of passivity, Mazaud (an arrogant little cockerel) that of a grotesque conceit, and Orsano (an effeminate loony who enters the ring in a pink and blue robe), the doubly spicy version of a vindictive *salope* (bitch: I suspect the Élysée-Montmartre public follows Littré in refusing to grant the term *salope* a masculine gender).

Thus the wrestlers' physique establishes a basic sign containing in germ the whole fight. But this germ proliferates, for at each moment of the combat, in each new situation, the wrestler's body affords the public the marvelous diversion of a humor that finds its natural function in a gesture. The various lines of signification illuminate each other, forming the most intelligible of spectacles. Wrestling is a sort of diacritical writing: above the fundamental signification of his body, the wrestler arrays episodic but always welcome explanations, constantly aiding the reading of the combat by certain gestures, certain attitudes, certain mimicries which afford the intention its utmost meaning. Sometimes the wrestler triumphs with a nasty grin as he kneels on his vulnerable opponent, sometimes he woos the crowd with a self-satisfied smile, announcing his imminent vengeance, and sometimes, immobilized on the floor of the ring, he pounds the boards with both arms to signify to everyone the intolerable nature of his situation; and sometimes,

finally, he concocts a complicated set of signs to let it be understood that he legitimately incarnates the ever-entertaining image of the sorehead, endlessly confabulating his displeasure.

We're dealing here with a veritable Human Comedy where
the subtlest nuances of intense feeling (complacency, entitle-
ment, refined cruelty, retribution) invariably encounter the most
explicit signs which can express them triumphantly to the last
rows of the arena. Understandably, at this pitch, it no longer
matters whether or not the passion being expressed is authentic. There is no more a problem of truth in wrestling than in
the theater. In either world what is expected is the intelligible
figuration of moral situations ordinarily secret. Such draining
of interiority in favor of external signs, this exhaustion of content by form, is the very principle of a triumphal classic art.
Wrestling is an immediate pantomime, infinitely more effective
than pantomime onstage, for the wrestler's gesture needs no
fabulation, no decor, in short no transference in order to appear true.

Each moment of the wrestling match is therefore a kind of
algebra which instantaneously discloses the relation of a cause
with its figured effect. The fans certainly experience a kind of
intellectual pleasure at *seeing* the perfect functioning of the
moral mechanism: certain wrestlers, great comedians, enter-
tain us as much as any character in Molière, for they succeed
in imposing an immediate reading of their interiority: a wrestler
of arrogant and absurd character (as one says that Harpagon is
a character), Armand Mazaud always delights the audience by
the mathematical rigor of his transcriptions, carrying the design of his gestures to the extreme point of their signification
and giving his combat the kind of transport and precision of a
great scholastic dispute whose stake is at once the triumph of
pride and the formal concern with truth.

What is thus given to the public is the great spectacle of

Suffering, of Defeat, and of Justice. Wrestling presents human suffering with all the amplification of the tragic masks: the wrestler suffering under the effect of a hold reputedly cruel (an armlock, a twisted leg) presents the excessive countenance of Suffering; like a primitive Pietà, he allows us to see his face exaggeratedly distorted by an intolerable affliction. Understandably, all reserve would be out of place in a wrestling match, since it is contrary to the deliberate ostentation of the spectacle, to that Exhibition of Suffering which is the very finality of the fight. Hence all the actions generating suffering are particularly spectacular, like the gesture of a magician who holds his cards high in the air: we would not understand a suffering which would appear to be without an intelligible cause; a secret gesture which was actually cruel would transgress the unwritten laws of wrestling and would have no more sociological efficacy than a mad or parasitic gesture. Quite the contrary, suffering appears to be inflicted with emphasis and conviction, for everyone not only must observe that a man is suffering but also and above all must understand why he is suffering. What wrestlers call a hold, i.e., some figure which permits the indefinite immobilization of the adversary, holding him at one's mercy, has the specific function of preparing in a conventional hence intelligible fashion the spectacle of suffering, methodically installing the conditions of suffering: the defeated wrestler's inertia permits the (momentary) victor to establish himself in his cruelty and to transmit to the public the victor's terrifying sloth of a torturer certain of the consequence of his gestures: harshly rubbing his powerless adversary's face or scraping his spinal column with a deep and regular movement of his fist, accomplishing at least the visual surface of such gestures—wrestling is the only sport to present such an external image of torture. But here again, only the image is in the field of action, and the spectator does not desire the actual suffering of the losing combatant, he enjoys only the perfection of an iconography. It is not true that wrestling is a sadistic spectacle: it is merely an intelligible spectacle.

There is another figure still more spectacular than the hold, which is the *manchette*, that loud slap of the forearm, that masked blow of the fist which seems to be overwhelming the adversary's chest with a squashy sound during the exaggerated collapse of the defeated body. In this forearm smash, the catastrophe is brought to its maximum obviousness, to such a degree that ultimately the gesture no longer appears to be anything but a symbol; this is going too far, violating the moral rules of wrestling, in which every sign must be excessively clear but must not reveal its intention of clarity; the public then shouts, "Fake!"—not because the public regrets the absence of genuine suffering, but because it condemns artifice: as in the theater, one ceases to act properly as much by excess of sincerity as by excess of affectation.

We have already seen what store wrestlers set by a certain physical style, composed and exploited in order to develop before the public's eyes a total image of Defeat. The slackness of big white bodies collapsing to the floor in one piece or crashing into the ropes with flailing arms, the inertia of huge wrestlers pitifully reflected by all the elastic surfaces of the Ring—nothing can signify more clearly and more passionately the exemplary humiliation of the vanquished. Deprived of all resilience, the wrestler's flesh is nothing but an obscene mass spread on the ground and vulnerable to relentless insults and relentless jubilations. There is a paroxysm of signification in the style of antiquity which can only recall the luxury of intensions of the Roman triumphs. At other moments, there is another ancient figure which rises from the coupling of wrestlers, that of the suppliant, of the man at his opponent's mercy, on his knees, arms raised over his head, and slowly abased by the vertical tension of his conqueror. In wrestling, unlike judo, Defeat is not a conventional sign, abandoned once it is achieved: it is not a way out, but quite the contrary a duration, a showing forth, it resumes the oldest myths of public Suffering and Humiliation: the cross and the pillory. The wrestler is somehow crucified in broad daylight, all eyes watching. I've heard it said of a wrestler lying on the floor of the ring: "He's dead, poor little Jesus, lying there on his cross" and this ironic phrase revealed the deep roots of a spectacle which performed the same gestures of the most ancient purifications.

But what wrestling is especially supposed to imitate is a purely moral concept: justice. The notion of payment is essential to wrestling, and the crowd's "Make him suffer" signifies above all "Make him pay." What is involved, then, of course, is an immanent justice. The viler the "action of the bastard," the more satisfied the public is by the blow he receives in return: if the villain—who is of course a coward—takes refuge behind the ropes, claiming his right to do so by a brazen gesture, he is pitilessly cornered there, and the crowd roars its approval at seeing the rules broken for the sake of a deserved punishment. Wrestlers are good at flattering the crowd's powers of outrage, going to the very limits of the concept of Justice, this farthest zone of confrontation, where it takes only a trifle to open the gates to a frenzied world. For the fan of wrestling, nothing is finer than the vengeful rage of a betrayed combatant who passionately attacks not a successful adversary but the stinging image of foul play. Of course it is the image of Justice which matters here much more than its contents: wrestling is above all a quantitative series of compensations (an eye for an eye, a tooth for a tooth). This explains how the reversal of situations possesses in the public eye a kind of moral beauty: the crowd delights in it as if it were a well-timed episode in a novel, and the greater the contrast between the success of a stratagem and its collapse, the more satisfying the mimed performance is judged to be. Justice is therefore the body of a possible transgression; it is because there is a Law that the spectacle of the passions transgressing is so gratifying.

Which explains that out of five wrestling matches, only one is "proper." Again, it must be understood that a legal termination here is a usage or a genre, as in the theater: the rules don't constitute a real constraint, but instead the conventional appearance of regularity. So in actuality a regular fight is nothing but an exceptionally polite one: the combatants confront each other with zeal, not with rage, they manage to master their passions, nor do they deem it necessary to punish an already defeated opponent, they cease fighting once they are ordered to do so, and congratulate each other after a particularly arduous episode during which, however, they have not ceased to fight fair. Of course we must understand that all these polite actions are communicated to the public by the most conventional signs of propriety: shaking hands, raising arms, ostensibly avoiding a sterile hold which would ruin a fight's perfection.

Conversely, foul play exists here only by its excessive signs: giving a big kick to the loser's body, taking refuge behind the ropes by ostensibly invoking a purely formal privilege, refusing to shake hands with a partner before or after the match, taking advantage of an official pause to sneak up behind an opponent, or dealing an illicit blow when the referee isn't looking (such a blow is worth dealing only because half the crowd can observe it and be outraged). Evil is wrestling's natural climate, and a fair fight has mainly the value of an exception; the public is startled by such a thing and hails it in passing as an anachronistic and rather sentimental return to a tradition of sportsmanship ("Aren't they fighting fair, these two!"); the fans are suddenly moved by the vision of general kindness, but would probably die of boredom and indifference if the wrestlers failed to return pretty soon to the orgy of bad feelings which is the indispensable condition of good wrestling.

Extrapolated, wrestling as a fair fight could lead only to boxing or judo, whereas true wrestling sustains its originality by all the excesses which make it a spectacle and not a sport. The ending of a boxing match or a judo contest is as decisive as the conclusive point of a demonstration. Wrestling's rhythm is quite different, for its natural meaning is that of rhetorical amplification: the emphasis of passions, the constant renewal of paroxysms, the exasperation of retaliations can naturally lead on to the most baroque of confusions. Certain fights, and the most successful ones, are crowned with a final charivari, a kind of frenzied fantasia in which laws, rules of the game, the censure of referees, and the limits of the Ring are abolished, swept away in a triumphant disorder which overflows into the hall and carries away pell-mell the wrestlers, the seconds, the referee, and the spectators.

It has already been noted that in America wrestling represents a kind of mythological combat between Good and Evil (of a parapolitical nature, the "bad wrestler" always being presumed to be a Red). French wrestling is an altogether different heroization, of an ethical order and no longer a political one. What the public seeks here is the progressive construction of an eminently moral image: that of the perfect bastard. We go to a wrestling match to watch the renewed adventures of a single leading character, as permanent and multiform as Guignol or Scapin, inventive of unexpected faces yet ever faithful to his role. The bastard reveals himself like a character in Molière or a portrait by La Bruyère, which is to say like a classical entity, an essence whose actions are only signifying epiphenomena arranged in a temporal sequence. This stylized character belongs to no nation and to no party, whether the wrestler is named Kuzchenko (nicknamed Mustache because of Stalin), Yerpazian, Gaspardi, Jo Vignola, or Nollières, the fans assign him no other country but that of "the rules."

So what is a bastard for this public apparently composed

of men outside the rules? Essentially someone unstable, who acknowledges the rules only when they are of use to him and transgresses the formal continuity of attitudes—a man who is unpredictable, hence asocial. He takes refuge behind the Law when he supposes it favors him and betrays it when it seems useful to do so; sometimes he denies the formal limit of the Ring and continues to belabor an adversary protected legally by the ropes, sometimes he reestablishes that limit and claims the protection of what a moment ago he failed to respect. This inconsistency, much more than betrayal or cruelty, sends the public beside itself: offended not in its morality but in its logic, the public considers the contradiction of arguments the vilest of crimes. The forbidden hold becomes irregular only when it destroys a quantitative equilibrium and disturbs the rigorous calculation of compensations; what the public condemns is not at all the transgression of insipid official rules, but the lack of revenge, the lack of penality. Hence nothing is more exciting for the crowd than the emphatic kick given to a vanquished bastard; the joy of punishing reaches its peak when it is based on a mathematical justification, at which point contempt is unrestrained: we are no longer dealing with a *salaud*, a bastard, but with a *salope*, a swine, the oral gesture of ultimate degradation.

A finality so precise demands that wrestling be exactly what the public expects it to be. The wrestlers, men of great experience, know just how to inflect the spontaneous episodes of combat toward the image which the public creates out of the great marvelous themes of its mythology. A wrestler may irritate or disgust, he never disappoints, for he always ultimately achieves, by a gradual solidification of signs, what the public expects of him. In wrestling, nothing exists unless it exists totally, there is no symbol, no allusion, everything is given exhaustively; leaving nothing in shadow, the gesture severs every parasitical meaning and ceremonially presents the public with a pure and full signification, three-dimensional, like Nature. Such emphasis is nothing but the popular and ancestral image of the perfect intelligibility of reality. What is enacted by wrestling, then, is an ideal intelligence of things, a euphoria of humanity, raised for a while out of the constitutive ambiguity of everyday situations and installed in a panoramic vision of a univocal Nature, in which signs finally correspond to causes without obstacle, without evasion, and without contradiction.

When the hero or the bastard of the drama, the man who has been seen a few minutes earlier possessed by a moral fury, enlarged to the size of a kind of metaphysical sign—when this figure leaves the wrestling hall, impassive, anonymous, carrying a gym bag and his wife on his arm, who could doubt that wrestling possesses that power of transmutation proper to Spectacle and to Worship? In the Ring and in the very depths of their voluntary ignominy, the wrestlers remain gods, for they are, for a few minutes, the key which opens Nature, the pure gesture which separates Good and Evil and unveils the figure of a finally intelligible Justice.

THE HARCOURT ACTOR

In France you're not an actor if you haven't been photographed by Harcourt Studios. The Harcourt actor is a god; gods never *do* anything, they're caught *in repose*.

A euphemism borrowed from the society pages accounts for such postures: the actor is imagined "in town." Which means, of course, an ideal town, the Players' City, where nothing exists but festivities and love affairs, whereas onstage everything is work, that dangerous and demanding "gift." And this reversal must be surprising to the highest degree; we must be stricken with confusion to discover, posted in the theater lobby like a sphinx at the sanctuary entrance, the Olympian image of an actor who has shed the skin of the frantic, all-too-human monster and at last recovered his timeless essence. Here the actor takes his revenge: obliged by his sacerdotal function to mime on occasion old age, ugliness, in any case the dispossession of himself; he now recovers an ideal visage detached from the improprieties of the profession. Leaving the "stage" for "town," the Harcourt actor in no way abandons "dreams" for "reality." Quite the contrary: onstage, well built, bony, fleshy, thick-skinned under the greasepaint; in town, smooth, sleek, pumiced by the grace, and aerated by the Harcourt Studios glow. Onstage, sometimes old, at least indicating some age or other; in town, eternally young, fixed forever at beauty's apogee.

See illustration 1.

Onstage, betrayed by the materiality of a voice as muscle-bound as a dancer's overdeveloped calves; in town, ideally silent, i.e., mysterious, filled with the deep secrecy attributed to all beauty that does not speak. Onstage, lastly, necessarily engaged in trivial or heroic, in any case effective gestures; in town, reduced to a face purged of all movement.

Moreover, this pure countenance is rendered utterly useless—i.e., luxurious—by the aberrant angle from which it is shot, as if the Harcourt camera, privileged to capture this unearthly beauty, had had to take up its position in the most improbable zones of a rarefied space—as if this countenance, floating between the stage's crude earth and the town's radiant sky, could be only momentarily ravished from its intemporal nature and then devoutly abandoned to its solitary and regal course; sometimes materially plunged earthward, sometimes ecstatically upraised, the actor's face seems to unite with his celestial home in an ascension without haste and without muscles, quite contrary to an onlooking humanity which, belonging to a different zoological class and capable of movement only by legwork (and not by face), must return to its residence on foot. (What we need here is a historical psychoanalysis of truncated iconographies. Walking is perhaps—mythologically—the most trivial, hence the most human gesture. Every dream, every ideal image, every social preferment initially suppresses the legs, either by portrait or by automobile.)

Reduced to face, shoulders, hair, actresses thereby attest to the virtuous unreality of their sex—whereby they are manifestly angels in town, after having been mistresses, wives, bitches, and soubrettes onstage. As for the men, with the exception of the young leads, who admittedly belong more or less to the angelic species, since their faces remain, like the women's, in a posture of evanescence—the men promote their virility by some urban attribute, a pipe, a dog, eyeglasses, a mantelpiece to lean on, objects trivial but necessary to the expression of masculinity, an audacity permitted only to the males of the species and by which the actor "in town" manifests, in the fashion of gods and kings on a spree, that he has no fear of being, sometimes, a man like anyone else, furnished with certain pleasures (pipe), affections (dog), weaknesses (glasses), and even an earthly domicile (mantelpiece).

The Harcourt iconography sublimates the actor's materiality and prolongs a necessarily trivial "scene" (since it functions) by means of an inert and consequently ideal "town." A paradoxical status, it is this scene which is reality here; "town" is myth, dream, wonderland. The actor, rid of the too-fleshly envelope of his profession, rejoins his ritual essence as hero, as human archetype, located at the limit of other men's physical norms. Here the face is a fictional object; its impassivity, its divine dough, suspends everyday truth and bestows the confusion, the pleasure, and ultimately the security of a higher truth. By a scruple of illusion quite proper to a period and a social class too weak both for pure reason and for mythical powers, the intermission audience (evidently bored) declares these unreal faces to be those of "town" and thereby acquires the rationalist good conscience of assuming a man behind the actor; but at the very moment of despoiling the mime, the Harcourt studio summons up a god, and thereby, for this bourgeois public that is both blasé and living on lies, everything is satisfied.

As a consequence the Harcourt photograph is, for the young actor, an initiation rite, a guild diploma, his true professional *carte d'identité*. Is he properly enthroned if he has not yet encountered the sacred Harcourt Image? This rectangle which first reveals his ideal head, his intelligent, sensitive, or witty expression, depending on the role he offers to life, is the formal document by which the whole of society agrees to separate him from its own physical laws and assures him the perpetual revenue of a countenance which receives as a gift, on the day of this baptism, all the powers ordinarily denied, at least simultaneously, to ordinary flesh: a changeless splendor, a seduction pure of all wickedness, an intellectual power which is not the necessary accompaniment to the ordinary actor's art or beauty.

Which is why the photographic portraits by Thérèse Le Prat or Agnès Varda, for example, are avant-garde: they always bequeath the actor his fleshly face and enclose it frankly, with an exemplary humility, in its social function, which is to "represent" and not to lie. For a myth as alienated as that of actors' faces, this choice is quite revolutionary: not to embellish their lobbies with classic Harcourts—titivating, languishing, angelized or virilized (according to sex)—is an audacity few theater managers can afford.

ROMANS IN THE MOVIES

In Mankiewicz's *Julius Caesar*, all the male characters wear bangs. Some (bangs, not characters) are curly, some straight, others tufted, still others pomaded, all are neatly combed, and bald men are not allowed, though Roman History has a good number to its credit. Those with scant hair don't get off so easily, and the hairdresser, the film's principal artisan, always manages one last lock which joins the frieze along the top of the forehead—of those Roman foreheads whose exiguity has ever indicated a specific mixture of power, of virtue, and of conquest.

What can it be which is attached to these persistent fringes? Quite simply, the announcement of Romanity. So that we see the Spectacle's mainspring exposed here: the *sign*. These frontal locks flood us with evidence, henceforth there can be no doubt we are in Ancient Rome. And this certitude is continuous: the actors speak, act, torment themselves, struggle with "universal" questions without ever losing, thanks to this little flag spread across their foreheads, their historical verisimilitude: their generality can even expand, quite safely, across the Ocean and down through the ages, merging with the Yankee lineaments of the Hollywood extras: no matter, everyone is reassured, installed in the tranquil certainty of an unequivocal universe where Romans are Roman by the most legible of signs, that bit of toupee over the forehead.

A Frenchman, to whose eyes American faces still retain

something exotic, finds comical the mixture of these gangster-sheriffs with the little Roman fringe: rather like an excellent music-hall gag. It's because for us the sign functions to excess, discrediting itself by letting its purpose show. But that same fringe produced on the one naturally Latin forehead in the whole film, Marlon Brando's, "works" for us without earning a laugh, and it's not unlikely that a share of this actor's success is due to the perfect integration of Roman capillarity with the general morphology of the character. Conversely, Julius Caesar is incredible, with his Anglo-Saxon lawyer's phiz already familiarized by a thousand bit parts in thrillers or comedies, his compliant skull carefully raked by a stylist's hairpiece.

In the category of capillary significations, here is a subsign, that of nocturnal surprises: Portia and Calpurnia, wakened in the middle of the night, have ostensibly disheveled hair; the younger Portia's expressed by flowing locks, so that her disarray is, so to speak, primary; while the mature Calpurnia presents a more studied informality: a braid winds around her neck and hangs over her right shoulder, expressing the traditional sign of disorder, asymmetry. But these signs are at once excessive and absurd: they postulate a naturalness which they lack the courage to honor completely: they are not "open and above board."

Still another sign in this *Julius Caesar*: every face sweats unremittingly: workers, soldiers, conspirators all bathe their austere and tense features in an abundant perspiration (of vaseline). And the close-ups are so frequent that sweat here must be an intentional attribute. Like the Roman bangs or the midnight braid, sweat too is a sign. Of what? Of morality. Everyone sweats because everyone is arguing with himself about something; we are meant to be in a site of an agonizingly laborious virtue, i.e., in the very locus of tragedy, which perspiration is intended to represent. The populace, traumatized by Caesar's death, then by Mark Antony's arguments, the populace sweats, economically combining in this one sign the intensity of its emotion and the primitive nature of its condition. And the virtuous men, Brutus, Cassius, Casca, also perspire continually, thereby testifying to the enormous labor which virtue performs in them as they are about to give birth to a crime. To sweat is to think (which obviously is based on the postulate, quite proper to a populace of businessmen, that to think is a violent, cataclysmic operation of which thinking is the mildest sign). In the whole film, only one man fails to sweat, remains smooth-skinned, unperturbed, and watertight: Caesar. Of course, Caesar, the *object* of the crime, remains dry, for he doesn't know, *he doesn't think*, he alone must sustain the firm, polished texture of a judicial piece of evidence.

Here again, the sign is ambiguous: it remains on the surface yet does not renounce passing itself off as a depth; it seeks to make itself understood (which is praiseworthy) but at the same time presents itself as spontaneous (which is deceptive), it declares itself to be simultaneously intentional and irrepressible, artificial and natural, manufactured and yet discovered. Which serves to introduce us to a morality of the sign. The sign ought to present itself in only two extreme forms: either frankly intellectual, reduced by its distance to an algebra, as in the Chinese theater, where a flag signifies a regiment; or else deeply rooted, somehow invented on each occasion, presenting an inward and secret face, the signal of a moment and no longer of a concept (such, for instance, would be the art of Stanislavsky). But the intermediary sign (the bangs of Romanity or the perspiration of thought) betrays a degraded spectacle, one which fears the naïve truth as much as the total artifice. For if it is a good thing that a spectacle be created to make the world clearer, there is a culpable duplicity in confusing the sign with what is signified. And this is a duplicity peculiar to bourgeois art: between the intellectual sign and the visceral sign, this art hypocritically arranges an illegitimate sign, at once elliptical and pretentious, which it baptizes with the pompous name *natural*.

THE WRITER ON VACATION

Gide was reading Bossuet going down the Congo. This posture nicely sums up the ideal of our writers "on vacation," photographed by *Le Figaro*: to attach to banal leisure the prestige of a vocation nothing can halt or corrupt: a nice piece of journalism, quite effective sociologically, which candidly informs us about our bourgeoisie's notion of its writers.

What initially seems to surprise and delight that bourgeoisie is its own broad-mindedness in acknowledging that writers too are the kind of people who take vacations. "Vacations" are a recent social phenomenon whose mythological development it might be interesting to trace. Initially a feature of academic life, they have become, since "paid leaves," a part of the proletarian—or at least of the workingman's—world. To assert that this feature can henceforth concern writers, that the specialists of the human heart are also subject to the general status of contemporary labor, is a way of convincing our bourgeois readers that they are in step with their time: we flatter ourselves that we recognize the necessity of certain prosaic realities, that we are in touch with "modern" realities in the teachings of Fourastié and André Siegfried.

During the summer of 1954 the literary supplement to the right-leaning daily newspaper Le Figaro *published a series titled "Écrivains en vacances," for which it asked a selection of French writers to send a photograph from their vacation along with a brief commentary.*

Of course this proletarianization of the writer is only granted with a certain parsimony, all the better to destroy it subsequently. No sooner provided with a social attribute (of which vacations are a highly agreeable example), the man of letters quickly returns to the empyrean he shares with the professionals of the vocation. And the "naturalness" in which our novelists are eternalized is in fact instituted to translate a sublime contradiction: that of a prosaic condition, produced, alas, by a quite materialistic period, and the glamorous status which bourgeois society liberally grants to its spiritual representatives (provided they remain harmless).

What proves the writer's marvelous singularity is that during those famous vacations, which he fraternally shares with workmen and shop assistants, he never ceases, if not working, at least producing. A false worker, the writer is also a false vacationer. One of them writes his memoirs, another corrects his proofs, a third is preparing his next book. And the one who does nothing confesses he is indulging some truly paradoxical behavior, an avant-garde exploit only a strong-minded individual can permit himself to acknowledge. We know from this last piece of braggadocio that it is entirely "natural" for the writer always to write, in all situations. First of all, it assimilates literary production to a kind of involuntary, hence taboo, secretion, since it escapes human determinisms: to put it more nobly, the writer is the prey of an internal god who speaks at all times, without concern, tyrant that he is, for his medium's vacation. The writer is on vacation, but his Muse is wide awake, and gives birth nonstop.

The second advantage of this logorrhea is that by its imperative character it passes quite naturally for the writer's very essence. The latter doubtless concedes that he's provided with a human existence, with an old house in the country, with a family, with shorts, with a granddaughter, etc., but contrary to the other workers who change essence—who are no longer on the beach as anything but summer visitors—the writer always preserves his writer's nature; provided with a vacation, he raises the sign of his humanity; yet the god remains, one is a writer the way Louis XIV was king, even on the *chaise percée*. Hence the function of the man of letters is, compared to human labors, a bit what ambrosia is compared to bread: a miraculous, eternal substance which condescends to a social form in order to be more readily apprehended in its prestigious difference. All of which leads to the same idea of the writer as superman, a kind of differential being whom society puts in a glass case to profit by the factitious singularity such a being has conceded to it.

Hence the ordinary-guy image of "the writer on vacation" is nothing but another of those cunning mystifications which society practices in order to subjugate its writers: nothing reveals more clearly the singularity of a "vocation" than its contradiction—not its denial, far from that—by the matter-of-factness of its incarnation; it's an old trick known to every hagiographer. We see this myth of "literary vacations" extending very far, much farther than summertime: the techniques of contemporary journalism are increasingly employed to make the writer into a prosaic spectacle. But it would be a great mistake to take this effort for an attempt at demystification. Quite the contrary. No doubt it might strike me as touching and even flattering that I, simple reader that I am, could share such confidences in the everyday life of a race selected by genius: no doubt I would feel deliciously fraternal towards a humanity about which newspapers inform me that this particular great writer wears blue pajamas, and that young novelist has a weakness for "pretty girls, Reblochon, and lavender honey." All the same, the balance of the operation is that the writer becomes a little more of a star, leaves this earth of ours for a slightly more remote celestial habitat where his pajamas and his cheeses in no way prevent him from resuming the use of his noble demiurgic speech.

Publicly to endow the writer with a quite carnal body, to reveal that he enjoys dry white wine and rare beef is to make even more miraculous, of diviner essence, the products of his art. Far from the details of his daily life bringing me closer to and more familiar with the nature of his inspiration, it is all the mythic singularity of his condition that the writer emphasizes by such confidences. For I cannot help ascribing to some sort of superhumanity the existence of beings vast enough to wear blue pajamas just when they manifest themselves as a universal consciousness, or else still profess a love for Reblochon in the same breath with which they announce their forthcoming Phenomenology of the Ego. The spectacular alliance of so much nobility and so much futility signifies that we still believe in the contradiction: being totally miraculous, each of its terms is miraculous too: obviously it would lose all its interest in a world where the writer's work would be desacralized to the point of appearing as natural as his vestimentary or gustatory functions.

THE "BLUE BLOOD" CRUISE

Ever since the Coronation, the French have been yearning for evidences of the monarchic reality they so dearly loved; the embarkation of nearly a hundred princes on the Greek yacht *Agamemnon* afforded a satisfying follow-up. If Elizabeth's Coronation was a touching, indeed a sentimental theme, the cruise of so many blue bloods afforded a diverting variation: kings playing at being men, as if in a comedy by Flers and Caillavet, from which results a host of absurd situations of the Marie-Antoinette-playing-milkmaid variety. The pathology of such diversions is somewhat oppressive: since we are amused by a contradiction, it's because we assume the terms are far apart; in other words, kings are of a superhuman essence, and when they temporarily assume certain forms of democratic life, the resulting incarnation must be *contra naturam*, possible only as a result of condescension. To feign that kings are capable of such prosaic behavior is to acknowledge that such conduct is no more natural to them than angelism to ordinary mortals, in other words, that kings are still kings by divine right.

Consequently the neutral gestures of everyday life have assumed, on the *Agamemnon*, an exorbitantly audacious character, like those creative fantasies in which Nature transgresses her own realm: kings shave themselves! This apparently habit-

---

In August 1954, Queen Frederika of Greece invited more than a hundred members of European royalty on a cruise around the Cyclades.

ual behavior was reported by our national press as an action of incredible singularity, as if in performing it, kings consented to risk the whole of their royalty, thereby professing their faith in its indestructible nature. King Paul wore a short-sleeved shirt, Queen Frederika a *print* dress, that is, a dress no longer unique but whose pattern can be seen on the bodies of simple mortals: in former days, kings disguised themselves as shepherds; nowadays, to wear garments from a chain store for two weeks is for them the sign of that kind of disguise. Another democratic sign: getting up at six a.m. All such things inform us, by antiphrasis, about a certain ideal nature of everyday life: wearing long-sleeved shirts with cuffs, being shaved by a valet, sleeping late. By renouncing such privileges, kings force them to recede to the heaven of dreams: their sacrifice—temporary as it is—establishes the eternal status of everyday happiness.

What is more curious still, this mythic character of our kings is nowadays laicized yet not in the least eliminated by the expedient of a certain scientism: kings are defined like puppies by the purity of their breeding (Blue Blood), and the ship, privileged site of any "closure," is a sort of modern Ark which preserves the main variants of the monarchic species. Here on shipboard the likelihood of certain couplings can be openly computed; confined aboard their floating stud farm, the thoroughbreds are protected from any mongrel weddings, everything is (annually?) prepared so they can reproduce with each other exclusively; securing their rarity like that of Lhasa apsos on Earth, the ship collects and immobilizes them, constituting an exclusive temporary community where such ethnographic curiosities may be as carefully perpetuated and as well protected as on a Sioux reservation.

The two age-old themes merge, that of the God-King and the King-Object. Yet this mythological heaven is not so harmless as the real one to our Earth. The most ethereal mystifications, the amusing details of the Blue Blood cruise, the entire anecdotal jabber on which the national press intoxicates its readers, are not proffered without damage: fortified in their restored divinity, our princes democratically engage in politics: the Comte de Paris abandons the *Agamemnon* and comes to Paris to "keep watch" on the European Defense Community, and young Prince Juan of Spain is sent to the rescue of Spanish fascism.

CRITICISM BLIND AND DUMB

Critics (literary critics, theater critics) often employ two rather singular arguments. The first consists in suddenly deciding that the object of criticism is ineffable and consequently that criticism is useless. The other argument, which also reappears periodically, consists in confessing that one is too stupid, too ignorant to understand a so-called philosophical work: Henri Lefebvre's play about Kierkegaard has thus provoked from our best critics (and I am not speaking of those who openly profess stupidity) a panic of imbecility (whose purpose was evidently to discredit Lefebvre by relegating him to the ridicule of pure cerebrality).

Why do critics thus periodically proclaim their impotence or their incomprehension? Surely not out of modesty: no one is more at ease than a critic confessing he understands nothing about existentialism; and no one is more ironic and therefore more self-assured than a critic confessing quite shamefacedly that he has not had the occasion to be initiated into the philosophy of the Extraordinary; and who could be more military than a third critic pleading for poetic ineffability?

All of which means that one considers oneself of sufficiently sure intelligence for the admission of incomprehension to call into question an author's clarity and not that of one's own

---

Henri Lefebvre's play Le Maître et la servante *was produced in Paris in September 1954. It was based on Søren Kierkegaard's brief engagement to Regine Olsen.*

mind: one mimics stupidity the better to make the public pro-test and then convert from a complicity in helplessness to a complicity in intelligence. This is a favorite operation in salons like that of Madame Verdurin: "Well, it's my métier to be in-telligent, and I don't understand a word; and you won't under-stand a word either; that's proof you're every bit as intelligent as I am."

The truth behind these seasonally professed inadequacies of intelligence is the old obscurantist myth which holds that an idea is noxious if it is not controlled by "common sense" and "feeling": Knowledge is Evil, both grow on the same tree: culture is permitted, provided one periodically proclaims the vanity of its purposes and the limits of its power (see also on this subject Mr. Graham Greene's ideas about psychologists and psychiatrists); ideal culture should be nothing but a sweet rhetorical effusion, the art of words to bear witness to a tran-sient moistening of the soul. Yet that old romantic couple, heart and head, has no reality except in an imagery of vaguely Gnos-tic origin, in those opiated philosophies which have always, ultimately, formed the backbone of strong regimes, the kind that get rid of intellectuals by telling them to run along and busy themselves with emotion and the ineffable. In fact, any reservations about culture is a terrorist position. To be a critic by profession, and to proclaim one doesn't understand a thing about existentialism or Marxism (as a matter of fact it is pre-cisely these two philosophies which are declared incompre-hensible), is to erect one's blindness or one's dumbness into a universal rule of perception—it is to reject Marxism and exis-tentialism from the world: "I don't understand, therefore you are idiots."

But if you so fear or despise a work's philosophical founda-tions, and if you so loudly proclaim your right to understand nothing about them and to say nothing about them, why be-come a critic? After all, isn't it your profession to understand, to enlighten? Of course you can judge philosophy in the name of common sense; the trouble is, if "common sense" and "feeling" understand nothing about philosophy, philosophy understands them perfectly. You don't explain philosophers, but they explain you. You have no desire to understand that play by the Marxist Lefebvre, but you can be sure that the Marxist Lefebvre understands your incomprehension perfectly, and above all that he understands (for I myself suspect you to be more subtle than stupid) the delightfully "harmless" confession you make of it.

SAPONIDS AND DETERGENTS

The first World Detergent Conference (Paris, September 1954) authorized the world to commit itself to the euphoria of *Omo*: not only do detergent products have no harmful effect on human skin, but they may even be able to save miners from silicosis. In recent years such products have been the object of an advertising campaign so massive that they are now part of that level of French daily life which the various schools of psychoanalysis would do well to pay some attention to if they want to keep up-to-date. One could then usefully contrast with the psychoanalysis of purifying fluids (the bleach *Javel*) that of saponid powders (*Lux, Persil*) or detergents (*Rai, Paic Crio, Omo*). The relations between the remedy and the evil, between dirtiness and these products, are very different in each case.

For instance, the fluids of *Javel* have always been felt to be a sort of liquid fire whose action must be carefully measured, or else the object itself is affected, "burned"; the implicit legend of this type of product rests on a violent, abrasive modification of matter: the results are of a chemical or mutilating order: the product "kills" dirt. Quite the contrary, the various powders are separating elements; their ideal role is to liberate the object from its circumstantial imperfection: dirt is "driven away," and killing no longer occurs; in *Omo* imagery, dirt is a sickly little enemy which flees from good clean linens at the first sign of *Omo*'s judgment. Products based on chlorine and ammonia are indeed the delegates of a sort of total fire, a savior but a blind one; powders, on the other hand, are selective, they force dirt through the meshes of a garment's material—a police action, not all-out warfare. This distinction has its ethnographic translation: chemical liquids are equivalent to the peasant laundress's hostile gesture of actually beating soiled clothes against the stones in a streambed, whereas powders imply a housewife's squeezing and rolling her laundry against the length of a sloping board at the riverside.

But even within the order of powders, we must again oppose to advertising on a psychological basis a procedure I should call psychoanalytic (I employ this word without attaching to it the signification of any particular school). For example, *Persil Whitener* bases its prestige on the evidence of a result; vanity is called into play, a certain social status offering for comparison two objects of which one is *whiter* than the other. *Omo*'s advertising also indicates its product's effect (in a superlative form, moreover), but chiefly emphasizes the mode of its action; the consumer is thereby engaged in a sort of experiential mode of substance, one that makes him the accomplice of a deliverance and no longer merely the beneficiary of a result: substance itself is here provided with value states.

Of these, *Omo* uses two, quite new in the order of detergents: the deep and the foamy. To say that *Omo* cleans in depth (see the Cinéma-Publicité playlet) is to suppose that linen is deep, which nobody had ever supposed, and what then proceeds to magnify it beyond contestation, to establish it as an object flattering to those obscure impulses of caressing envelopment which are inside every human body. As for foam, its signification of luxuriousness is well known: first of all, it has an appearance of uselessness; secondly, its ready, abundant, and almost infinite proliferation suggests that in the substance from which it issues there is a vigorous seed, a healthy and powerful essence, a great wealth of active elements proceeding from a tiny original volume; and finally it flatters in the consumer an airy imagination of substance, a mode of contact at once light and vertical, pursued like a sort of bliss in the gustative order (foie gras, delicacies, wines) as well as in the vestimentary (chiffons, tulles) and in the cosmetic order of soaps (the film star taking her bath). Foam can even be the sign of a certain spirituality, insofar as the spirit is reputed to be capable of producing everything from nothing, a great surface of effects from a tiny volume of causes (creams have an altogether different psychoanalysis, of a sopitive order: they abolish wrinkles, pain, itching, etc.). The important thing is to have successfully masked the abrasive function of the detergent under the delicious image of a substance at once deep and airy which can control the molecular order of substances without damaging them. A consequent euphoria must not allow us to forget that there is one level on which *Persil* and *Omo* are just alike: the level of the Anglo-Dutch trust *Unilever*.

THE POOR AND THE PROLETARIAT

Charlie Chaplin's ultimate joke was to have transferred half of his Soviet prize money into the coffers of Abbé Pierre. At bottom this comes down to establishing an equality in nature between the proletarian and the poor man. Chaplin has always seen the proletariat under the features of the poor: hence the human power of his representations, but also their political ambiguity. This is clearly visible in that admirable film *Modern Times*. Here Chaplin repeatedly approaches the proletarian theme, but never assumes it politically: what he allows us to see is the proletarian still blind and mystified, defined by the immediate nature of his needs and his total alienation at the hands of his masters (bosses and policemen).

For Chaplin, the proletarian is still a man who is hungry: representations of hunger are always epic in Chaplin: excessive size of sandwiches, rivers of milk, pieces of fruit hardly bitten into and carelessly thrown away; in mockery, the food-dispensing machine (part of the bosses' world) furnishes only cut up pieces, evidently stale. Snared in his hunger, Chaplin-Man is always located just below political awareness: for him,

---

Abbé Pierre, founder of the Emmaüs charity movement, made a call for help in the extremely cold winter of 1954. The call triggered what became known as the uprising of kindness, raising a total of five hundred million francs in donations, of which Charlie Chaplin gave two million. Charlie Chaplin received the World Peace Prize in 1954 from the Communist-sponsored World Peace Council.

the strike is a catastrophe because it threatens a man actually blinded by his hunger; this man rejoins the workingman's condition only at the moment when the poor and the proletariat coincide under the gaze (and the blows) of the police. Historically, Chaplin gradually regains the position of the worker of the French Restoration, rebelling against the machine, helpless in the face of strikes, fascinated by the breadwinner's problem (in the literal sense of the word), but still incapable of acceding to the consciousness of political causes and to the demand of a collective strategy.

But it is just because Chaplin portrays a sort of primitive proletarian, still external to the Revolution, that his representative strength is so great. No socialist work has yet managed to express the worker's humiliated condition with as much violence and as much generosity. Only Brecht, perhaps, has perceived the necessity, for a socialist art, of always showing man on the eve of the Revolution, which is to say, man alone, still blind, on the point of being accessible to revolutionary light by the "natural" excess of his miseries. By showing the worker already engaged in a conscious combat, subsumed under the Cause and the Party, other versions account for a necessary political reality, but without aesthetic force.

Now Chaplin, in accord with Brecht's idea, presents a man's blindness so that the public sees both the blind man and what is in front of his eyes. To see someone not seeing is the best way of seeing intensely what he doesn't see: thus at a Punch and Judy show, it is the children in the audience who tell Punch what he pretends not to see. For example, Chaplin in his cell, pampered by his wardens, is leading the ideal life of the American petit bourgeois: legs crossed in his easy chair, he reads his newspaper under a portrait of Lincoln, but the adorable self-satisfaction of such a posture utterly discredits it, makes it no longer possible to take refuge in it without noticing the new alienation it contains, and even a poor man is constantly cut off from his temptations. In short, this is why Chaplin's poor man triumphs over everything: because he eludes every temptation, rejects every partnership, and never invests in man except in man alone. His anarchy, arguable politically, represents perhaps the most efficacious form of revolution artistically.

MARTIANS

The mystery of Flying Saucers was at first terrestrial: supposedly the saucer came from the Soviet unknown, that world as deprived of explicit intentions as another planet. And already this form of the myth contained in germ its planetary development: if the saucer of Soviet contrivance so readily became a Martian one, it was because in fact Western mythology attributes to the Communist world the very alterity of a planet: the USSR is a world intermediate between Earth and Mars.

Only, in its evolution, the marvelous has changed meaning, has shifted from a myth of combat to one of judgment. Mars indeed, for the time being, is impartial. It lands here to judge Earth, but before condemning, Mars seeks to observe, to understand. The great USSR-USA contestation is therefore perceived from now on as a guilty state, because here the danger bears no relation to reason; hence the mythic resort to a celestial consideration, sufficiently powerful to intimidate both parties. Analysts of the future will be able to explain the figurative elements of this power, the oneiric themes composing it: the rondure of the spaceship, the gloss of its metal, that superlative state of the world which would be a substance

---

In the fall of 1954, more than a hundred cases of UFO sightings were registered around the country. Investigations by the French police and the Air Force failed to identify their provenance. By October 1954, suspicions had been raised that the flying engines came from the Soviet Union.

without seams: *a contrario*, we better understand everything which in our perceptive field participates in the theme of Evil: the irregular planes, the noise, the discontinuity of surfaces. All that has already been meticulously posited in the novels of anticipation, whose Martian psychosis merely retraces the descriptions with remarkable exactitude.

What is more significant is that Mars is implicitly endowed with a historical determinism modeled on that of Earth. If the saucers are vehicles of Martian historians here to observe Earth's configuration, as has been loudly reported by one American scientist, and as many others discreetly concur, this is because Martian history has ripened at the same rhythm as that of our world and produced geographers in exactly the same period that we ourselves have discovered aerial geography and photography. The only advance is that of the vehicle itself, Mars thus being only an Earth of dreams, endowed with perfect wings as in any dream of idealization. Most likely if we were to disembark in our turn on the Mars we have designed, we should find there merely Earth itself, and between these two products of the same history we should be unable to determine which is our own. For in order that Mars be given to geographical lore, it too must have had its Strabo, its Michelet, its Vidal de la Blache and, step by step, the same nations, the same wars, the same scientists, and the same men as ourselves.

Logic compels it also to have had the same religions and of course, singularly, our own, those of us Frenchmen. For the Martians, according to the newspaper *Le Progrès de Lyon*, have necessarily had a Christ; consequently they've also had a pope (and had as well, moreover, an open schism): lacking which they couldn't be civilized to the point of inventing the interplanetary saucer. For, according to this newspaper, religion and technological progress being equally qualified as precious perquisites of civilization, the one could not occur without the other: *it is inconceivable,* writes this authority, *that beings having attained such a degree of civilization that they could arrive among us by their own means, would be "pagans." They would have to be deists, acknowledging the existence of a god and having their own religion.*

Thus this whole psychosis is based on the myth of the Identical, i.e., of the Double. But here, as always, the Double is ahead, the Double is a Judge. The confrontation of East and West is already no longer the pure combat of Good and Evil, it is a sort of Manichaean melee, cast under the eyes of a third Onlooker; it postulates the existence of a Super-Nature at the level of heaven, because it is in heaven that the Terror abides: heaven is henceforth, without metaphor, the field of apparition of atomic death. The judge is born in the same place where the executioner threatens.

Again this Judge—or rather this Inspector—has just been seen carefully reinvested by a common spirituality and differing very little, all in all, from a pure terrestrial projection. For this impotence to imagine the Other is one of the constant features of all petit bourgeois mythology. Alterity is the concept most antipathetic to "common sense." Every myth inevitably tends to a narrow anthropomorphism and, what is worse, to what might be called a class anthropomorphism. Mars is not only Earth, it is a petit bourgeois Earth, it is the little district of mentality cultivated (or expressed) by what in France is called *la grande presse illustrée.* No sooner formed in the heavens, Mars is thereby *aligned* by the most powerful of appropriations, that of identity.

OPERATION ASTRA

To insinuate into Order the accommodating spectacle of its servitudes has of late become a paradoxical but peremptory means of its inflation. Here is the schema of this new demonstration: take any rank of order you want to restore or develop, first manifest at length its various inadequacies, the bullying it gives rise to, the injustices it produces, immerse it in the imperfections of its nature; then at the last minute save it *despite* or rather *with* the heavy fatality of its defects. Examples? No lack of them.

Take an army: manifest plainly the militarism of its leaders, the narrow, unjust character of its discipline, and into this stupid tyranny thrust an average being, fallible but sympathetic, archetype of the onlooker. And then, at the last moment, reverse the magic helmet, and out of it draw the image of a triumphant army, flags flying, adorable, to which, like Sganarelle's wife, you can only be faithful, though beaten (*From Here to Eternity*, a novel by James Jones).

Take another army: expose the scientific fanaticism of its engineers, their blindness; show all that such an inhuman rigor destroys: men, couples. And then bring out your flag, save the army by progress, attach the former's grandeur to the latter's triumph (*Les Cyclones*, a novel by Jules Roy).

Lastly, the Church: speak in a sufficiently brilliant way of its hypocrisy, the narrow-mindedness of its bigots, show how all this can be murderous, hide none of the miseries of the faith. And then, in extremis, reveal that the Letter, however ungrateful, is a way to salvation for even its victims, and justify such moral rigorism by the sanctity of those it overwhelms (*The Living Room*, a play by Graham Greene).

This is a kind of homeopathy: doubts about the Church, about the Army, are cured by the very evils of the Church and the Army. A contingent evil is inoculated to forestall or cure an essential evil. To take arms against the inhumanity of the values of Order, one supposes, is a common disease, quite natural, pardonable; not to be directly opposed, rather to be exorcised as if one were possessed: one shows the patient the representation of his sickness, one leads him to know the very countenance of his rebellion, and the rebellion vanishes all the more surely if set aside, distanced, Order being no more than a Manichaean mixture, hence fatal, winning on all counts and consequently beneficent. The imminent evil of servitude is redeemed by the transcendent good of religion, of fatherland, of the Church, etc. A small dose of evil "avowed" spares the recognition of a great deal of evil hidden.

One recognizes in advertising a novelistic schema which neatly employs this new vaccine. Consider the Astra advertisements. The little story always begins with an indignant outcry against margarine: "A mousse made with margarine? Unthinkable! Your uncle will be furious!" And then eyes are opened; conscience is soothed; margarine is a delicious nourishment, pleasant-tasting, digestible, economical, always useful. The moral at the end is familiar: "And now you're rid of a prejudice that used to cost you dear!" In the same way Order delivers you from your "progressive" prejudices. The Army an ideal value? Unthinkable! Look at all that bullying, that militarism, that inevitable blindness of the leaders. The Church infallible? Unfortunately that's very doubtful: look at its bigots, its powerless priests, its murderous conformism. And then common sense adds up its columns: What are those minor clinkers within any Order compared to its advantages? They're all well worth the cost of one vaccine. What does it matter, *after all*, that margarine is nothing but grease if its efficiency is superior to that of butter? What does it matter, *after all*, that an Order is somewhat brutal, somewhat blind, if it allows us to live inexpensively? There we are, rid of a prejudice that used to cost us dear, too dear, that used to cost us too many scruples, too many rebellions, too many battles, and too much solitude.

CONJUGALS

A lot of marrying goes on in our tabloids these days: grand weddings (Marshal Juin's son and the daughter of a Finance Inspector, the duc de Castries's daughter and the baron de Vitrolles, love matches (Miss Europe '53 and her childhood friend), (future) weddings of stars (Marlon Brando and Josiane Mariani, Raf Vallone and Michèle Morgan). Naturally, all these weddings don't come about at the same instant, for their mythological virtue is not always the same.

The grand wedding (aristocratic or bourgeois) corresponds to the ancestral and exotic function of the nuptial: both potlatch between two families and spectacle of that potlatch in the eyes of the crowd surrounding the consumption of riches. The crowd is necessary; hence the grand wedding is always celebrated in the public square, in front of the church; it is here that money is burned, and with it the assembly is blinded; into the brazier are cast uniforms and dress suits, steel and decorations (of the Legion of Honor), the Army and the Government, all the high offices of the bourgeois theater, military attachés (eyes shining with emotion), a Captain of the Legion (himself blind), and the Parisian crowd (deeply moved). Power, the Law, the mind, the heart, all these values of Order are flung together in the nuptial, consumed in the potlatch but thereby instituted more solidly than ever, heavily prevaricating the

See illustrations 2 and 3.

natural wealth of every union. A "grand wedding," it must not be forgotten, is a fruitful operation of bookkeeping which consists in shifting to nature's credit the heavy debit of Order, absorbing in the public euphoria of the Couple "the sad and savage history of men": Order is fed on Love; mendacity, exploitation, cupidity, all social bourgeois evils "funded" by the truth of the couple.

The union of Sylviane Carpentier, Miss Europe '53, and her childhood friend, the electrician Michel Warembourg, permits the development of a different image, that of the happy hearth. Thanks to her title, Sylviane would have been able to manage the brilliant career of a star, to travel, make movies, earn a great deal of money; wise and modest, she has renounced "ephemeral fame" and, faithful to her past, she has married an electrician from Palaiseau. The young spouses are here presented to us in the postnuptial phase of their union, in the process of establishing the felicity of their habits and installing their lives in the anonymity of minor comfort: the two-rooms-and-kitchen are furnished and arranged; they breakfast together, go to the movies or the market.

Here the operation evidently consists in putting at the service of the petit bourgeois model all the glory of the couple: that this happiness, by definition a meager affair, can nevertheless be *chosen* to sustain the millions of French men and women who participate in this condition. The petite bourgeoisie can be proud of Silviane Carpentier's adherence, just as in other days the Church derived power and prestige from some aristocratic taking-of-the-veil: the modest wedding of Miss Europe, her touching entrance, after such fame, in the two-rooms-and-kitchen in Palaiseau are also M. de Rancé choosing La Trappe, or Louise de La Vallière, Carmel: great glory for La Trappe, for Carmel, and for Palaiseau.

Love-stronger-than-glory here renews the morale of the social status quo: it is not wise to leave one's condition, it is glorious to return to it. In exchange for which, the condition itself can develop its advantages, which are essentially those of flight. Happiness, in this universe, is to act out a sort of domestic confinement: "psychological" questionnaires, shortcuts, household devices, and timesavers, that whole implemental paradise of magazines, like *Elle* or *L'Express*, which glorifies the closure of the hearth, its aproned and slippered introversion, everything which busies home life, infantilizes it, accentuates its innocence, and severs it from a widened social responsibility. "Two hearts, one hearth." The world still exists, of course, but love spiritualizes the hearth and the hearth masks the slum: indigence is exorcised by its ideal image, poverty.

As for the marriage of the stars, it is presented chiefly under its aspect of futurity. What it promotes is the virtually pure myth of the Couple (at least in the Vallone-Morgan case; for Brando, the social elements still prevail, as we shall soon see). Conjugality risks being superficial here, relegated without precaution to a problematic future: Marlon Brando *is going to* marry Josiane Mariani (but only after he has a dozen new films in the can); Michèle Morgan and Raf Vallone *may* become another married couple (but first of all, Michèle must get her divorce). Chance is always seen as a sure thing, to the point where its importance is marginal, subject to that very general convention which holds that marriage, publicly, is always the "natural" finality of the couple's situation. What matters is, on the security of a hypothetical marriage, to make the couple's carnal reality pass for the real thing.

The (future) marriage of Marlon Brando is still loaded with social complexes: it is the match of the shepherdess and her lord. Josiane, daughter of a "modest" fisherman from Bandol, is an accomplished young woman, since she has completed the first part of her high school degree and speaks English fluently (theme of the bride's "perfections")—Josiane has attracted the most mysterious man of the cinema, a sort of compromise between Hippolyte and some solitary and savage sultan. But this ravishment of a modest French girl by the Hollywood monster is complete only in its reciprocal movement: the hero enchained by love seems to transfer all his glamour to the little French town, the beach, the market, the cafés and grocery stores of Bandol; as a matter of fact, it is Marlon who is impregnated by the petit bourgeois archetype of all the readers of glossy monthlies. "Marlon," says *Une Semaine du monde*, "accompanied by his (future) mother-in-law and his (future) bride, like any petit bourgeois Frenchman, enjoys a peaceful predinner stroll." Reality imposes on the dream its decor and its class status, as today's French petite bourgeoisie manifestly enjoys a phase of mythic imperialism. To the first degree, Marlon's prestige is of a muscular, Venusian order; to the second degree, it is of a social order: Marlon is consecrated by Bandol, much more than he consecrates the town.

DOMINICI, OR THE TRIUMPH OF LITERATURE

The whole Dominici trial was performed according to a certain idea of psychology, which happens as if by accident to be that of the proprieties of bourgeois literature. Material proofs being uncertain or contradictory, recourse was had to mental proofs; and where to find these if not in the very mentality of the accusers? Therefore the motives and sequence of actions were reconstructed with a free hand but without the shadow of a doubt; a procedure like that of those archaeologists who gather old stones from all over an excavation site, and with their quite modern cement erect a delicate wayside altar to Sesostris, or even reconstruct a religion dead for two thousand years by consulting the remains of universal wisdom, which is in fact only their own wisdom elaborated in the academies of the Third Republic.

A comparable procedure was applied to obtain old Dominici's "psychology." Was it actually his? No one knows. But we can be sure it was the psychology of the Presiding Judge of the Assizes or of the Public Prosecutor. Do these two mentalities, that of the old peasant from the Alps and that of the

---

Gaston Dominici, a farmer in the southern Alps, was accused of the murder of Sir Jack Drummond, his wife, and their daughter, found dead in August 1952 near La Grand'Terre, home of the Dominicis. Both the police investigation and the conduct of the trial were widely criticized. Gaston Dominici was sentenced first to death, then to life imprisonment. President Charles de Gaulle later ordered Dominici's release.

judiciary personnel, function in the same way? Nothing is less likely. Yet it is in the name of a "universal" psychology that old Dominici was condemned: descending from the charming empyrean of bourgeois novels and essentialist psychology, Literature has just condemned a man to the scaffold. Listen to the Public Prosecutor: *Sir Jack Drummond, as I have told you, was afraid. But he knows that the best way to defend yourself is always to attack. He therefore hurls himself on this savage creature and takes the old man by the throat. Not one word is exchanged between them. But for Gaston Dominici, the simple fact that someone wants to hold him down by the shoulders is unthinkable. He is not physically able to oppose the strength that is suddenly pitted against him.* This is plausible, as the temple of Sesostris is plausible, or the Literature of Monsieur Genevoix. Merely to base an archaeological reconstruction or a novel on a "Why not?" harms no one. But Justice? Periodically, some trial, and not necessarily a fictional one like the one in Camus's *L'Étranger*, comes to remind you that Justice is always ready to lend you a spare brain in order to condemn you without a second thought, and that like Corneille it depicts you as you ought to be and not as you are.

This appearance of Justice in the world of the accused is possible thanks to an intermediary myth, always made good use of by officialdom, whether the Court of Assizes or literary tribunals: the myth of the transparency and the universality of language. The Presiding Assize Judge, who reads *Le Figaro*, obviously has no scruples about exchanging words with an old "illiterate" goatherd. Don't they share the same language, and the clearest one there is, French? Wonderful assurance of a classical education, where shepherds converse with judges without embarrassment! But here, too, behind the prestigious (and grotesque) morality of Latin translations and French essays, a man's head is at stake.

Still, the disparity of languages, their impenetrable barriers, have been emphasized by several journalists, and Jean Giono himself has given numerous examples of this in his accounts of court sessions. Such observations show that there is no need to imagine mysterious barriers, misunderstandings à la Kafka. No, syntax, vocabulary, most of the elementary, analytical materials of language blindly seek one another without ever meeting, but no one pays the slightest attention: *Etes-vous allé au pont? —Allée? Il n'y a pas d'allée, je le sais, j'y suis été.** Of course everyone pretends to believe that it is the official language which is common sense, Dominici's being merely an ethnological variant, picturesque in its poverty. Yet this juridical language is just as peculiar, loaded with unreal clichés, a language for school compositions, not for concrete psychology (unless the majority of students are obliged, alas, to receive the psychology of language they are taught). The fact of the matter is that there are two particular uses of language confronting each other. But one has honors, law, and force on its side.

And this "universal" language comes at just the right time to reinforce the psychology of the masters: it permits that psychology always to take other men as objects, to describe and to condemn at the same time. It is an adjectival psychology, knowing only how to endow its victims with attributes, being ignorant of their actions except for the culpable categories into which they are made to fit. These categories are those of classical comedy or of a treatise of graphology: boastful, irritable, selfish, cunning, lecherous, hard; in its eyes a man exists only by the "character" which designates him to society as an object of more or less easy assimilation, as a subject of a more or less respectful submission. Utilitarian, setting aside any state of consciousness, such psychology yet claims to base any

*"Did you go [*allé*] to the bridge?" "Alley? There is no alley. I know that for a fact, I've been there."

action on a previous interiority, it postulates "the soul"; it judges man as a "conscience," without being troubled by having previously described him as an object.

Now this particular psychology, in whose name you can easily be decapitated, comes straight out of our traditional literature, which is called in bourgeois style the literature of the Human Document. It is in the name of the human document that old Dominici was condemned. Justice and literature have entered into an alliance, have exchanged their old techniques, thereby revealing their basic identity and impudently compromising one another. Behind the judges in curule thrones, the writers (Giono, Salacrou). At the prosecutor's desk, a magistrate? No, an "extraordinary storyteller," endowed with an "incontestable wit" and a "dazzling verve" (to quote the shocking *satisfecit* accorded to the prosecutor by *Le Monde*). Even the police here are seen to be practicing their style. (A Police Superintendent: "Never have I seen such a jocular liar, such a wary gambler, such a merry storyteller, such a crafty trickster, such a giddy septuagenarian, such a self-assured despot, such a cunning calculator, such a deceptive dissimulator . . . Gaston Dominici is a quick-change artist juggling with human souls and bestial thoughts. He has not a few faces, this false patriarch of the Grand'Terre, he has a hundred!" Antitheses, metaphors, flights of oratory, it is the whole of classical rhetoric which accuses the old shepherd here. Justice has clapped on the mask of realist literature, of the rustic tale, while literature itself came into court in search of new "human" documents, innocently culling on the accused's countenance and on those of the suspects the reflexion of a psychology which, however, it had been the first to impose on them all by the arm of the law.

Only, confronting the literature of repletion (always passed off as the literature of the "real," of the "human") there is a literature of anguish: the Dominici trial has also been that literature. There have not been here only writers hungering for reality and storytellers whose "dazzling verve" takes off a man's head; whatever the degree of the accused's guilt, there has also been the spectacle of a terror by which all of us are threatened, that of being judged by a power which will hear only the language it lends us. We are all potential Dominicis, not murderers but as the accused deprived of language or, worse, dressed up, humiliated, condemned in that of our accusers. To steal his language from a man in the very name of language: every legal murder begins here.

ICONOGRAPHY OF ABBÉ PIERRE

His myth has one priceless asset: his looks. A fine head, which offers unmistakable signs of apostleship: the compassionate expression, the Franciscan haircut, the missionary's beard, all confirmed by the worker-priest's duffle coat and the pilgrim's staff. Every winning clue to both Legend and Modernity.

That haircut, for example: rather closely sheared, without affectation and above all without any particular shape, indeed quite artless, not even trying for technique, a sort of zero degree of barbering; of course hair must be cut, but at least this inevitable operation need not imply any particular mode of existence: let it be without being something special. Abbé Pierre's haircut, visibly conceived to achieve a neutral equilibrium between short hair (an indispensable convention to avoid notice) and shaggy hair (a suitable condition to manifest scorn for other conventions), here joins the capillary archetype of sanctity: the saint is above all a being without formal context; the idea of fashion is antipathetic to the idea of sanctity.

But where things get complicated—unknown to the abbé, one hopes—is that here as elsewhere neutrality ends up by functioning as the *sign* of neutrality, and if you really wanted to go unnoticed you'd be back where you started. The zero haircut, then, quite simply *means* Franciscanism; at first conceived negatively in order not to contradict the appearance of

---

See illustration 4.

sainthood, it quite soon becomes a superlative mode of signification, it *disguises* the abbé as Saint Francis. Hence the rising
iconographic fortune of this haircut in magazines and films
(where it will suffice for the actor Reybaz to adopt it in order
to be completely identified with the abbé).

The same mythological circuit operates in the case of the
beard, which may of course be no more than the attribute of a
free man, detached from the everyday conventions of our
world and reluctant to waste his time shaving: a fascination
with charity may reasonably lead to such kinds of contempt;
but we are obliged to notice that the ecclesiastical beard too
has a little mythology of its own. For among priests it is not by
chance that one is bearded or not; beards are chiefly the attribute of missionaries or of Capuchins, they cannot do otherwise
than *signify* apostolate and poverty; they somewhat abstract
their wearer from the secular clergy: clean-shaven priests are
supposedly more temporal, bearded ones more evangelical: the
wicked Frolo was clean-shaven, good Father Foucauld bearded;
behind a beard, one belongs a little less to one's bishop, to the
hierarchy, to the political Church; one seems freer, more independent, more primitive perhaps, benefiting from the prestige of the first hermits, availing oneself of the blunt candor
of the founders of monachism, depositories of the spirit against
the letter: wearing a beard means exploring with the same
conviction the slums, the realm of the ancient Britons, or
Nyasaland.

Obviously the problem is not to know how this forest of
signs has been able to cover the Abbé (though it is actually
rather surprising that the attributes of goodness should be
like some sort of transferable coins, objects of easy exchange
between reality, the Abbé Pierre of *Match*, and fiction, the
Abbé Pierre of film, and that in a word the apostolate should
present itself from the very first minute quite prepared, entirely equipped for the great voyage of reconstitutions and

legends). I merely wonder at the enormous consumption of such signs that the public makes. I see people reassured by the spectacular identity of a morphology and of a vocation; in no doubt about the latter because it recognizes the former; having no more access to the real experience of the apostolate than by its bric-a-brac, and growing quite used to acquiring a clear conscience by merely looking in the shopwindows of sanctity; and I'm troubled that a society which so greedily consumes the posters of charity forgets to ask itself questions about its consequences, its uses, and its limits. And I begin to wonder if the lovely and touching iconography of the Abbé Pierre is not the alibi by which a sizable part of the nation authorizes itself, once again, to substitute the signs of charity for the reality of justice.

NOVELS AND CHILDREN

According to *Elle*, which lately assembled in the same photograph seventy women novelists, the *femme de lettres* constitutes a remarkable zoological species which produces both novels and children. *Elle*'s list includes, for example: *Jacqueline Lenoir (two daughters, one novel); Marina Grey (one son, one novel); Nicole Dutreil (two sons, four novels)*, etc.

Which means? This: to write is a glorious but bold undertaking; the writer is an "artist" who is granted a certain right to bohemianism. Since artists are duty-bound, at least in *Elle*'s France, to justify their qualifications, their services must of course be remunerated: they are tacitly accorded the right to lead some sort of personal life. But make no mistake: women must not suppose they can enjoy the advantages of this arrangement without first submitting to the eternal status of femininity. Women are on earth to give men children; let them write all they like, let them ornament their condition, but on no account must they leave it: their biblical destiny is not to be disturbed by the advantage which has been shared with them, and they must forthwith pay, by the tribute of their maternity, for this bohemianism naturally attached to the writer's life.

Therefore be courageous, be free: play at being men, write as they do; but never get far away from them; live under their gaze, compensate for your novels by your children; enjoy your freedom, but be sure to come back to your condition. A novel, a child, a little feminism, a little conjugality, fasten art's adventure to the solid pillars of the home: both will greatly profit from the reciprocation; where myths are concerned, mutual help is always fruitful.

For instance, the Muse will bestow her sublimity on the humblest household functions; and in return, as a sort of thanks for these good offices, the myth of natality will lend the Muse, whose reputation is sometimes rather licentious, the guarantee of her respectability, the touching decor of the nursery. And so all is for the best in the best of worlds—*Elle*'s world: women, be confident you can very likely accede as well as men to the superior status of creation. But husbands too should quickly be reassured: their wives will not be taken away from them for all that, but remain no less a natural and available genitrix. *Elle* puts on its nimble show right out of Molière, says Yes on one side and No on the other, careful to upset no one; like Don Juan between his two peasant girls, *Elle* says to women: you're worth just as much as men; and to men: your wives will never be anything but women.

At first men seem absent from this double parturition; children and novels appear to come by themselves, and both belong only to the mother; well, after seeing seventy editions of works and offspring in the same parentheses, you might suppose they were all fruits of the imagination and of dreams, miraculous products of an ideal parthenogenesis which would present a woman with both the Balzacian joys of creation and the tender joys of maternity. Where is the man in this family portrait? Nowhere and everywhere, like a sky, a horizon, an authority which simultaneously determines and limits a condition. Such is the world of *Elle*: here women are always a homogeneous species, a constituted body jealous of its privileges, even more enamored of its servitudes; here men are never on the inside, femininity is pure, free, powerful; but men are everywhere outside, exerting pressure on *all* sides, making everything exist; they are eternally the creative absence, that of the Racinian god: a world without men but entirely constituted by the male gaze, the feminine world of *Elle* is precisely that of the gynoeceum.

In all of *Elle*'s functions we find this double movement: close the gynoeceum, then and only then release women inside. Love, work, write, be *femmes de lettres* or businesswomen, but always remember that men exist, and that you are not made as they are: your order is free on condition that it depends on his; your freedom is a luxury, possible only if you first acknowledge the obligations of your nature. Write if you like, we shall always be quite proud; but don't forget, on the other hand, to produce children, for that is your destiny. A Jesuit morality: come to terms with the morality of your condition, but never compromise about the dogma on which it rests.

TOYS

French toys are the best example one can find that toys are essentially an adult microcosm; all are miniature reproductions of human objects, as if to the public eye the child were, all told, nothing but a littler man, a homunculus who must be furnished with objects his own size.

Invented forms are very rare: a few sets of blocks, appealing to a passion for construction, offer the only dynamic options. For the rest, the French toy *always signifies something*, and that something is always entirely socialized, constituted by the myths or techniques of modern adult life: the Army, Broadcasting, the Post Office, Medicine (miniature instrument kits, operating rooms for dolls), School, Hairdressing (dryers for permanent waves), Aviation (parachutists), Transportation (trains, cars, motorcycles, gas stations), Science (Martian toys).

The fact that French toys *literally* prefigure the universe of adult functions can only prepare the child to accept them all, constituting for him even before he can think about it the alibi of a Nature which has created for all time soldiers, postmen, and Vespas. The toy here delivers the catalog of everything the grown-up does not find surprising: war, bureaucracy, ugliness, Martians, etc. But it is not so much imitation which is the sign of abdication, as its literalness: the French toy is like a shrunken Jivaro head, where you can find in an object the size of an apple the adult's hair and the adult's wrinkles. There exist, for example, dolls that urinate; they have an esophagus, and they can be made to drink from a bottle, they then wet their nappies; soon, I have no doubt, the milk in their belly will turn to water. By which means the little girl can be prepared for household causality, "conditioned" for her future role as mother. Only, confronted with this universe of faithful and complicated household objects, the child cannot constitute himself as anything but an owner, a user, never as a creator; he does not invent the world, he utilizes it; gestures are prepared for him without adventure, without surprise, and without joy. He is turned into a little stay-at-home householder who needs not even invent the springs of adult causality; they are furnished for him ready-made: all he has to do is help himself, he is never given anything he must get through from start to finish. The most elementary set of building blocks, if not too refined, implies an altogether different apprenticeship to the world: with them the child creates no significant objects, to him it matters little that they have no grown-up name: his actions are not those of a user but those of a demiurge: he creates forms which walk, which roll, he creates a life, not property; objects move of their own accord, they are no longer an inert, complicated substance in the palm of his hand. But this is now a rare event: the French toy is usually a toy of imitation, meant to make child users, not creative children.

The embourgeoisement of the toy is recognizable not only from its forms, all functional, but from its substance as well. Contemporary toys are made of unpromising materials, products of chemistry, not of nature. Many are now molded from elaborate compounds; the plastics out of which they are made look both crude and hygienic, they eliminate the pleasure, the gentleness, the humanity of touch. An alarming sign is the gradual disappearance of wood, an ideal substance for its firmness and comparative softness, the natural warmth of its contact; in whatever form it takes, wood avoids the wounding quality of overly sharp angles, the chemical chill of metal;

when the child handles it and bumps or drops it, a wooden toy neither vibrates nor grates, it makes a sound that is both muffled and distinct; wood is a familiar and poetic substance which allows the child a continuity of contact with the tree, the table, the floor. Wood neither wounds nor goes to pieces; it doesn't break, it wears down and can last a long time, can live with the child, gradually modifying relations of hand and object; if it dies, it is by diminishing, not by swelling, like those mechanical toys which vanish under the hernia of a broken spring. Wood makes essential objects, lasting objects. Yet there are scarcely any wooden toys left, like those sheepfolds from the Vosges, only possible, it's true, in the days of craftsmen. Henceforth toys will be chemical, in substance and in color; their very material introduces us to a coenesthesia of use, not of pleasure. Such toys die, moreover, very quickly, and once dead, they have no posthumous life for the child.

PARIS NOT FLOODED

Despite the difficulties or the disasters it may have inflicted on thousands of French people, the flood of January 1955 was actually more of a celebration than a catastrophe.

First of all, it displaced certain objects, thereby refreshing the perception of the world by introducing into it unaccustomed and yet explicable points of view: one saw cars reduced to their roofs, streetlamps truncated so that only their tops remained above the surface like water lilies, houses cut up like children's blocks, a cat marooned for several days in a tree. All these everyday objects suddenly seemed separated from their roots, deprived of that reasonable substance par excellence, Earth. This rupture had the merit of remaining curious, without being magically threatening: the sheet of water behaved like a successful but familiar special effect, people had the pleasure of seeing certain shapes modified but on the whole "natural," their minds could remain fixed on the effect without regressing in anguish toward the obscurity of causes. The rising waters overwhelmed the everyday optic without diverting it toward the fantastic; objects were partially obliterated, not deformed: the spectacle was singular but reasonable. Any rather ample rupture of the everyday introduces festivity: now the rising waters not only selected and displaced certain objects, they upset the very coenesthesia of the landscape, the

See illustration 5.

ancestral organism of horizons: the habitual lines of the ca-
dastre, the curtains of trees, the rows of houses, the streets,
the riverbed itself, that angular stability which so well prepares
the shapes of property, all that was erased, extended from angle to plane; no more roads or riverbanks, no more directions;
a level surface going nowhere, thereby suspending human becoming, detaching it from any right decision, from a utensility
of sites.

The most troubling phenomenon is certainly the river's
very disappearance: the actual cause of all this disturbance no
longer exists, the water takes no course, the river's ribbon,
that elementary form of all geographical perception, of which
children, precisely, are so fond, shifts from a line to a plane,
the accidents of space now have no context, there is no longer
a hierarchy among the river, the road, the fields, the scree, the
empty lots; the panoramic view loses its major power, which is
to organize space as a juxtaposition of functions. Hence it is to
the very center of the optic reflexes that the rising water bears
its disturbance. Yet this disturbance is not *visually* threatening
(I'm talking about the press photos, sole means of the flood's
truly collective consummation): the appropriation of space is
suspended, perception is astonished, but the total sensation
remains gentle, peaceful, immobile, and friendly; one's gaze
is put into infinite dilution; the rupture of quotidian vision is
far from the order of tumult: this is a mutation of which one
sees only the completed version, thereby doing away with its
horror.

To this pacification of vision, engaged by the overflow of
calm rivers in a suspension of the functions and the *names* of
terrestrial topography, corresponds of course a whole happy
myth of retrogradation: examining photographs of the flood,
each spectator feels himself conveyed by proxy. Whence the
great success of scenes showing boats moving down streets:
such scenes are numerous, newspapers and readers have shown

their eagerness to enjoy them. This is because we are seeing fulfilled in reality the great mythic and childish dream of walking on water. After millennia of navigation, the boat still remains a surprising object: it produces desires, passions, dreams: children in their play or workers fascinated by a passing steamer see it as the instrument of deliverance, the always astonishing solution of a problem inexplicable to common sense: to walk on water. The flood revives this theme, makes it a lively frame for the everyday street: the housewife takes a boat to the grocer, the curé travels by canoe to his church, a family goes shopping by dinghy.

To this kind of unlikelihood is added the euphoria of reconstructing one's village or neighborhood, of giving it new roads and somehow making use of it as a theatrical site, varying the childish myth of the hut or cabin by the arduous approach to the-house-as-refuge protected by water itself, like a moated castle or a Venetian palazzo. Paradoxically, the flood has created a world that is more accessible, controllable with the same kind of delectation a child takes in arranging his toys, experimenting with them, enjoying them anew. Houses are now no more than cubes, rails are isolated lines, herds of cattle shifting masses, and the little boat, superlative toy of the childhood universe, becomes the means of possessing this now rearranged, outspread, and no longer rooted space.

Turning from myths of sensation to myths of value, the flood retains the same attitude of euphoria: the press easily develops a dynamic of solidarity and quite spontaneously reconstitutes the rising waters as an event unifying mankind. This essentially relates to the *foreseeable* nature of the problem: for instance, there was something warm and active in the way newspapers assigned *in advance* the day of the rising water's maximum height; the virtually scientific delay imparted to the disaster's attack united people in a rational elaboration of the remedy: dikes, landfills, evacuations. It is the same kind of industrious euphoria which brings in a harvest or even a laundry before a storm, which raises a drawbridge in an adventure novel, in short, combats nature by the sole weapon of time.

Threatening Paris, the flood even acquired something of the quality of the myth of '48: Parisians raised "barricades," defended their city by cobblestones against the enemy waters. This mode of legendary resistance proved very seductive, sustained by a whole imagery of barrier walls, glorious trenches, ramparts of sand erected by children on the beach in their struggle for time against the tides. This seemed nobler than pumping out cellars, an activity the newspapers could not celebrate to great effect, the concierges failing to see the point of checking the water's onset by dumping it back into the flooding river. Better to develop the image of an armed mobilization, the teamwork of troops, motorized life rafts, rescues of "children, old people, and invalids," the biblical stabling of herds of cattle, all the frenzy of Noah filling the Ark. For the Ark is a happy myth: in it humanity stands aloof from the elements, concentrates and elaborates the necessary consciousness of its own powers, making disaster itself give evidence that the world is manageable.

BICHON AMONG THE BLACKS

Match has told us a tale which says a lot about the petit bourgeois myth of Blacks: a family of young academics has been exploring Cannibal country to do some painting; they've brought
along their seven-month-old son, Bichon. A good deal of en-
thusiasm is lavished on the courage of all three.

First of all, nothing is more irritating than heroism without
an object. It is a serious matter for a society to start developing
the *forms* of its virtues gratuitously. If the dangers incurred by
young Bichon (floods, wild animals, diseases, etc.) were real, it
was simply stupid to impose them, on the sole pretext of going to Africa to paint and to acquire the dubious distinction
of spreading on canvas "a debauch of sun and light"; it would
be even more reprehensible to pass off such stupidity as a fine
piece of audacity, so decorative *and* so touching. One sees
how courage functions here: it is a formal and hollow act (the
more unmotivated it is, the more respect it inspires); we are at
the heart of Boy Scout civilization, where the code of sentiments and values is completely detached from concrete problems of solidarity or progress. It is the old myth of "character,"
in other words, "training." Bichon's exploits are of the same
sort as spectacular feats of mountain climbing: demonstra-
tions of an ethical order, which receive their ultimate value from
the publicity they are given. In our culture, there frequently

See illustration 6.

corresponds to the socialized forms of collective sport a superlative form of star sport: here physical effort does not institute
man's apprenticeship to his group, but instead an ethic of vanity, an exoticism of endurance, a minor mystique of risk, mon-
strously severed from any concern with sociability.

The trip Bichon's parents made into a region situated quite
vaguely and significantly labeled the Country of the Red Ne-
groes, a kind of fictional site whose actual characteristics are
skillfully attenuated but whose legendary name already suggests a terrifying ambiguity between the color of their painted
skins and the human blood they supposedly drink—this jour-
ney is presented to us in the vocabulary of conquest: our travelers set out unarmed, no doubt, but "armed with palette and
brush," just as if the occasion were a hunting safari or a military expedition, made under ungrateful material conditions
(the heroes are always poor, our bureaucratic society not favor-
ing noble departures) but rich in courage—and in a superb (or
grotesque) uselessness. Young Bichon himself plays the Parsifal
role, and with his blondness, his innocence, his curls, and his
smile confronts the infernal world of black and red skins with
all their scarifications and their hideous masks. Naturally it is
the white child's gentleness which is victorious: Bichon sub-
dues "the man-eaters" and becomes their idol (Whites are decidedly cut out to be gods). Bichon is a good little Frenchman,
he assuages and overcomes the savages without firing a shot: at
the age of two, instead of going to the Bois de Boulogne, he
is already working for his country, just like his papa, who, for
some unknown reason, shares the life of a troop of legion-
naires and tracks down "looters" in the bush.

We have already divined the image of the Negro taking
shape throughout this quite tonic little tale: at first he is terrifying, he is a cannibal; and if Bichon is considered heroic, it
is because he risks actually being eaten. Without the implicit
presence of this risk, the tale would lose all its shock value, the

reader would not be scared, hence many are the confrontations where the white child is alone, abandoned, insouciant, and exposed to a circle of potentially threatening Blacks (the only completely reassuring image of the Negro will be that of the *boy*, the domesticated barbarian, coupled, moreover, with that other fixture of all good African stories: the *thieving boy* who disappears with the master's belongings). With each image, one shudders of course at what could have happened: it is never specified, the narration is "objective"; but actually it rests on the pathetic collusion of white flesh and black skin, of innocence and cruelty, of spirituality and magic: Beauty enchains the Beast, Daniel is nuzzled by lions, and a civilization of the soul subjects the barbarism of instinct.

The profound resourcefulness of Operation Bichon is always to reveal the Black world through the eyes of the white child: everything here looks like a puppet show. And since this reduction exactly corresponds to the image common sense provides of exotic arts and costumes, the reader of *Match* is confirmed in his infantile vision, installed a little deeper in that impotence to imagine *the other*, which I have already indicated apropos of petit bourgeois myths. Indeed, the Black has no full and autonomous life: he is a peculiar, a bizarre object, reduced to a parasitical function, which is to divert the white man by his vaguely threatening baroque: Africa is a more or less dangerous puppet show.

And now, if you will be so good as to contrast this general imagery (*Match*: about one and a half million readers) with the ethnologists' efforts to demystify the Negro phenomenon, their rigorous precautions, long since observed when obliged to use such ambiguous notions as "Primitive" or "Archaic," the intellectual probity of men like Mauss, Lévi-Strauss, or Leroi-Gourhan at grips with old, scarcely camouflaged racial terms, you will have a better understanding of one of our major servitudes: the oppressive divorce of knowledge and mythology.

Science proceeds straight and fast in its course, but collective representations do not follow suit, they are centuries behind, kept stagnant in their errors by the press and by the values of Order.

We still live in a pre-Voltairean mentality; that is what must be constantly repeated. For since the time of Montesquieu or of Voltaire, if we were astonished by the Persians or the Hurons, at least it was to grant them the benefits of ingenuity. Today, Voltaire would not write the adventures of Bichon the way *Match* has done: instead he would imagine some cannibal (or Korean) Bichon contending with the napalmed puppet show of the West.

A SYMPATHETIC WORKER

Kazan's film *On the Waterfront* is a good example of mystification. It concerns, as you doubtless know, a handsome, indolent, slightly brutal longshoreman (Marlon Brando), whose consciousness is gradually awakened to Love and to the Church (in the form of a shock priest, Spellman style). Since this awakening coincides with the elimination of a fraudulent and abusive union and appears to involve the longshoremen in resisting their exploiters, some viewers have supposed we've been shown a courageous film, a "leftist" film determined to reveal the worker's problem to the American public.

Actually, we are dealing once again with that truth vaccine whose very modern mechanism I have indicated apropos of other American films: a small gang of mobsters is made to symbolize the entire body of employers, and once this minor disorder is acknowledged and dealt with like a trivial and disgraceful pustule, the real problem is evaded, is never even named, and is thereby exorcised.

Yet it is sufficient to describe objectively the "roles" in Kazan's film to establish its mystifying power beyond a doubt: the proletariat here is constituted by a group of weaklings submitting to a servitude they clearly recognize but lack the courage to shake off; the (capitalist) State is identical with absolute Justice and is the only possible recourse against the crime of exploitation: if the worker can make contact with the State (for instance, by communicating with the police and its investigative agencies), he is saved. As for the Church, in its phony modernist guise, it is merely a mediating power between the worker's constitutive poverty and the boss State's paternal power. Ultimately, moreover, this minor irritation of justice and conscience is soon resolved in the grand stability of a beneficent order, in which the workers resume their labor, the bosses fold their arms, and the priests bless both sides in their manifestly just functions.

It is the ending, however, which betrays the film, at the very moment when many supposed Kazan had cunningly insinuated his progressivism: in the very last sequence we see Brando, by a superhuman effort, managing to present himself as a conscientious good worker to the boss waiting to meet with him. Now this boss is obviously a caricature, and the audience murmurs: See how Kazan has managed to ridicule the capitalists.

Here or nowhere is the occasion to apply the demystification method proposed by Brecht and to examine the consequences of the attachment we feel for the film's main character. It is obvious that Brando is our positive hero to whom, despite his faults, the public gives its heart, according to that participation phenomenon without which, in general, we are reluctant to consider any entertainment possible. When this hero, all the greater for having rediscovered his conscience and his courage, exhausted, injured, yet still tenacious, heads for the boss who will give him work, our communion knows no bounds, we identify ourselves totally and unhesitatingly with this new Christ and participate unreservedly in his Calvary. Yet Brando's painful Assumption actually conduces to the passive acknowledgment of the eternal boss: what is orchestrated for us here, despite all the caricatures, is the *restoration of order;* with Brando, with the longshoremen, with all the workers of America, we put ourselves, with a sense of victory and relief, back in the boss's hands which it serves no further purpose to portray as tainted: we have long since been snared in a fatal communion with this longshoreman who discovers a sense of social justice only to bestow it as a homage to American capital.

As we see, it is the *participational* nature of this scene which objectively makes it an episode of mystification. Trained to love Brando from the start, we can no longer at any point criticize him or even admit we are conscious of his objective stupidity. Now it is precisely against the danger of such mechanisms that Brecht proposed his method of *alienation*. Brecht would have asked Brando to *show* his naïveté, to make us understand that despite all the sympathy we may feel for his misfortunes, it is still more important that we see their causes and their remedies. We can sum up Kazan's mistake by saying that what should have been judged was much less the capitalist than Brando himself. For there is much more to expect from the rebellion of victims than from the caricature of their executioners.

GARBO'S FACE

Greta Garbo still belongs to that moment in cinema when the apprehension of the human countenance plunged crowds into the greatest perturbation, where people literally lost themselves in the human image as if in a philter, when the face constituted a sort of absolute state of the flesh which one could neither attain nor abandon. Some years earlier, Valentino's face caused suicides; Garbo's still participates in that same realm of *amour courtois* when the flesh develops certain mystical sentiments of perdition.

It is without a doubt an admirable face-as-object; in *Queen Christina*, a film shown again here in recent years, the star's makeup has the snowy density of a mask; it is not a painted face but a face in plaster, protected by the surface of its shadows and not by its lineaments; in all this fragile and compact snow, only the eyes, black as some strange pulp but not at all expressive, are two rather tremulous wounds. Even in its extreme beauty, this face not drawn but instead sculptured in something smooth and friable, which is to say both perfect and ephemeral, matches somehow Chaplin's flour-white complexion, those vegetally dark eyes, his totemic visage.

Now, the temptation of the total mask (the mask of antiquity, for example) may imply less the theme of secrecy (as is the case with the Italian half mask) than that of an archetype

---

See illustration 7.

of the human face. Garbo produced a sort of Platonic idea of
the human creature, which accounts for her own face being
virtually sexless without being at all "dubious." It's true that
the film (Queen Christina is alternately a woman and a young
cavalier) lends itself to this indeterminacy; but Garbo does not
give any kind of travestied performance; she is always herself,
frankly revealing under her crown or her wide-brimmed felt
hats the same countenance of snow and solitude. Her nick-
name, Divine, probably intended to suggest less a superlative
state of beauty than the essence of her corporeal person, descended from a heaven where things are formed and finished
with the greatest clarity. She herself knew this: How many
actresses have consented to let the crowd watch the disturbing
maturation of their beauty? Not Garbo: the Essence must not
degrade, her visage could never have any other reality than
that of its intellectual perfection, even more than its plastic
one. The Essence has gradually dimmed, progressively veiled
by dark glasses, hooded capes, and various exiles; but it has
never altered.

Still, in that deified countenance, something sharper than
a mask appears: a sort of deliberate and therefore human relation between the curve of the nostrils and the superciliary ar-
cade, a rare, individual function between two zones of the
face; the mask is merely an addition of lines, the face is above
all a thematic recall of the former to the latter. Garbo's face
represents that fragile moment when cinema is about to ex-
tract an existential beauty from an essential beauty, when the
archetype will be inflected toward the fascination of perish-
able figures, when the clarity of carnal essences will give way
to a lyric expression of Woman.

As a moment of transition, Garbo's face reconciles two iconographic ages, assures the passage from terror to charm. We
know that in our own moment we are at the other pole of this
evolution: Audrey Hepburn's face, for instance, is individualized

not only by its specific thematics (woman-as-child, woman-as-cat), but also by her person, by a virtually unique specification of the face, which has nothing essential left in it but is constituted by an infinite complexity of morphological functions. As a language, Garbo's singularity was of a conceptual order, Audrey Hepburn's of a substantial order. Garbo's face is an Idea, Hepburn's an Event.

POWER AND "COOL"

Our crime and detective films have now arrived at an adequate gestuary of "cool": slack-lipped molls exhaling their smoke rings under male assault; Olympian fingers snapping the clear and parsimonious signal for a burst of gunfire; imperturbable knitting continued by a gang boss's wife amid impossibly explosive circumstances . . . *Grisbi* had already institutionalized this gestuary by furnishing it the guarantee of utterly French ordinariness.

The gangster world is primarily a world of sangfroid. Phenomena which ordinary philosophy still judges to be considerable, such as the death of a man, are reduced to a blueprint, presented in the volume of a tiny gesture: a minor disturbance in the calm displacement of lines, two fingers snapped, and at the other end of the perceptive field a man falls in the same convention of movements. This universe of litotes, which is always constructed as an icy mockery of melodrama, is also, we know, the last universe of the fairy tale. The exiguity of the decisive gesture enjoys an entire mythological tradition, from the numen of the old gods, whose nod of the head would topple the destiny of mortals, to the touch of the fairy's (or the magician's) wand. Firearms have doubtless distanced death, but in a fashion so visibly rational that the gesture has had to be refined in order to manifest once again the presence of destiny, which precisely defines the "cool" of our gangsters: the residue of a tragic movement which succeeds in identifying gesture with action within the slenderest volume.

I shall insist further on the semantic precision of this world, on the spectacle's intellectual (and not just emotive) structure. The Colt's abrupt extraction from the jacket in an impeccable parable does not at all *signify* death, for usage has long since indicated that this is merely a threat, whose effect can be miraculously reversed: the revolver's emergence has no tragic value here, but only a cognitive one; it signifies the appearance of a new peripety, the gesture is argumentative, not strictly terrifying; it corresponds to a certain inflection of reasoning in a Marivaux comedy: the situation is altered; what had been the object of conquest is abruptly lost; the ballet of revolvers makes time more labile, arranging in the narrative's itinerary certain returns to zero, regressive leaps analogous to those of the Monopoly board. The Colt is language, its function is to maintain a pressure of life, to elude time's closure; it is Logos, not praxis.

The gangster's "cool" gesture has, on the contrary, all the concerted power of a halt; without any sort of excitement, swift in the infallible quest for its terminal point, it severs time and questions rhetoric. Any "cool" affirms that only silence is effective: knitting, smoking, raising a finger, all these operations impose the notion that real life is in silence, and that action has the rights of life and death over time. The spectator thereby has the illusion of a positive world which is modified only under the pressure of actions, never under that of words; if the gangster speaks, it is in images, for him language is only poetry, the world has in itself no demiurgic function: to speak is his way of being idle and of showing it. There is an essential universe which is that of well-oiled gestures, always halted at a specific and foreseen point, a sort of summa of pure efficacity: and then, over and above that, there are certain festoons of slang, which are like the useless (and thereby aristocratic) luxury of an economy whose sole exchange value is gesture.

But this gesture, in order to signify that it is identical with action, must refine any extravagance, compress itself to the perceptual sill of its existence; it must have no more than the density of a liaison between cause and effect; here "cool" is the most artful sign of efficacity; by it each of us regains the ideality of a world at the mercy of a purely human gestuary, a world which will no longer slacken under the fetters of language: gangsters and gods do not speak, they nod their heads and all is done.

WINE AND MILK

Wine is felt by the French nation to be a possession as much its own as its 360 kinds of cheese and its culture. It is a totem drink, corresponding to the milk of Dutch cows or to the tea ceremonially taken by the British royal family. Bachelard has already provided a "substantial psychoanalysis" of this liquid at the end of his essay on the reveries of the will, and shows that wine is the juice of the sun and the earth, that its basic state is not wet but dry, and that on this basis the mythic substance most contrary to it is water.

Actually, like every lively totem, wine supports a varied mythology which is not embarrassed by contradictions. This galvanic substance is always considered, for instance, the most effective of thirst quenchers—at least thirst serves as an initial alibi for its consumption ("It's thirsty weather"). In its red form it has, as a very old hypostasis, blood, that dense and vital fluid. As a matter of fact, its humoral form matters very little; above all, it is a conversion substance, capable of reversing states and situations, of extracting from objects their actual contraries: of making, for instance, a weakling strong, a chatterbox silent; whence its ancient alchemical heredity, its philosophical power to transmute or to create ex nihilo.

Being in essence a function, whose terms can change, wine

In 1954, President Pierre Mendès-France introduced a health campaign promoting milk to fight against malnutrition and alcoholism.

possesses apparently plastic powers: it can serve as an alibi for dreams as well as for reality, depending on the users of the myth. For the worker, wine will be a qualifier, a demiurgic facility for the task ("heart for the work"). For the intellectual, it will have the opposite function: the writer's "little white wine" or "Beaujolais" will be responsible for separating him from the all too natural world of cocktails and expensive drinks (the only ones that snobbishness attempts to offer him); wine will deliver him from myths, free him from his intellectuality, make him a proletarian as good as the rest; by wine the intellectual approaches a natural virility, believing he can thereby escape the curse a century and a half of romanticism still imposes on pure cerebrality (one of the favorite myths of the modern intellectual is the obsession with "having what counts").

But what is special to France is that the power of conversation is never openly given as a goal: other countries drink to get drunk, a procedure everyone acknowledges; in France intoxication is a consequence, never a goal; drinking is felt as the exposure of a pleasure, not as the necessary cause of a sought-for effect: wine is not only a philter but also a durational act of drinking: the gesture here has a decorative value, and wine's power is never separated from its modes of existence (contrary to whiskey, for example, drunk for its intoxication—"the most agreeable effects with the least painful aftereffects," gulped down and repeated, and whose administration is reduced to a causal act).

All of which is widely known, rehearsed a thousand times in folklore, proverbs, conversations, and literature. Yet this very universality involves a conformism: to believe wine is a coercive collective act; the Frenchman who keeps his distance from the myth exposes himself to minor but specific problems of integration, the first of which is precisely the obligation to explain himself. The principle of universality functions here in full, in the sense that society *labels* sick, infirm, or vicious anyone who does not believe in wine: such a person is not *comprehended* (in both the intellectual and spatial senses of the word). Conversely a diploma of proper integration is awarded to a practicing wine drinker: knowing *how to drink* is a national technique which serves to qualify the Frenchman, to prove at once his performative power, his control, and his sociability. Wine thus provides a collective morality, within which everything is redeemed: excesses, disasters, crimes are of course possible with wine, but not wickedness, perfidy, or ugliness; the evil it can engender is in the nature of fate and therefore escapes penalization, it is a theatrical evil, not a temperamental one.

Wine is socialized because it provides a basis not only for a morality but also for a decor; it embellishes the merest ceremonial occasions of French daily life, from a snack (the *gros rouge* with a piece of Camembert) to a feast, from a conversation at a bar to a speech at a banquet. It exalts every kind of atmosphere, in cold weather associates with every warming myth and in dog days with all the images of cool shade and refreshment. There is no situation of physical constraint (temperature, hunger, boredom, compulsion, disorientation) which fails to inspire dreams of wine. Combined as a basic substance with other alimentary figures, it can cover all a Frenchman's spaces and all his times. Once you reach a certain detailed awareness of everyday life, absence of wine is shocking, like something exotic: Monsieur Coty, early in his seven-year term as president of France, having allowed himself to be photographed at home in front of a coffee table where a bottle of beer seemed on this one occasion to be replacing the liter of red wine, the entire nation was upset; it was as intolerable as a bachelor king. Wine here was a part of the raison d'état.

Bachelard was certainly right to say that water was the opposite of wine: mythically, this is true; sociologically, at least today, it is less so; economic or historical circumstances have given this role to milk, which is now the true antiwine: and not only because of Monsieur Mendès-France (who had a deliberately mythological look when he drank his milk during speeches to the Chamber: drinking milk up there was like Popeye eating spinach) but also because, in the grand morphology of substances, milk is contrary to fire by its entire molecular density, by the creamy and therefore sopitive nature of its emulsive surface; wine is mutilating, surgical, it transmutes and brings to birth; milk is cosmetic, it fastens, covers up, restores. Moreover, its purity, associated with a child's innocence, is a sign of nonrevulsive, noncongestive strength, but calm, white, lucid, quite the equal of reality. Several American films, in which the tough yet pure hero did not hesitate to take a glass of milk before drawing his avenging Colt, have set the stage for this new Parsifalian myth: even more recently certain gangster and hoodlum circles in Paris have been seen occasionally drinking a strange milk-and-grenadine cocktail imported from America. But milk remains an exotic substance; wine is the national drink.

Actually, wine's mythology can help us understand the habitual ambiguity of our daily life. For it is true that wine is good, a fine substance, but it is no less true that its production is heavily involved in French capitalism, both that of private distillers and that of the big Algerian settlers who impose on the Muslims, on the very land of which they have been dispossessed, a crop for which they have no use, while they actually lack bread. There are indeed very engaging myths which are nonetheless anything but innocent. And the truth about our present alienation is precisely the fact that wine cannot be an entirely happy substance, unless we wrongfully forget that it is also the product of an expropriation.

STEAK-FRITES

Steak participates in the same sanguinary mythology as wine. Steak or *bifteck* is the heart of a cut of meat, mythologically it is meat in the pure state, and whoever eats it assimilates a taurine strength. Apparently steak's prestige relates to its semi-rawness: blood is visible in it, natural, dense, compact yet sectile; ancient ambrosia can easily be imagined as this kind of heavy matter which diminishes under one's teeth so as to make one aware of its original strength and at the same time of its plasticity in pouring into man's very blood. Full-bloodedness is steak's raison d'être: the degrees to which it is cooked are expressed not in calorie units but in images of blood, rare steak is *saignant* when it is said to suggest the arterial blood of the animal whose throat has been cut, or *bleu*, which is the plethoric blood of the veins suggested by the purplish color, a superior degree of redness. Even a moderate degree of cooking cannot be explicitly expressed; such an unnatural state requires a euphemism: a medium-cooked steak is said to be *à point*, an expression intended more as a limit than as a degree of perfection.

To eat steak *saignant* therefore represents both a nature

Christian de Castries was the French commander at the battle of Dien Bien Phu (1954), which effectively put an end to the First Indochina War and the French presence in Southeast Asia. Castries was held prisoner for several months while an armistice agreement was reached.

and a morality: a "nature" because it is supposed to benefit all temperaments, the sanguinary because it is identical, the nervous and lymphatic because it is complementary. And just as wine becomes for many intellectuals a mediumistic substance that leads them in the direction of the original force of nature, in the same way steak for them is a redemptive element thanks to which they make a sort of prose of their cerebrality and exorcise, by means of blood and soft pulp, the sterile dryness of which they are incessantly accused. The vogue of steak tartare, for example, is an operation by which a spell is cast against the romantic association of sensibility with sickliness; in this preparation are to be found all the germinative states of matter: the bloody pulp of beef and egg whites, a regular harmony of soft and living substances, a sort of signifying compendium of images of parturition.

Like wine, steak is, in France, a basic element, nationalized even more than socialized; it figures in every setting of alimentary life: flat, yellow-edged, somewhat shoe-leathery in cheap restaurants; thick, juicy, in specialized bistros: cubical, the core moistened throughout beneath a charred papery crust in haute cuisine establishments; it participates in all rhythms, comfortable bourgeois meals and bohemian bachelor snacks; it is a foodstuff both dense and expeditious, creates the best possible rapport between economy and efficacity, as well as both the mythology and the plasticity of its consumption.

Moreover, it is a French possession (circumscribed nowadays, it is true, by the invasion of American steaks). As with wine, there is no alimentary constraint which doesn't make a Frenchman dream of steak. No sooner abroad than his nostalgia for it is declared, here steak is endowed with a supplementary virtue of elegance, for in the apparent complication of exotic cuisines, it is a nourishment which is thought to combine succulence with simplicity. National, it follows the index of patriotic values: it rises with them in wartime, becoming the very lifeblood of the French combatant, the inalienable possession which can fall into enemy hands only by treason. In an old movie, *Deuxième Bureau contre Kommandantur,* the patriotic curé's housekeeper serves a meal to a German spy disguised as a French underground fighter: "Oh, it's you, Laurent: let me give you some steak!" And then, when the spy is unmasked: "And to think I gave him some of my steak!" Supreme abuse of confidence.

Usually associated with fries, steak transmits to them its national luster: fries are as nostalgic and patriotic as steak. *Match* has taught us that after the Indochinese armistice "For his first meal General de Castries ordered French fried potatoes." And the president of the Indo-Chinese Veterans, commenting subsequently on this information: "General de Castries's gesture of ordering French fries for his first meal has not always been properly understood." What we were being asked to understand was that the General's order was certainly not a vulgar materialistic reflex, but a ritual episode of approval of French ethnicity recovered. The general was well aware of our national symbolism, he knew that fries were the alimentary sign of Frenchness.

THE *NAUTILUS* AND THE *BATEAU IVRE*

Jules Verne's oeuvre (whose fiftieth anniversary was recently celebrated) would be a good subject for structuralist study; it is a richly thematic oeuvre. Verne constructed a sort of closed cosmogony which has its own categories, its time, its space, its plenitude, and even its existential principle.

This principle seems to me to be a continuous gesture of enclosure, and the sympathy between this author and childhood derives not from a banal mystique of adventure but, on the contrary, from a mutual delight in the finite, which we also find in the childhood passion for cabins and tents: to enclose oneself inside something—that is the existential dream of childhood and of Jules Verne. The archetype of this dream is that almost perfect novel *The Mysterious Island*, in which the man-child reinvents the world, fills it, encloses it, and himself within it, and crowns this encyclopedic effort by the bourgeois posture of appropriation: pipe, slippers, and fireside, while outside the storm—i.e., infinity—rages to no avail.

Verne was a maniac of plenitude: he unceasingly finished and furnished the world, filling it full as an egg; his impulse was exactly that of an eighteenth-century encyclopedist or of a Dutch painter: the world is finite, crammed with numerable and contiguous substances. The artist can have no other task than to make catalogs, inventories, to discover empty little corners in order to stuff them, in serried ranks, with the creations and instruments of mankind. Verne belongs to the progressist lineage of the bourgeoisie: his oeuvre proclaims that nothing can elude mankind, that the world, however remote, is like an object in his hand, and that ownership is, all in all, only a dialectical moment in the general enslavement of Nature. It never occurred to Verne to enlarge the world according to the romantic escape routes or the mystical blueprints of infinity: he constantly seeks to contract it, to populate it, to reduce it to a known and enclosed space which mankind can then comfortably inhabit: the world can derive everything from itself; it needs, in order to exist, no one but mankind.

Beyond the innumerable resources of science, Jules Verne invented an excellent novelistic means of glamorizing this appropriation of the world: wagering space against time, constantly uniting these two categories, risking them on a single cast of the dice or on a single, always successful intellectual notion. The peripeties themselves have the task of imprinting on the world a sort of elastic condition, releasing then narrowing closure, blithely playing with cosmic distances, and quite mischievously testing human powers over space and time. And on this planet triumphantly devoured by the Vernean hero, a kind of bourgeois Antaeus whose nights are innocent and "restorative," often loiters some desperado or other, a prey to remorse or to spleen, vestige of a bygone romantic age, who by contrast strikingly shows up the health of the world's true owners, those who have no other concern but to adapt themselves as perfectly as possible to situations whose complexity, neither metaphysical nor even ethical, derives quite simply from some provocative caprice of geography.

Jules Verne's profound gesture, then, is incontestably *appropriation*. The image of the boat, so important in his mythology, in no way contradicts this, quite the contrary: the boat may well be the symbol of departure; it is, more profoundly, the figure of enclosure. Verne's love of ships is always the joy of perfect self-enclosure, including the greatest possible number of objects. To possess an absolutely finite space: to love a ship is first of all to love a superlative house, one that is unremittingly enclosed, and certainly not loving great vague departures: a ship is a habitat phenomenon before being a means of transport. Indeed all of Verne's ships are ideal "firesides," and the immensity of their periplus further adds to their enclosure, to the perfection of their interior humanity. The *Nautilus* in this regard is an adorable cavern: the delights of enclosure attain their paroxysm when, from the bosom of this unfissured interiority, it is possible to see through a huge pane the vague exterior of the waters and thereby to define, in one and the same gesture, its interior by its contrary.

Most boats of legend or fiction enact, in this regard like the *Nautilus,* the theme of a beloved enclosure, for it suffices a man to conceive his ship as a human habitat for him to organize the delights of a smooth, round universe of which, moreover, an entire nautical morality immediately makes him into the god, master, and owner (*sole master on board*, etc.). In this mythology of navigation, there is only one means of exorcising man's possessive nature over the ship, which is to suppress the man altogether and to leave the ship on its own; then the boat ceases to be a crate, a habitat, a possessed object; it becomes a voyaging eye, an intimate of infinities: it ceaselessly produces departures. The really contrary object to Verne's *Nautilus* is Rimbaud's *Bateau ivre*, the boat which says "I" and, liberated from its concavity, can make mankind proceed from a psychoanalysis of the cavern to a true poetics of exploration.

DEPTH ADVERTISING

Today, as I have indicated elsewhere, the advertising of detergents essentially flatters a notion of depth: dirt is no longer stripped from the surface, it is expelled from its most secret cells. All advertising of beauty products is similarly based on a kind of epic representation of the intimate. Those little scientific prefaces, meant to introduce (and to promote) the product, ordain that it clean *in depth*, feed *in depth*, relieve *in depth*, at all costs *infiltrate*. Paradoxically, it's insofar as the skin is first of all a surface, but a living, hence a mortal surface, likely to dry out and to age, that it readily assumes its role as the tributary of deep roots, of what certain products call *the basic layer of renewal*. Moreover, medicine makes it possible to give beauty a *deep space* (dermis *and* epidermis) and to persuade women that they themselves are the product of a sort of germinative surface where the beauty of efflorescences depends on the nutrition of the roots.

Hence the notion of depth is a general one, present in every advertisement. About the substances which infiltrate and convert *within* this depth, a total blank; all we are told is that it is a matter of (vivifying, stimulating, nutritive) *principles* or (vital, revitalizing, regenerative) *essences*, a whole Molièresque vocabulary, updated perhaps by a touch of scientism (*bactericide agent r-51*). No, the real drama of this whole little psychoanalysis of advertising is the conflict of two warring substances subtly opposed to the advance of "essences" and "principles" toward the field of depth. These two substances are water and grease.

Both are morally ambiguous: water is beneficent, for anyone can see that old skin is dry and young skin cool, pure ("of a cool moisture," says one product); firmness, smoothness, all the positive values of a fleshly substance are spontaneously perceived as made taut by water, swelled like a sheet on the line, established in that ideal state of purity, cleanness, and coolness to which water is the usual key. In advertising terms, hydration of the depths is therefore a necessary operation. And yet the infiltration of an opaque body appears anything but easy for water: we imagine that water is too volatile, too light, too impatient to reach altogether reasonably those cryptal zones where beauty is elaborated. Then, too, water, in this physics of the flesh and in a free state, water scours, irritates, returns to air, becomes part of fire; water is beneficent only when imprisoned, contained.

Greasy substances have the inverse qualities and defects: they do not refresh; their softness is excessive, too lasting, artificial; we cannot base a beauty campaign on the pure notion of cream, whose very density is perceived as an unnatural state. Doubtless grease (more poetically known as *oils*, as in the Bible or the Orient) contains a notion of nutriment, but it is safer to exalt it as a vehicular element, a euphoric lubricant conducting water to the skin's depths. Water is posited as volatile, aerial, fugitive, precious; oil, on the contrary, holds fast, weighs down, slowly forces its way into surfaces, impregnates, slides one way only through the "pores" (essential characters in beauty advertising). Every beauty product campaign therefore prepares a miraculous conjunction of these enemy liquids, henceforth declared complementary; diplomatically respecting all the positive values of the mythology of substances, this conjunction manages to impose the happy assurance that grease is conveyed by water, and that there exist certain aqueous creams, certain leniences without luster.

Most of the new creams are therefore nominally *liquid*, *fluid*, *ultrapenetrating*, etc.; the notion of grease, for so long consubstantial with the very idea of a beauty product, is masked, or complicated, corrected by liquidity, and sometimes even vanishing, giving way to the fluid *lotion*, to the spiritual *tonic*, gloriously *astringent* if it is to combat the skin's waxiness, modestly *special* if, on the contrary, it is to nourish those voracious depths whose digestive phenomena are pitilessly exposed. This public opening of the human body's interiority is moreover a general feature of the advertising of beauty products. "Decay is expelled (from the teeth, the skin, the blood, the breath)": France is experiencing a great yen for cleanliness.

A FEW WORDS FROM MONSIEUR POUJADE

What the petite bourgeoisie respects most in the world is immanence: any phenomenon which bears its own term within itself by a simple mechanism of return—i.e., to put it literally, any *paid* phenomenon—is agreeable to this class. Language is made to accredit, in its figures, in its very syntax, this morality of the retort. For example, Monsieur Poujade says to Monsieur Edgar Faure: "You take responsibility for the breakdown, you'll suffer its consequences," and the world's infinity is spirited away, everything is restored to a brief but complete and airtight order, the order of payment. Beyond the sentence's mere contents, there is in the very balance of the syntax the affirmation of a law according to which nothing is achieved without an equal consequence, in which every human action is rigorously countered, recouped, in short a whole mathematics of the equation reassures the petit bourgeois, makes him a world to the measure of his own commerce.

This rhetoric of retaliation has its own figures, which are all figures of equality. Not only must every offense be averted by a threat, but even every action must be forestalled. The

---

Pierre Poujade, a populist politician, created the Union de Défense des Commerçants et des Artisans (UDCA) in 1953. The movement, soon to be called Poujadism, articulated the financial grievances of shopkeepers and other small businesses facing economic and social change. The main themes of Poujadism were nationalism, tax cuts, and defense of "the common man" against the elites. Poujade ran against Edgar Faure, then prime minister, for the cantonal election of 1955.

pride of "not being fooled" is none other than the ritual respect for a numerative order in which to foil is to annul. Thus the world reduced to a pure equality, the observance of quantitative relations between human actions are both triumphant states. To pay back, to counter, to generate the event from its reciprocal, either by turning the opponent's argument against himself or by foiling him by your own—all this closes the world upon itself and produces a certain happiness; so that it is only natural we should pride ourselves on such moral bookkeeping: the petit bourgeois flourish consists in eluding qualitative values, in opposing processes of transformation by a statics of equalities (an eye for an eye, effect vs. cause, merchandise vs. money, penny for penny, etc.).

Monsieur Poujade is well aware that the capital enemy of this tautological system is the dialectic, which he more or less confuses, in fact, with sophistry: he defeats the dialectic only by an incessant return to calculation, to the computation of human behavior, to what Monsieur Poujade, in agreement with etymology, calls Reason ("Will the rue de Rivoli be stronger than Parliament? the dialectic stronger than Reason?"). Indeed the dialectic risks opening this world he has so carefully closed over its equalities; insofar as the dialectic is a technique of transformation, it contradicts the numerative structure of ownership, it escapes the petit bourgeois limits and is therefore first anathematized, then declared a pure illusion: once again degrading an old romantic theme (which was once a bourgeois one), Monsieur Poujade dispenses with all the techniques of the intelligence, asserting petit bourgeois "reason" against the dreams and sophisms of academics and intellectuals discredited by their mere position outside a computable reality. ("France is stricken with an overproduction of men with diplomas, polytechnicians, economists, philosophers and other dreamers who have lost all contact with the real world.")

We know now what petit bourgeois reality really is: it is not even what is seen, it is what is counted; now this reality, the narrowest any society has been able to define, has its philosophy all the same, it is "common sense," the famous common sense of the "little people," Monsieur Poujade says. *La Petite bourgeoisie*, at least Monsieur Poujade's bourgeoisie (the butcher stall, the corner grocery), possesses common sense in its own right, in the fashion of a splendid physical appendage, a special organ of perception: a curious organ, moreover, since in order to see clearly it must first blind itself, refuse to go beyond appearances, to take for granted the propositions of "reality" and declare anything which risks substituting an explanation for a retort to be null and void. Its role is to posit simple equalities between what is seen and what is, and to assure a world without stages, without transition, and without progression. Common sense is the watchdog of petit bourgeois equations: it blocks any dialectical outlets, defines a homogeneous world in which we are at home, sheltered from the disturbances and the leaks of "dreams" (by which we are to understand an uncountable vision of things). Human behavior being pure talion, common sense is that selective reaction of the mind which reduces the ideal world to certain direct mechanisms of retort, of what the French call *riposte*.

Thus Monsieur Poujade's language shows, once more, that the whole petit bourgeois mythology implies the refusal of alterity, the negation of the different, the happiness of identity, and the exaltation of the similar. In general, this equational reduction of the world prepares an expansionist phase in which the "identity" of human phenomena quickly establishes a "nature" and thereupon a "universality." Monsieur Poujade is not yet at the point of defining *common sense* as the general philosophy of humanity; it is still, in his eyes, a class virtue, already given, it is true, as a universal reinvigorant. And this is precisely what is sinister in Poujadism: that it has laid claim from the start to a mythological truth and posited culture as a disease, which is the specific symptom of all fascisms.

ADAMOV AND LANGUAGE

As we have just seen, our Poujadist common sense consists in establishing a simple equivalence between what is seen and what is. When an appearance is decidedly too peculiar, this same common sense still has a means of reducing that excess without relinquishing the mechanism of equalities. This means is symbolism. Each time that something seen appears unmotivated, common sense orders up the heavy cavalry of the symbol, admitted to the petit bourgeois heaven insofar as, despite its abstract tendency, it unites the visible and the invisible in the form of a quantitative equality (this *is worth* that): calculation is saved, and the world still abides.

Artur Adamov having written a play about pinball machines, an unwonted object in our bourgeois theater, which in the matter of stage properties knows little more than the adulterous bed, our popular press has hastily spirited away the unaccustomed object by reducing it to a symbol. As soon as it *meant something* it was less dangerous. And the more apparently the criticism of *Ping-Pong* was addressed to a mass audience (*Match*, *France-Soir*), the more it has insisted on that play's symbolic character: be reassured, it's only a symbol, the pinball machine simply *signifies* "the complexity of the social

---

Ping-Pong *by Arthur Adamov, one of the foremost exponents of the Theater of the Absurd, was produced in 1955 in Paris.*

system." This strange stage property is thereby exorcised since it means something—since it is *worth* something.

Now the pinball machine in *Ping-Pong* symbolizes nothing at all; it does not express, it produces; it is a literal object whose function is to engender, by its very objectivity, certain situations. But once again our criticism is misled, in its thirst for depth: these situations are not psychological, they are essentially *language situations*. Here is a dramatic reality which we must admit, ultimately, alongside the old arsenal of plots, actions, characters, conflicts, and other elements of the classic theater. *Ping-Pong* is a masterfully mounted network of language situations.

What is a language situation? A configuration of words likely to engender what *at first glance* seem to be psychological relations, not so much false as frozen in the compromise of a previous language. And it is this paralysis which, finally, annihilates psychology. To parody the language of a class or of a character is still to keep a certain distance, to lay claim to a certain *authenticity* (that virtue beloved of psychology). But if this borrowed language is in general use, always situated below caricature and covering the play's entire surface with a variable pressure but without any fissure through which some cry, some invented speech might emerge, then human relations, despite their apparent dynamism, are as though vitrified, ceaselessly deflected by a kind of verbal refraction, and the problem of their "authenticity" vanishes like a lovely (and false) dream.

Ping-Pong is entirely constituted by a block of this language under glass, analogous, if you like, to those frozen vegetables which permit the British to enjoy in their winter the acidities of spring; this language, entirely woven out of tiny commonplaces, partial truisms, scarcely discernible stereotypes hurled with all the force of hope—or of despair—like the particles of a Brownian movement, this language is not, to tell the truth, a canned language, as was, for example, the concierge's jargon reconstituted by Henri Monnier; it is rather a delayed-action language, fatally formed in the characters' social life and thawing, real yet a little too acid or virid, in a later situation where its slight glaciation, a touch of vulgar, *learned* emphasis, produces incalculable effects. *Ping-Pong*'s characters are a little like Michelet's Robespierre: *they think everything they say!* A profound observation which underlines man's tragic plasticity with regard to his language, especially when—final and astounding aspect of the misunderstanding— that language is not even quite his.

This will perhaps account for *Ping-Pong*'s apparent ambiguity: on one hand, a mockery of language is obvious, and on the other, this mockery is continually creative, producing perfectly living beings endowed with a density of time which can even conduct them through an entire existence to death. This means precisely that in Adamov the language situations altogether resist both symbol and caricature: it is life which is parasitical to language, that is what *Ping-Pong* declares.

Hence Adamov's pinball machine is not a key—it is not D'Annunzio's dead lark or the door of one of Maeterlinck's palaces; it is an object which generates language; like a catalytic element, it constantly affords the actors a fragment of speech, makes them exist in the proliferation of language. *Ping-Pong*'s clichés, moreover, do not all have the same density of memory, the same relief; that depends on who says them: Sutter the faker, who makes up fine speeches, displays certain caricatural acquisitions, parades a parodic language which produces laughter at once ("Words, they're all traps"). The paralysis of Annette's language is slighter, and also more pathetic ("Someone else's turn, Mr. Roger").

Each character in *Ping-Pong* seems thereby doomed to his verbal rut, but each rut is dug differently, and these differences of pressure create precisely what in the theater is called situations, i.e., possibilities and choices. Insofar as *Ping-Pong*'s language is altogether acquired, having come from the theater of life, i.e., from a life itself given as theater, *Ping-Pong* is theater of the second degree. It is the very contrary of naturalism, which always proposes to amplify the insignificant; here, on the contrary, the spectacular aspect of life, of language, *sets* onstage (as we say that ice *sets*). This mode of congelation is the very mode of all mythic speech: like *Ping-Pong*'s language, myth itself is a speech frozen by its own doubling. But since we are concerned with theater, the reference of this second language is different: the mythic language plunges into Society, into a general History, while the language Adamov has experimentally constituted can double only a first individual language, for all its banality.

In all our theatrical literature I see only one of whom it can be said, to some extent, that he too has constructed his theater in a free proliferation of language situations: this is Marivaux. Conversely, the theater most opposed to this dramaturgy of language situations is, paradoxically, a verbal theater: Giraudoux, for instance, whose language is sincere, i.e., plunges into Giraudoux himself. Adamov's language has its roots in the air, and everyone knows that in the theater whatever is exterior flourishes.

EINSTEIN'S BRAIN

Einstein's brain is a mythical object: paradoxically, it is the greatest intelligence which constitutes the image of the world's most perfected machine; the all too powerful man is separated from psychology, introduced into a world of robots; as we know from science-fiction novels, there is always something reified about a superman. Einstein too: as is commonly expressed by his brain, an anthological organ and a veritable museum piece. Perhaps because of his mathematical specialization, the superman is in this instance stripped of all magical character whatsoever; in him, no diffuse power, no mystery other than mechanical: he is a superior, prodigious organ but real, even physiological. Mythologically, Einstein is matter, his power does not spontaneously tend in the direction of spirituality, it requires the help of an independent morality, the reminder of the scientist's "conscience" ("Science without conscience . . ." the saying goes).

Einstein himself has somewhat abetted the legend by bequeathing his brain, the possession of which two hospitals disputed as if it were some strange machine which could finally be taken apart. A picture shows him lying prone, his head bristling with electric wires: his brain waves are being recorded while he is being asked to "think of relativity." (Actually, what does it mean "to think of . . ."?) Probably we are meant to understand that the seismograms will be all the more violent since "relativity" is a strenuous subject. Thought itself is thus represented as an energetic form of matter, the measurable product of a complex (virtually electric) apparatus which transforms the cerebral substance into power. The mythology of Einstein makes him a genius so little magical that his thinking is spoken of as a functional labor analogous to the mechanical production of sausages, the grinding of corn, or the crushing of some mineral: he produced thought continuously, as a mill produces flour, and death, for him, was chiefly the cessation of a localized function: "The world's most powerful brain has stopped thinking."

What this machine of genius was supposed to produce was equations. By the mythology of Einstein, the world delightedly recognized the image of a formula for knowledge. Paradoxically the more the man's genius materialized in the guise of his brain, the more the product of his invention attached itself to a magical condition, reincarnated the old esoteric image of a science entirely confined in a handful of letters. There is one secret in the world, and this secret resides in a word, the universe is a safe whose combination humanity is looking for: Einstein almost found this combination, and that is the myth of Einstein; in it can be perceived all the gnostic themes: the unity of nature, the ideal possibility of a fundamental reduction of the world, the aperient power of a word, the age-old struggle of a secret and an utterance, the notion that total knowledge can only be discovered all at once, like a lock which suddenly yields after a thousand ineffectual attempts. The historic equation $E = mc^2$, by its unexpected simplicity, nearly embodies the pure idea of the key, naked, linear, made of a single metal, opening with utterly magical facility a door mankind had struggled with for centuries. The imagery accounts nicely for these circumstances: Einstein, *photographed*, stands beside a blackboard covered by mathematical signs of an evident complexity; but Einstein *drawn*, i.e., signifying he has entered into legend, stands with a piece of chalk still in his hand in front of an empty blackboard on which he has just written, quite spontaneously, the magical formula of the world. In this way mythology respects the nature of the tasks: research proper mobilizes a series of mechanical gears, and relies on an entirely material organ which has about it nothing monstrous but its cybernetic complication; discovery, on the contrary, is of a magical essence, it is simple as a primordial body, a principial substance, the hermetists' philosophical stone, Berkeley's tar water, Schelling's oxygen.

But since the world still continues, since research still flourishes, and since God's share must be preserved, a certain failure is necessary for Einstein: Einstein died, we are told, without having been able to verify "the equation containing the secret of the world." So in the end, the world has resisted; no sooner disclosed than the secret closed once more, the code was incomplete. Thus Einstein utterly satisfies the myth, which derides all contradictions, provided it establishes a euphoric security: at once magus and machine, permanent seeker and unfulfilled finder, unleashing both the best and the worst, brain and conscience, Einstein satisfies the most contradictory dreams, mythically reconciles man's infinite power over nature and the "fatality" of a rite which man cannot yet reject.

THE JET-MAN

The Jet-Man is the pilot of a jet plane. *Match* has specified that he belongs to a new race in aviation, closer to a robot than to a hero. Yet there is some Parsifalian residue in the jet-man, as we shall soon see. But what is immediately striking in jet-man mythology is the elimination of speed: nothing in his legend makes any substantial allusion to speed. Here we have a paradox everyone readily acknowledges and even takes as proof of modernity; this paradox states that excessive speed turns into repose; the hero-pilot was remarkable for a whole mythology of apparent speed, of space devoured, of intoxicating movement; but the jet-man is defined by a coenesthesia of motionlessness (*at 2,000 km in level flight, no impression of speed whatever*), as if the extravagance of his vocation precisely consisted in *overtaking* movement, in going faster than speed. Here mythology abandons an entire imagery of external friction and approaches a pure coenesthesia: movement is no longer an optical perception of points and surfaces; it has become a sort of vertical disturbance consisting of contractions, of blackouts, terrors, and loss of consciousness; it is no longer gliding, but internal devastation, monstrous upheaval, motionless crises of corporeal consciousness.

Naturally, if it reaches this point, the myth of the aviator loses any appearance of humanism. The hero of classical speed remained just that so long as movement was sustained as an episodic performance for which courage alone was requisite;

he resorted to speed in bursts as a daring amateur, not as a professional, seeking "intoxication," he approached movement armed with an ancestral morality which sharpened perception and permitted him to abide by a certain philosophy. It was to the degree that speed was an *adventure* that it linked the aviator to a whole series of human roles.

The jet-man no longer seems to know adventure or fate, but merely a condition; even this condition is at first glance less human than anthropological: mythically the jet-man is defined less by his courage than by his weight, his diet, and his habits (temperance, frugality, continence). His racial identity can be read in his morphology: the anti-G inflatable nylon suit and the polished helmet encase the jet-man in a new skin in which "not even his mother would recognize him." This suggests a veritable racial conversion all the more plausible in that science fiction has already accredited this transferal of species: everything occurs as if there had been a sudden transmutation between the old creatures of propeller-humanity and the new ones of jet-humanity.

In fact, and despite the scientific apparatus of this new mythology, there has been a simple displacement of the sacred: the hagiographic era (Saints and Martyrs of propeller aviation) has been succeeded by a monastic period: and what at first passed for simple dietetic prescriptions soon appeared armed with a sacerdotal signification: continence and temperance, abstention from pleasures, shared lives, shared *fashions*, in the jet-man's mythology everything concurs to manifest the plasticity of the flesh, its submission to collective ends (moreover modestly vague), and it is this submission which is offered as a sacrifice to the glamorous singularity of an inhuman condition. Society ultimately rediscovers in the jet-man the old theosophical pact which has always compensated power by ascesis, paying for semidivinity by the coin of human "happiness." The jet-man's situation so severely involves a vocational aspect that it is itself the price of previous macerations, of initiatic ceremonies, intended to test the postulant (time in the altitude chamber and in the centrifuge). There is even the gray-haired, anonymous, and impenetrable instructor who perfectly represents the necessary mystagogue. As for endurance, we are carefully instructed that, as in any initiation, it is not of a physical order: the triumph over previous ordeals is actually the fruit of a spiritual gift, one is endowed by jet flight as others are called to God.

All of which would be banal if we were dealing with a traditional hero, whose whole value was that he performed the tasks of aviation without abandoning his humanity (Saint-Exupéry a writer, Lindbergh in a casual suit). But the mythological peculiarity of the jet-man is that he keeps none of the romantic and individualized elements of the sacred role, though without forsaking the role itself. Assimilated by his name to pure passivity (what could be more inert and more utterly dispossessed than a re*jected* object?), he nonetheless recovers the ritual through the myth of a fictive, celestial race which retains its special features from its ascesis and achieves a sort of anthropological compromise between humans and Martians. The jet-man is a reified hero, as if even today men could conceive of heaven populated only by semiobjects.

RACINE IS RACINE

Taste is taste.   —*Bouvard and Pécuchet*

I have elsewhere discussed the petit bourgeois predilection for tautological reasoning ("business is business," etc.). Here is a splendid example, one quite frequent in the order of the arts: "*Athalie* is a play by Racine," a Comédie-Française actress reminds us before presenting her new production.

First of all, we might notice here a little declaration of war (against the "grammarians, controversialists, annotators, priests, writers, and artists" who have commented on Racine). And it is true that tautology is always aggressive: it signifies a choleric break between the intelligence and its object, the arrogant threat of an order in which we are not to think. Our tautologists are like masters tugging sharply on their dogs' leashes; thought must not range too widely, the world is filled with suspect and futile alibis, we must play our common sense close to the chest, reduce our leash to the distance of a computable reality. And if someone were to set about thinking about Racine? A great danger: the tautologist furiously cuts down whatever is growing around him, for it might smother him.

Recognizable in our actress's declaration is the language of that familiar enemy we have often encountered here, which

---

Racine's play Athalie *was performed at the Comédie-Française in 1955, under the direction of Véra Korène, who also acted in it.*

is anti-intellectualism. We know the old saws: too much intelligence is ruinous, philosophy is a useless jargon, you must leave room for feeling, intuition, innocence, simplicity, art dies from too much intellectuality, intelligence is not an artist's virtue, powerful creators are empirical, the work of art escapes all systems—in short, cerebrality is sterile. We know that the war against intelligence is always waged in the name of *common sense*, and here we are essentially applying to Racine that kind of Poujadist "understanding" I have already discussed. Just as the general economy of France is merely a dream with regard to French fiscality, the only reality revealed to Monsieur Poujade's common sense, so the history of literature and of thought, and *a fortiori* of history itself, is merely an intellectual hallucination with regard to a very simple Racine, a Racine as "concrete" as the Internal Revenue Service.

Our tautologists employ another weapon of anti-intellectualism as well: the recourse to innocence. Armed with a divine simplicity, they claim a true apprehension of the true Racine; we all know this old esoteric theme: the virgin, the child, simple and pure beings, see more clearly. In Racine's case, this invocation to "simplicity" has a double power as an alibi: on the one hand, it opposes the vanities of intellectual exegesis, and on the other (moreover, the point is virtually uncontested), it claims for Racine an aesthetic *ascesis* (the famous Racinian purity) which obliges all who approach him to accept a *discipline* (to the tune of *art is born of constraint . . .*).

Lastly our actress's tautology contains what we might call the myth of critical rediscovery. Our essentialist critics spend their time rediscovering the "truth" of past geniuses, literature for them is a huge warehouse of lost objects through which they go hunting . . . or fishing. What they rediscover there no one knows, and that is precisely the major advantage of the tautological method: not to have to tell. Our tautologists would be quite embarrassed, moreover, to advance further:

Racine himself, Racine degree zero, doesn't exist. There are only Racine-adjectives, Racine-pure-poetry, Racine-lobster (Montherlant), Racine-Bible (Madame Véra Korène), Racine-Passion, Racine-Realist, etc. In short, Racine is always something besides Racine, and this is what renders the Racinian tautology so illusory. We understand at least what such vacuity in definition affords those who brandish it so proudly: a kind of minor ethical salvation, the satisfaction of having militated in favor of a truth of Racine without having to assume the risks which any somewhat positive search involves: tautology dispenses us from having ideas, but at the same time prides itself on making this license into a stern morality; whence its success: laziness is promoted to the rank of rigor. Racine is Racine: admirable security of nothingness.

BILLY GRAHAM AT THE VEL' D'HIV'

So many missionaries have regaled us with the religious practices of "Primitives" that it is entirely regrettable that a Pap-
uan witch doctor was not at the Vel' d'Hiv' to describe the
ceremony presided over by Dr. Graham under the name of an
evangelizing campaign. There is a splendid piece of anthropological raw material here, which seems, moreover, to be inherited from certain "savage" cults, for we recognize in it under an
immediate aspect the three great phases of every religious action: Expectation, Suggestion, Initiation.

Billy Graham makes us wait for him: hymns, invocations,
any number of futile little speeches entrusted to supernumer-
ary pastors or to American impresarios (jovial introduction of
the troupe: pianist Smith, from Toronto, soloist Beverly, from
Chicago, "an artist of the American radio who sings the Gospel
so marvelously"), a good deal of boosting precedes Dr. Graham,
who is constantly announced and who never appears. Here he
is at last, but only to lead our curiosity further, for his first
speech is not the right one: he is merely preparing the advent
of the *Message*, which, according to the best traditions of such
spectacles, begins by making itself desired in order to exist all
the more readily afterward.

---

*The American Christian evangelist Billy Graham, who had conducted crusades since
1948, preached from June 5 to June 9, 1955, at the Vel' d'Hiv' stadium in Paris, gathering more than five thousand people every night.*

We recognize in this first phase of the ceremony that great sociological recourse of Expectation which Mauss has studied and of which Paris has already had a very up-too-date example in the hypnotism séances of Le Grand Robert. Here, too, the Mage's appearance was postponed as long as possible, and by repeated false starts the public was wrought up to that troubled curiosity which is quite ready to see in fact what it is being made to wait for. Here, from the first minute, Billy Graham is presented as a veritable prophet, into whom we beg the Spirit of God to consent to descend, on this very evening in particular: it is an Inspired Being who will speak, the public is invited to the spectacle of a possession: we are asked in advance to take Billy Graham's speeches quite literally for divine words.

If God is really speaking through Dr. Graham's mouth, it must be acknowledged that God is quite stupid: the Message stuns us by its platitude, its childishness. In any case, assuredly, God is no longer a Thomist, He shrinks from logic: the Message is constituted by an outburst of discontinuous affirmations without any kind of link, each of which has no content that is not tautological (*God is God*). The merest Marist brother, the most academic pastor would figure as decadent intellectuals next to Dr. Graham. Some journalists, deceived by the Huguenot decor of the ceremony (hymns, prayer, sermon, benediction), lulled by the lenitive compunction proper to Protestant worship, have praised Dr. Graham and his team for their sense of proportion, their restraint: we were expecting an outré Americanism, girls, jazz, jovial and modernist metaphors (there were two or three of these, all the same). Billy Graham has doubtless purged his sessions of anything picturesque, and the French Protestants have been able to accommodate him. Still, Billy Graham's manner breaks with a whole tradition of the sermon, Catholic or Protestant, inherited from ancient culture, a tradition which is that of a requirement to persuade. Western Christianity has always submitted for its exposition to the general context of Aristotelian thought, has always consented to deal with reason, even when accrediting the irrationality of faith. Breaking with centuries of humanism (even if the forms may have been hollow and petrified, the concern for a subjective Other has rarely been absent from Christian didacticism), Dr. Graham brings us a method of magical transformation: he substitutes suggestion for persuasion: the pressure of the delivery, the systematic eviction of any rational content from the proposition, the grandiloquent designation of the Bible held at arm's length like the universal can opener of a quack peddler, and above all the absence of warmth, the manifest contempt for others, all these operations belong to the classic material of the music hall hypnotist: I repeat, there is no difference between Billy Graham and Le Grand Robert.

And just as Le Grand Robert ended the "treatment" of his public by a particular selection, picking out and calling up to the stage beside him the elect of hypnosis, confiding to certain privileged individuals the responsibility of manifesting a spectacular trance state, so Billy Graham crowns his Message by a material segregation of the Awakened: the neophytes who this evening at the Vel' d'Hiv', among the posters for Super Dissolution and Cognac Polignac, "received Christ" under the action of the magic Message, are led to a private hall, and even—if they are English-speakers—to a still more secret crypt: whatever it is that happens there—inscription on the conversion lists, new sermons, spiritual conferences with "counselors," or collections—this new episode is an ersatz form of Initiation.

All this concerns us quite directly: first of all, Billy Graham's "success" manifests the mental fragility of the French petite bourgeoisie, a class from which the public for these meetings, it appears, is chiefly recruited; the plasticity of this public as to alogical and hypnotic forms of thought suggests that there exists in this social group what we might call a situation of risk: a portion of the French petite bourgeoisie is no longer even protected by its famous "common sense," which is the aggressive form of its class consciousness. But that is not all: Billy Graham and his team have insisted heavily and repeatedly on the goal of this campaign: "to awaken" France ("We have seen God do great things in America; an awakening in Paris would have an enormous influence throughout the world"; "We want something to happen in Paris which will have repercussions throughout the world"). From all appearances, the optic is the same as Eisenhower's in his declarations concerning French atheism. France has made herself known the world over by her rationalism, her indifference to faith, the irreligion of her intellectuals (a theme common to America and the Vatican; moreover, a theme vastly overrated): it is from this bad dream that she must be awakened. The "conversion" of Paris would obviously have the value of a worldwide example: Atheism defeated by Religion in its own lair.

Clearly we are dealing with a political theme: France's atheism interests America only because atheism is seen as the incipient phase of Communism. "To awaken" France from atheism is to awaken her from the Communist fascination. Billy Graham's campaign has been merely a McCarthyist episode.

THE DUPRIEZ TRIAL

The trial of Gérard Dupriez (who murdered his father and mother without known motive) exposes the crude contradictions in which our Justice is imprisoned. This has to do with the fact that History advances unequally; the idea of man has changed a great deal in the last 150 years, new sciences of psychological exploration have appeared, but this partial promotion of History has not yet produced any change in the system of penal justifications, because Justice is a direct emanation of the State, and because our State has not changed masters since the promulgation of the penal code.

It happens that crime is always *constructed* by Justice according to the norms of classical psychology: the phenomenon exists only as an element of a linear notionality, must be *useful*, or else it loses its essence, cannot be recognized. To be able to name Gérard Dupriez's action, we had to find an origin for it; hence the entire trial was committed to the search for a cause, however small; there was nothing left for the defense, paradoxically, except to claim for this crime a sort of absolute state, stripped of all qualifications—to make it, precisely, a *crime without a name*.

The prosecution, for its part, had found a motive— subsequently belied by the testimony: Gérard Dupriez's parents had apparently opposed his marriage, and it was for this reason that he killed them. Here we have the example of what Justice regards as criminal causality: the murderer's parents happen to be in the way; he kills them in order to suppress the obstacle. And even if he kills them out of anger, this anger does not cease being a rational state, since it directly serves a purpose (which signifies that, in the eyes of Justice, the psychological facts are not yet compensatory, pertaining to a psychoanalysis, but still utilitarian, pertaining to an economy).

Hence it suffices that the action be abstractly useful for the crime to receive a name. The prosecution admitted the parents' refusal to countenance Gérard Dupriez's marriage only as the motive of a quasi-demential state, anger; it does not matter that rationally (in terms of that same rationality which a moment before established the crime) the criminal cannot hope for any profit or benefit from his action (the marriage is more certainly destroyed by the murder of the parents than by their resistance, for Gérard Dupriez did nothing to conceal his crime): we are content here with an amputated causality; what matters is that Dupriez's anger be motivated in its origin, not in its effect; we impute to the criminal a mentality sufficiently logical to conceive the abstract utility of his crime, but not its real consequences. In other words, it suffices that madness have a *reasonable* origin for us to be able to call it a crime. I have already described, in the Dominici case, the quality of penal reason: it is of a "psychological" and thereby "literary" order.

As for the psychiatrists, they have not admitted that an inexplicable crime thereby ceases to be a crime, they have left the accused his entire responsibility, thereby seeming at first glance to oppose the traditional penal justifications: for them the absence of causality in no way prevents us from calling the murder a crime. Paradoxically, it is psychiatry which here defends the notion of an absolute self-control, and leaves the criminal his guilt, even beyond the limits of reason. Justice (the prosecution) establishes the crime on the cause and thus leaves room for the possibility of madness; whereas psychiatry, at least our official psychiatry, seems to want to postpone the definition of madness as long as possible; it grants no value to determinism and revives the old theological category of free will; in the Dupriez trial, it plays the role of the Church handing over to the secular arm (Justice) the accused whom it cannot include in any of its "categories"; it even creates for this purpose a privative, purely nominal category: perversion. Hence, confronting a Justice born in the bourgeois era, and as such trained to rationalize the world by reaction against divine or monarchic arbitrary action, and showing as an anachronistic vestige the progressive role it might have played, official Psychiatry revives the very old notion of a responsible perversion, whose condemnation must be indifferent to any effort of explanation. Far from seeking to enlarge its domain, legal psychiatry hands over to the executioner the madmen whom Justice, more rational though timorous, asks for nothing better than to abandon.

Such are some of the contradictions of the Dupriez trial: between Justice and the defense; between psychiatry and Justice; between the defense and psychiatry. Other contradictions exist at the very heart of each of these powers: Justice, as we have seen, irrationally dissociating the cause from the result, tends to excuse a crime in proportion to its monstrosity; legal psychiatry readily renounces its own and sends the murderer back to the executioner precisely when the psychological sciences are daily accounting for a greater share of man; and the defense itself hesitates between the claim of an *advanced psychiatry* which would recuperate each criminal as a madman, and the hypothesis of a magical "force" which apparently seized upon Dupriez, as in witchcraft's finest hour (plea of Maître Maurice Garçon).

SHOCK PHOTOS

In her book on Brecht, Geneviève Serreau referred to a photograph from *Match* showing the execution of Guatemalan Communists; she noted accurately that this photograph is not terrible in itself, and that the horror comes from the fact that *we are looking at it* from inside our freedom; an exhibition of Shock Photos at the Galerie d'Orsay, very few of which, precisely, manage to shock us, paradoxically confirms Serreau's remark: it is not enough for the photographer to *signify* the horrible for us to experience it.

Most of the photographs exhibited to shock us have no effect at all, precisely because the photographer has too generously substituted himself for us in the formation of the subject: he has almost always *overconstructed* the horror he is proposing, adding to the *fact*, by contrasts or parallels, the intentional *language* of horror: one of them, for instance, places side by side a crowd of soldiers and a field of skulls; another shows us a young soldier looking at a skeleton; another catches a column of prisoners passing a flock of sheep. Now, none of these photographs, all too skillful, touches us. This is because, as we look at them, we are in each case dispossessed of our judgment: someone has shuddered for us, reflected for us, judged for us; the photographer has left us nothing—except a simple right of intellectual acquiescence: we are linked to these images only

---

See illustrations 8 and 9.

by a technical interest; overindicated by the artist himself, for us they have no history, we can no longer *invent* our own reception of this synthetic nourishment, already perfectly assimilated by its creator.

Other photographers have tried to surprise, having failed to shock us, but the mistake in principle is the same; they have attempted, for example, to catch, with great technical skill, the rarest moment of a movement, its extreme point, the leap of a soccer player, the levitation of objects in a haunted house . . . But here again the spectacle, though direct and not at all composed of contrasting elements, remains too constructed; capture of the unique moment appears gratuitous, too intentional, the product of an encumbering will to language, and these successful images have no effect on us; the interest we take in them does not exceed the interval of an instantaneous reading: it does not resound, does not disturb, our reception closes too soon over a pure sign; the perfect legibility of the scene, its *formulation* dispense us from receiving the image in all its scandal; reduced to the state of pure language, the photograph does not disorganize us.

Painters have had to solve this same problem of the acme of movement, but they have had far greater success. Under the Empire, for example, having to reproduce certain instantaneous views (a horse rearing, Napoleon extending his arm on the battlefield, etc.), painters have left to movement the amplified sign of the unstable, what we might call the numen, the solemn shudder of a pose nonetheless impossible to fix in time; it is this motionless overvaluation of the ineffable— which will later, in the cinema, be called *photogeny*—which is the very site where art begins. The slight scandal of those exaggeratedly rearing horses, of that Emperor frozen in an impossible gesture, that persistence of expression we might also call rhetorical, add to the reading of the sign a kind of disturbing challenge, sweeping the reader of the image into an astonishment less intellectual than visual precisely because it fastens him to the surface of the spectacle, to his optical resistance and not immediately to its signification.

Most of the shock photos we have been shown are false, just because they have chosen an intermediate state between literal fact and overvalued fact: too intentional for photography and too exact for painting, they lack both the letters' scandal and art's truth: the photographer has made them into pure signs, without consenting to give these signs at least the ambiguity, the delay of a density. Hence it is logical that the only true shock photos of the exhibition (whose principle remains quite praiseworthy) should be the news-agency photographs, where the fact, surprised, explodes in all its stubbornness, its literality, in the very obviousness of its obtuse nature. The executed Guatemalans, the grief of Aduan Malki's fiancée, the murdered Syrian, the policeman's raised truncheon—these images astonish because at first glance they seem alien, almost calm, inferior to their legend: they are visually diminished, dispossessed of that numen which the painters would not have failed to add to them (and rightly, since they were making paintings). Deprived of both its song and its explanations, the *naturalness* of these images compels the spectator to a violent interrogation, commits him to a judgment which he must elaborate himself without being encumbered by the demiurgic presence of the photographer. Here we are indeed concerned with that critical catharsis Brecht demands, and no longer, as in the case of painting, with a emotive purgation: thus perhaps we can rediscover the two categories of the epic and the tragic. The literal photograph introduces us to the scandal of horror, not to horror itself.

TWO MYTHS OF THE NEW THEATER

If we are to judge by a recent festival of young companies, the new theater angrily inherits the myths of the old (so that it is hard to tell what it is that distinguishes the one from the other). We know, for example, that in the bourgois theater the actor, "devoured" by his role, is supposed to seem fired by a veritable conflagration of passion. She must seethe at all costs, i.e., burn and at the same time spill over, whence the moist forms of this combustion. In one new play (which won a prize), the two male partners spread themselves in liquids of all kinds, tears, sweat, and saliva. It was as if we were watching a dreadful psychological labor, a monstrous torsion of the internal tissues, as if passion were a huge wet sponge squeezed by the playwright's implacable hand. The intention of this visceral tempest is comprehensible enough: to make "psychology" into a quantitative phenomenon, to compel laughter or suffering to assume simple metrical forms, so that passion, too, becomes a merchandise like any other, an object of commerce inserted in a numerical system of exchange: I give my money to the theater, in return for which I demand a clearly visible, almost computable passion; and if the actor gives full measure, if he can make his body work before my eyes without cheating, if I cannot doubt the trouble he takes, then I shall declare the actor to be excellent, I shall evidence my joy at having invested my money in a talent worthy of it, returning it to me a hundredfold in the form of real tears, real sweat. Combustion's great advantage is of an economic order: my spectator's money has a verifiable yield at last.

Naturally the actor's combustion decks itself out in spiritualized justifications: the actor gives himself over to the demon of the theater, he sacrifices himself, allows himself to be eaten up from inside by his role: his generosity, the gift of his body to Art, his physical labor are worthy of pity and admiration; this muscular labor is acknowledged, and when, exhausted, drained of all his humors, he appears in front of the curtain at the end, we applaud him like a champion weight lifter or hunger artist, and we secretly suggest he go and restore himself somewhere, renew his inner substance, replace all that water by which he has measured out the passion we have bought from him. No bourgeois public resists so obvious a "sacrifice," and I suppose that an actor who knows how to weep or sweat onstage is always certain to triumph: the obviousness of his labor makes it unnecessary to judge further.

Another unfortunate element in the heritage of the bourgeois theater is the myth of the "find." Veteran directors make their reputation out of it. Playing *La Locandiera*, one young troupe flies the furniture from the ceiling for each act. Of course this is unexpected, everyone marvels at the invention: the trouble is, there is no reason for it, the device is evidently directed by an imagination at bay, craving something new at any price; since by now we have exhausted all artificial methods for setting the stage, since modernism and the avant-garde have saturated us with these scene changes in full view where some servant comes—supreme audacity—and sets down three chairs before our very eyes, the director now resorts to the last free space, the ceiling. The method is quite gratuitous, a matter of pure formalism, but nevertheless: in the bourgeois public's eyes, staging is never anything but a technique of such finds, and certain "animators" are very indulgent as to these requirements: for them it is enough to invent. Here again, our theater relies on the harsh law of exchange: it is necessary and sufficient that the director's provisions be visible and that each of us can verify the yield on his investment: whence an art that seeks the swiftest possible issue and chiefly manifests itself as a discontinuous—and therefore computable—series of formal successes.

Like the actor's combustion, the "find" has its disinterested justification: the effort is to give it the warrant of a "style": flying the furniture from the ceiling will be presented as an offhand operation, in harmony with that climate of lively irreverence traditionally ascribed to commedia dell'arte. Of course, style is almost always an alibi, meant to elude the play's profound motivations: to give a Goldoni comedy a purely "Italian" style (harlequinade, mime, bright colors, half masks, dance movements, and the rhetoric of nimbleness) is a cheap way of avoiding any social or historical content, thwarting the acute subversion of civic relationships—in a word, it is a mystification.

It would be difficult to overstate the ravages of "style" on our bourgeois stages. Style excuses everything, absolves us from everything, notably any historical reflection; it imprisons the spectator in the servitude of a pure formalism, so that the revolutions of "style" are themselves no more than formal: the avant-garde director will be the one who dares substitute one style for another (without ever resuming contact with the play's real basis), converting, like Barrault's production of *The Oresteia*, our tragic academicism into a voodoo festival. But this comes down to the same thing; it gets us no further to replace one style by another: Aeschylus the Bantu author is no less false than Aeschylus the bourgeois one. In the art of the theater, style is a technique of evasion.

THE TOUR DE FRANCE AS EPIC

There is an onomastics of the Tour de France which in itself tells us that these races are a great epic. The racers' names seem for the most part to come from a very old ethnic period, an age when the "race" indeed was audible in a little group of exemplary phonemes (*Brankart le Franc, Bobet le Francien, Robic le Celte, Darrigade le Gascon*). Then, too, these names keep recurring; they form certain fixed points in the great risk of the ordeal, whose task is to fasten an episodic, tumultuous duration to the stable essence of the great characters, as if man were, above all, a name which enables him to master events: Brankart, Geminiani, Lauredi, Antonin Rolland, these patronymics are read as algebraic signs of valor, loyalty, treachery, or stoicism. It is insofar as the racer's Name is both nutriment and ellipsis that it forms the chief figure of a veritable poetic language, making legible a world in which description is finally useless. This slow concretion of the racer's virtues in the audible substance of his name ends, moreover, by absorbing all adjectival language: at the outset of their glory, the racers are provided with some epithet indicative of their nature. Later on, this is futile. One says: *elegant Coletto* or *Batavian Van Dongen*; for *Louison Bobet* nothing more need be said.

In reality, entrance into the epic order is made by the name's diminution: Bobet becomes Louison, Lauredi becomes

---

See illustrations 10 and 11.

Nello, Raphael Geminiani—a hero twice-crowned because he is both *good* and *valorous*—is sometimes called Raph and sometimes Gem. These names are trivial enough, somewhat affectionate and somewhat servile; they account in one and the same syllable for a superhuman value and an utterly human intimacy which the journalist approaches familiarly, a little the way the Latin poets approached the intimacy of Caesar or Maecenas. In the cyclist's diminutive there is that mixture of servility, admiration, and prerogative which posits the people as a voyeur of its gods.

Diminished, the Name becomes truly public; it permits placing the racer's intimacy on the heroes' proscenium. For the true epic site is not the combat but the tent, the public threshold where the warrior elaborates his intentions, from which he hurls his insults, his challenges, and his confidences. The Tour de France is thoroughly familiar with this glory of a false private life in which affront and accolade are the intensified forms of human relation: in the course of a hunting trip in Brittany, generous Bobet publicly offers to shake hands with Lauredi, who no less publicly refuses to do so. These Homeric quarrels have as their counterpart the praises which the great racers address to each other over the crowd's head. Bobet says to Koblet: "You're being missed," and this remark all by itself traces the epic universe in which the enemy exists only in proportion to the esteem in which he is held. This is because there subsist in the Tour de France many vestiges of infeudation, that status which joined man to man in a virtually carnal manner. They embrace a good deal during the Tour. Marcel Bidot, technical director of the French team, embraces Gem following his victory, and Antonin Rolland presses a fervent kiss on the hollow cheek of this same Geminiani. Here the accolade is the expression of a magnificent euphoria experienced in the presence of the heroic world in all its closure and perfection. On the contrary, we must avoid attaching to this fraternal happiness all the sentiments of gregarity seething among the members of *the same team*; these sentiments are much murkier. Indeed, the perfection of public relations is possible only among the great stars: as soon as the "domestics" come onstage, the epic declines to a novel.

The Tour's geography, too, is entirely subject to the epic necessity of ordeal. Elements and terrain are personified, for it is against them that man measures himself, and as in every epic it is important that the struggle should match equal measures: man is therefore naturalized, Nature humanized. The gradients are *wicked*, reduced to difficult or deadly percentages, and the stages—each of which has the unity of a chapter in a novel (we are given, in effect, an epic duration, and an additive sequence of absolute crises and not the dialectical progression of a single conflict, as in tragic duration)—the stages are above all physical characters, successive enemies, individualized by that combination of morphology and morality which defines an epic Nature. The stage is *hairy*, *sticky*, *burned out*, *bristling*, etc., all adjectives which belong to an existential order of qualification and seek to indicate that the racer is at grips not with some natural difficulty but with a veritable theme of existence, a theme of substance in which he engages by a single impulse both his perception and his judgment.

In Nature the racer finds an animated milieu with which he sustains exchanges of nutrition and subjection. A certain maritime stage (Le Havre–Dieppe) will be "iodized," will afford energy and color; another (the North), consisting of paved roads, will constitute an opaque, rugged nourishment: it will be literally "hard to swallow"; still another (Briançon–Monaco), being schistose, prehistoric, will entrap the racer. All posit a problem of assimilation, all are reduced by a strictly poetic movement to their profound substance, and confronting each of them the racer dimly seeks to define himself as a total man at grips with a Nature-as-substance, and no longer merely with a

Nature-as-object. Hence it is the movements of approach to the substance which count: the racer is always represented in a state of immersion and not of advance: he plunges, he crosses, he flies, he sticks, it is his link to the ground which defines him, often in anguished or apocalyptic circumstances (the *terrifying* descent above Monte Carlo).

The stage which undergoes the strongest personification is that of Mont Ventoux. The main passes, Alpine or Pyrenean, difficult as they are, remain, despite everything, passages, they are perceived as objects to pass over; the pass is a *trou*, it accedes, albeit with difficulty, to the person; but Ventoux has the mountain's plenitude, it is a god of Evil to which sacrifice must be made. A veritable Moloch, despot of the cyclists, it never forgives the weak and exacts an unjust tribute of sufferings. Physically, Ventoux is dreadful: bare, bald (stricken with a dry seborrhea, according to *L'Équipe*), it is the very spirit of the Dry, its absolute climate (it is much more an essence of climate than a geographical space) makes it an accursed terrain, a test site for the hero, something like a higher hell in which the cyclist will define the truth of his salvation: he will vanquish the dragon either with the help of a god (Gaul, *Phoebus's friend*) or else by a pure Prometheanism, opposing this god of Evil by a still harsher demon (Bobet, *Satan of the bicycle*).

The Tour thus possesses a veritable Homeric geography. As in the *Odyssey*, the race is here both a periplus of ordeals and a total exploration of the earth's limits. Ulysses reached the ends of the Earth several times. The Tour, too, frequently grazes an inhuman world: on Mont Ventoux, we are told, the racers have already left planet Earth, encountering unknown stars. By its geography the Tour is thus an encyclopedic survey of human space; and if we were to refer to some Viconian schema of History, the Tour would represent in it that ambiguous moment when man strongly personifies Nature in order to confront it more readily and to free himself from it more completely.

Of course, the racer's adherence to this anthropomorphic Nature can only be fulfilled by semireal means. The Tour commonly practices an energetics of Spirits. The strength the racer possesses in order to confront Earth-as-Man may assume two aspects: *form*, a state more than an impulse, a privileged equilibrium between quality of muscles, acuity of intelligence, and force of character; and *leap*, a veritable electric influx which erratically possesses certain racers beloved of the gods and causes them to accomplish superhuman feats. *Leap* implies a supernatural order in which man succeeds insofar as a god assists him: it is for *leap* that Brankart's mother prays to the Virgin in Chartres Cathedral, and Charlie Gaul, glamorous beneficiary of grace, is precisely a *leap* specialist; he receives his electricity from an intermittent commerce with the gods; sometimes the gods inhabit him and he works wonders; sometimes the gods abandon him, his *leap* is exhausted. Charlie can do nothing more of any use.

Leap has a hideous parody, *doping*: to dope the racer is as criminal, as sacrilegious as trying to imitate God; it is stealing from God the privilege of the spark. God, moreover, knows how to take revenge on such occasions: as the wretched Malléjac knows, a provocative *doping* leads to the gates of madness (punishment for the theft of fire). Bobet, on the contrary, cool and rational, has no experience of *leap*: he is a strong spirit who does his work on his own; a specialist in form, Bobet is an entirely human hero who owes nothing to supernature and derives his victories from purely earthly qualities, promoted by that humanist sanction par excellence: the will. Gaul incarnates the Arbitrary, the Divine, the Marvelous, Election, complicity with the gods; Bobet incarnates the Just, the Human, Bobet denies the gods, illustrating an ethic of man-by-himself. Gaul is an archangel, Bobet is Promethean, a Sisyphus who refuses to dump his rock on those very gods who have doomed him to be, so magnificently, merely a man.

The dynamics of the Tour itself are obviously presented as a battle, but its confrontation being of a special kind, this battle is dramatic only by its decor or its advances, not strictly speaking by its shocks. No doubt the Tour is comparable to a modern army, defined by the importance of its matériel and the number of its servants; it knows murderous episodes, national funks (France encircled by the *corridori* of Signor Binda, director of the Italian Squadra), and the hero confronts his ordeal in a Caesarian state, close to the divine calm familiar to Hugo's Napoleon ("Gem plunged, clear-eyed, into the dangerous descent above Monte Carlo"). Still, the very action of the conflict remains difficult to grasp and does not permit itself to be established in duration. As a matter of fact, the dynamics of the Tour knows only four movements: *to lead, to follow, to escape, to collapse*. *To lead* is the most difficult action, but also the most useless; to lead is always to sacrifice oneself; it is pure heroism, destined to parade character much more than to assure results; in the Tour, panache does not pay directly, it is usually reduced by collective tactics. *To follow*, on the contrary, is always a little cowardly, a little treacherous, pertaining to an ambition unconcerned with honor: to follow to excess, with provocation, openly becomes a part of Evil (shame to the "wheel-suckers"). *To escape* is a poetic episode meant to illustrate a voluntary solitude, though one unlikely to be effective, for the racer is almost always caught up with, yet glorious in proportion to the kind of useless honor which sustains it (solitary escapade of the Spaniard Alomar: withdrawal, haughtiness, the hero's Castilianism à la Montherlant). *To collapse* prefigures abandon, it is always horrifying and saddens the public like a disaster: on Mont Ventoux, certain collapses have assumed a "Hiroshimatic" character. These four movements are obviously dramatized, cast in the emphatic vocabulary of *crisis*; often it is one of them, in the form of an image, which gives its name to the stage, as to the chapter of a novel (title: *Kübler's Tumultuous Grind*). Language's role is enormous here, it is language which gives the event—ineffable because ceaselessly dissolved into duration—the epic promotion which allows it to be solidified.

The Tour possesses an ambiguous ethic: certain knightly imperatives constantly mingle with the brutal demands of the pure spirit of success. It is an ethic which cannot or will not choose between the commendation of devotion and the necessities of empiricism. A racer's *sacrifice* to his team's success, whether self-generated or imposed by an arbiter (the technical director), is always exalted but always argued as well. Sacrifice is great, noble, testifies to a moral plenitude in the exercise of a team sport, of which it is the great justification; but it also contradicts another value necessary to the complete legend of the Tour: realism. *There is no place for sentiment in the Tour*, this is the law which enlivens the spectacle's interest. Here the knightly ethic is perceived as the risk of a possible submission to fate; the Tour resolutely rejects anything which might seem to affect in advance the naked, brutal risks of combat. *The die is not cast*, the Tour is a confrontation of characters, it requires a morality of the individual, of solitary combat for life: the journalists' problem and preoccupation is to contrive for the Tour *an uncertain future*: throughout the 1955 Tour, protests were made against the general belief that Bobet was certain to win. But the Tour is also a sport, it requires an ethic of the collectivity. It is this contradiction, in truth one never resolved, which obliges the legend constantly to discuss and to explain sacrifice, to recall each time the generous ethic which sustains it. It is because sacrifice is perceived as a sentimental value that it must tirelessly be justified.

Here the technical director plays an essential part: he guarantees the link between end and means, conscience and pragmatism; he is the dialectical element that unites in a single laceration the reality of evil and its necessity: Marcel Bidot is a specialist in these Cornelian situations which require the sacrifice, in one and the same team, of one racer to another, sometimes even, more tragically, of one brother to another (Jean to Louison Bobet). In fact, Bidot exists only as the real image of a necessity of an intellectual order, for this reason, in a universe emotional by nature, requires independent personification. Labor is carefully distributed among each group of ten racers, there must be a pure mind, whose role, moreover, is in no way privileged, for here intelligence is functional, its sole task to represent to the public the competition's strategic nature. Marcel Bidot is therefore reduced to the figure of a meticulous analyst, his role is *to meditate*.

Sometimes a racer takes the cerebral burden upon himself: this is precisely the case with Louison Bobet and constitutes the entire originality of his "role." In general, the racers' strategic power is slight, rarely exceeding the art of a few clumsy feints (Kübler's faking in order to deceive his adversary). In Bobet's case, this monstrous lack of distribution among the roles engenders an ambiguous popularity, much more doubious than that of a Coppi or of a Koblet: Bobet thinks too much, he is a *winner*, not a *player*.

This mediation of the intelligence between the pure ethic of sacrifice and the harsh law of success translates a composite mental order, at once utopian and realistic, consisting of vestiges of a very old ethic, feudal or tragic, and of new requirements proper to the world of total competition. It is in this ambiguity that the essential signification of the Tour consists: the masterly amalgam of the two alibis, idealist and realist, permits the legend to mask perfectly, with a veil at once honorable and exciting, the economic determinism of our great epic.

But whatever the ambiguity of the sacrifice, it ultimately reintegrates an order of clarity insofar as the legend ceaselessly returns it to a purely psychological disposition. What saves the Tour from the discomforts of freedom is that it is by definition *the world of characterial essences*. I have already indicated how these essences were posited by a sovereign nominalism which makes the racer's name the stable depository of an eternal value (Coletto, elegance; Geminiani, regularity; Lauredi, treachery; etc.). *The Tour is an uncertain conflict of certain essences*; nature, customs, literature, and rules successively relate these essences to each other: like atoms they graze each other, hook together, repel each other, and it is from this interplay that the epic is born. I supply below a characterial lexicon of the racers, at least of those who have acquired a reliable semantic value; we can count on this typology, it is stable, we are indeed dealing with essences. One might say that here, as in classical comedy, and singularly in commedia dell'arte, though according to an entirely different order of construction (comic duration remains that of a theater of conflict, whereas the Tour's duration is that of fictive narrative), the spectacle is generated by an astonishment of human relations: the essences collide according to every possible figure.

I believe that the Tour is the best example we have ever encountered of a total, hence an ambiguous myth; the Tour is at once a myth of expression and a myth of projection, realistic and utopian at the same time. The Tour expresses and liberates the French people through a unique fable in which the traditional impostures (psychology of essences, ethics of combat, magism of elements and forces, hierarchy of supermen and servants) mingle with forms of a positive interest, with the utopian image of a world stubbornly seeking reconciliation by the spectacle of a total clarity of relations between man, men, and nature. What is vitiated in the Tour is the basis, the economic motives, the ultimate profit of the ordeal, generator of ideological alibis. This does not keep the Tour from being a fascinating national phenomenon insofar as the epic expresses that fragile moment of history in which man, however clumsy and deceived, nonetheless contemplates through his impure fables a perfect adequation between himself, the community, and the universe.

RACER'S LEXICON (1955)

BOBET (Jean). Louison's double is also his negative; he is the great victim of the Tour. He owes to his elder the total sacrifice of his person, "as a brother." This racer, ceaselessly demoralized, suffers from a serious infirmity: he thinks. His quality as an established intellectual (he is an English teacher and wears enormous glasses) commits him to a destructive lucidity: he analyzes his suffering and loses by introspection the advantage of a musculature superior to his brother's. He is *complicated*, hence unlucky.

BOBET (Louison). Bobet is a Promethean hero; he has a magnificent fighter's temperament, an acute sense of organization, he is a calculator, he aims realistically at *winning*. His problem is a touch of cerebrality (though less than his brother, being only a high school graduate); he has experienced anxiety and wounded pride: he is bilious. In 1955 he had to face a heavy solitude. Without Koblet or Coppi, having to struggle with their ghosts, without declared rivals, powerful and solitary, everything was a threat to him, danger could appear from anywhere and everywhere ("I need the Koblets and the Coppis, it's too difficult being the only favorite"). *Bobetism* consecrates a very special type of racer, in whom energy is paired with an analytical and calculating interiority.

BRANKART. Symbolizes the rising younger generation. Has caused his elders some anxiety. Magnificent on the straight stretches, of an ever-lasting, offensive humor.

COLETTO. The most elegant racer in the Tour.

COPPI. Perfect hero. On the bike, he has every virtue. Formidable ghost.

DARRIGADE. Repellent Cerberus, but useful. Zealous servant of the Tricolor's cause, and for this reason forgiven for being a wheel sucker, an intractable jailer.

DE GROOT. Solitary rider, taciturn Batavian.

GAUL. New archangel of the mountain. Carefree ephebe, slender cherub, beardless boy, delicate and insolent, inspired youth, he is the Rimbaud of the Tour. At certain moments, Gaul is inhabited by a god; his supernatural gifts then suspend a mysterious threat over his rivals. The divine gift given to Gaul is lightness: by grace, elevation, and soaring (the mysterious absence of effort), Gaul suggests a bird or a plane (he perches lightly on the spurs of the Alps, and his pedals turn like propellers). But sometimes, too, the god abandons him, his gaze then becomes "strangely blank." Like every mythic being that has the power of vanquishing air or water, Gaul, on earth, becomes clumsy, impotent; the divine gift encumbers him ("I can race only in the mountains. And even then, only uphill. Coming down, I'm clumsy, *or perhaps too light*").

GEMINIANI (called Raph or Gem). Races with the loyal and slightly obtuse regularity of a motor. Uninspired yet earnest in the mountains. Out of favor and sympathetic. Talkative.

HASSENFORDER (called Hassen the Magnificent or Hassen the Corsair). A combative and conceited racer ("I've got a Bobet in each leg"). The ardent warrior who knows nothing but fighting, cannot fake.

KOBLET. Charmed racer who could permit himself anything, even not calculating his efforts. The anti-Bobet, for whom he remains, even absent, a formidable ghost, like Coppi.

KÜBLER (called Ferdi or the Eagle of the Adziwil). Angular, ungainly, dry, and whimsical, Kübler participates in the theme of the galvanic. His *leap* is sometimes suspected of artificiality (does he use drugs?). An actor (coughs and limps only when you're looking). As a German-speaking Swiss, Kübler has the right and the duty to talk baby talk, like Balzac's Teutons and the Countess de Ségur's foreigners ("Ferdi unlucky. Gem always behind Ferdi. Ferdi not get away").

LAUREDI. The traitor, the villain of the Tour this year. This situation permits him to be openly sadistic: he tried to make Bobet suffer by becoming a fierce leech behind him. Forced to give it up: was this a punishment? In any case a warning.

MOLINERIS. The man of the last kilometer.

ROLLAND (Antonin). Mild, stoical, sociable. A good racer in the clinch, regular in his performances. Bobet's confidant. Cornelian debate: must he be offered up? Typical sacrifice, since it is unfair and necessary.

THE *BLUE GUIDE*

The *Blue Guide* scarcely knows landscape save in the form of the picturesque. Picturesque means what is more or less uneven. We recognize here that bourgeois promotion of mountains, that old alpestrine myth (dating mostly from the nineteenth century) which Gide correctly associated with Helvetico-Protestant morality and which has always functioned as a bastardized mixture of nature worship and puritanism (regeneration by pure air, ethical convictions in the presence of mountain peaks, climbing as a civic function, etc.). Among the numerous sights (really *views*) promoted by the *Guide* to aesthetic existence, we rarely find plains (redeemed only when they can be said to be fertile), never plateaus (or even *plateaux*). Only mountains, gorges, defiles, and of course torrents can accede to the travelers' pantheon, doubtless to the degree where they appear to sustain a morality of effort and of solitude. A trip according to the *Blue Guide* is thus revealed as an economic management of work, the ready substitution for the moralizing walk. Which already signifies that the *Blue Guide*'s mythology dates back to the previous century, from that historical phase when the bourgeoisie enjoyed a sort of new-minted euphoria in *buying* effort, retaining its image and its virtue without suffering any of its discomforts. Thus it is, quite logically and quite stupidly, the landscape's thanklessness, its lack of spaciousness or humanity, so contrary to the happiness of travel, which accounts for its interest. The *Guide* might go as far as to write, quite coldly: "The road becomes very picturesque (tunnels)": it makes no difference that one can see nothing at all, since the word *tunnel* has here become the sufficient sign of mountains, a sign expressive enough for its encasement to be of no interest.

In the same way that hilliness is flattered to the point of annihilating any other kind of horizon, similarly a country's humanity disappears to the exclusive benefit of its monuments. For the *Blue Guide*, men exist only as "types." In Spain, for instance, the Basque is an adventurous sailor, the Levantine a carefree gardener, the Catalan a cunning tradesman, and the Cantabrian a sentimental mountaineer. Here we recognize this disease of *essence*, which is the basis of all of mankind's bourgeois mythology (which is why one encounters it so often). The Hispanic ethnic reality is thereby reduced to a vast classical ballet, a sort of very well-behaved commedia dell'arte whose improbable typology serves to mask the real spectacle of conditions, classes, and trades. Socially, for the *Blue Guide*, people exist only on trains, where they populate a very "mixed" third class. Apart from that, they are only "introductory," they constitute a charming romantic decor destined to impose on the country's essential nature: its collection of monuments.

Apart from its wild defiles, suitable for moral ejaculations, the Spain of the *Blue Guide* knows only one kind of space, the one which weaves, across any number of unnamable spaces, a close-knit chain of churches, sacristies, altarpieces, crosses, altar curtains, spires (always octagonal), sculptural groups (Family and Labor), Romanesque porches, naves, and life-size crucifixes. It leaps to the eye that all these monuments are religious, for from a bourgeois point of view it is virtually impossible to imagine a History of art which is not Christian and Catholic. Christianity is the chief purveyor of tourism, and one travels only to visit churches. In the case of Spain, this imperialism is a joke, for Catholicism here often looks like a barbaric force which has stupidly degraded the previous successes of Muslim civilization: the mosque at Córdoba, whose marvelous forest of columns is constantly obstructed by crude clumps of altars, or else some site denatured by the aggressive domination of a monumental Virgin (put there by Franco), all of which should help the French bourgeois to glimpse at least once in his life that there is also, historically speaking, quite another side to Christianity.

In general, the *Blue Guide* testifies to the vanity of all analytic descriptions, those which reject both explanation and phenomenology: it answers in fact none of the questions which a modern traveler might ask in crossing any terrain which is real and *which requires time to cross.* The choice of monuments suppresses both the reality of the landscape and that of the people native to it, it takes no account of anything present, i.e., historical, and thereby the monument itself becomes indecipherable, hence stupid. The spectacle is constantly in the process of disappearing, and the *Guide* becomes, by an operation common to any mystification, the very contrary of its own publicity, an instrument of blindness. By reducing geography to the description of a monumental and uninhabited world, the *Blue Guide* offers a mythology dated by a portion of the bourgeoisie itself: it is incontestable that travel has become (or become again) a human and no longer a "cultural" means of approach: it is once again (perhaps as in the eighteenth century) the manners of everyday life which are nowadays a principal object of travel, and these are the human geography, the urbanism, the sociology, and the economy which trace today's actual and even most profane questions. The *Guide* has remained at the stage of a partially dated mythology, the kind which postulated (religious) art as a fundamental value of culture, but considered its "wealth" and its "treasures" only a comforting accumulation of merchandise (a creation of museums). Such behavior expressed a double requirement: to offer a cultural alibi as "escapist" as possible and yet to insist on maintaining this alibi in the toils of a numerable and appropriative system, so that the ineffable could be evaluated at any moment. It follows that this myth of travel has become entirely anachronistic, even in the heart of the bourgeoisie, and I presume that if we were to entrust the elaboration of a new tourist guide, to the editors, say, of *L'Express* or of *Match*, we would see, arguable as they would still be even now, quite different countries: the Spain of Anquetil or Larousse would be succeeded by the Spain of André Siegfried, followed by that of Fourastié. Already, consider how, in the *Michelin Guide*, the number of bathrooms and of restaurant forks outnumbers that of "artistic curiosities": the bourgeois myths too have their differential geology.

It is true that for Spain, the blinkered and retrograde character of the description best suits the *Guide*'s latent Franco-oriented sympathies. Aside from some specifically historical narratives (moreover, rare and meager, for it is well known that History is hardly a good bourgeois), in which the Republicans are always "extremists" busily pillaging the churches (but nothing about Guernica), while the good "Nationalists" of course spend their time "liberating" solely by virtue of "skillful strategic maneuvers" and "heroic feats of resistance," I must mention the flowering of a superb alibi myth, that of the country's *prosperity*: of course this is a "statistical" and "total" or more exactly a "commercial" prosperity. The *Guide* does not tell us how this fine prosperity was distributed: doubtless hierarchically, since we are delightedly told that "the serious and patient effort of this nation has included the reform of its political system, in order to obtain the regeneration by the loyal application of solid principles of order and hierarchy."

AGONY COLUMNS

Journalism today is quite a technocracy, and our weekly press is the bench of a veritable magistracy of Conscience and Council, as in the Jesuits' finest days. The morality involved is a modern one, i.e., not emancipated but guaranteed by science, and for which we require less the advice of a universal sage than of a specialist. Thus each organ of the human body (for we must start with the concrete) has its technician, both pope and supreme scholar: the Colgate dentist for the mouth, the "Doctor, tell me" physician for nosebleeds, the Lux chemist for the skin, a Dominican father for the soul, and the agony columnist of certain women's papers for the heart.

The Heart is a female organ. To deal with it therefore requires a competence in the moral order as special as the gynecologist's in the physiological. The adviser consequently occupies her position thanks to the sum of her knowledge in moral cardiology; but a characterial gift is also required, a gift which is, as we know, the glorious mark of the French practitioner (contrasted, say, with her American colleagues): this gift is the alliance of extensive experience, implying a respectable age, with an eternal youth of the Heart, which here defines the right to knowledge, to science. The adviser thus participates in a powerful type, that of the *rough diamond*, endowed with healthy frankness (to the point of bullying), a great vivacity in repartee, an enlightened but confident wisdom, and whose knowledge, real and modestly hidden, is always sublimated by the open sesame of contentious bourgeois morality: common sense.

To the degree that the Column allows us to know them, women who consult it are carefully stripped of any specific condition: just as under the surgeon's impartial scalpel the patient's social origin is generously put between parentheses, so under the adviser's gaze the postulant is reduced to a pure cardiac organ. Only her quality as a woman defines her: social condition is here treated as a useless parasitical reality which might hamper the concern for an undiluted feminine essence. Only men, an exterior race which forms the column's "subject," in the logistical sense of the word (what is talked about), are entitled to be social (as they must, since they *earn*); hence a specific heaven can be established for them: in general, it will be that of the successful businessman.

The Column's humanity reproduces an essentially juridical typology: far from any romanticism and from any actual investigation of what has been experienced, it follows as closely as possible a stable order of essences, that of the Civil Code. Women's world is divided up into three classes, of distinct status: *puella* (virgin), *conjunx* (wife), and *mulier* (unmarried woman, widow, adulteress, but in any case presently alone and possessing a certain amount of experience). Confronting this distribution is external humanity, the one which resists or threatens: first of all, *parentes* (those possessing *patria potestas*); then *vir* (the husband or the male who also wields the sacred right to subjugate the woman). Recognizably, for all its fictive apparatus, the world of the Heart is not improvised: it always reproduces, for better or worse, fixed juridical relationships. Even when it says "I" in its most lacerating or naïve voice, the column's humanity exists a priori only as a small number of fixed, named elements, those of the familial institution: the column postulates the Family just when it seems to be taking as its liberating task the exposure of its interminable disputes.

In this world of essences, that of woman herself is threatened, sometimes by the parents, more often by the man; in
both cases, juridical marriage is salvation, the resolution of
the crisis; whether the man be adulterous or a seducer (moreover, an ambiguous threat), or reluctant, it is marriage as a
social contract of appropriation which is the panacea. But the
goal's very fixity compels, in cases of delay or failure (and this
is by definition the moment when the Column intervenes),
certain unreal procedures of compensation: the Column's vac-
cines against the man's aggressions or negligences all aim at
sublimating defeat, either by sanctifying it in the form of sacrifice (keeping silence, not thinking about it, being kind, hop-
ing) or by claiming it a posteriori as a pure freedom (keeping
one's head, working, flouting men, linking arms with women) .

Thus, whatever the apparent contradictions, the Column's
morality never postulates for Woman any condition but a parasitical one: only marriage, by naming her juridically, makes her
exist. Once again we find the very structure of the gynoeceum, defined as a closed freedom under man's external gaze.
The Column establishes Woman more solidly than ever as a
special zoological species, a colony of parasites with interior
movements of its own but whose limited amplitude is always
brought back to the fixity of the guardian element (*vir*). This
parasitism, maintained under trumpet calls of Female Independence, naturally involves a complete impotence with regard
to any opening onto the real world: under cover of a competence whose limits are loyally paraded, the adviser always refuses
to take sides about problems which appear to exceed the functions proper to the Feminine Heart; frankness comes to a halt,
modestly enough, at the threshold of racism or religious feeling; this is because such frankness constitutes a vaccine with a
very specific use; its role is to infuse a conformist morality of
subjection: onto the adviser is projected all the emancipatory

potential of the feminine species: in her, women are free by proxy. The apparent freedom of the advice makes unnecessary any real freedom of conduct: morality seems to be loosened a little, only to tighten a little more securely the constitutive dogmas of society.

ORNAMENTAL CUISINE

The periodical *Elle* (a veritable mythological treasure) gives us almost weekly a lovely color photograph of an elaborately prepared dish: gilded partridges studded with cherries, a pinkish jellied chicken, a mold of crayfish fringed with their own russet shells, a creamy trifle embellished with a frieze of candied fruit, multicolored sponge cakes, etc.

In this cuisine, the prevailing substantial category is surface sheen: visible effort has been made to produce glazed, carefully smoothed finishes, to conceal whatever aliment is underneath by a sleek deposit of sauces, icings, jellies, and creams. Such coatings derive, of course, from the very finality of superficies, vested in a primarily visual order. The magazine advocates a cuisine devoted to sight, that most distingué of the senses, for there is, in this insistence on *appearance*, a permanent craving for distinction. *Elle* is a journal of precious things, at least so legend has it, for its role is to offer its huge working-class public (described thus according to market research) the answer to everyone's dream of chic; hence a cuisine of surfaces and alibis which consistently endeavors to attenuate or even to disguise the primary nature of foodstuffs, the brutality of meats, or the abruptness of shellfish. A peasant dish is admitted only on occasion (an "authentic" family pot-au-feu), as the rustic whim of blasé city folk.

See illustration 12.

But above all, a shiny surface prepares and supports a major development in a cuisine of distinction: ornamentation. *Elle*'s glazes supply a fabric for frenzied minor embellishments: intricately incised mushrooms, a punctuation of cherries, sculptured lemons, truffle slivers, silver pastilles, arabesques of crystallized fruit, the underlying layer (which is why I called it a deposit, the aliment itself being no more than an uncertain stratum) intended as the page on which can be read an entire curlicued cuisine (pink being the favorite color).

Such ornamentation proceeds by two contradictory routes whose dialectical resolution can be readily discerned: on the one hand, to escape nature by a sort of delirious baroque (to stud a lemon with shrimps, to color a chicken shocking pink, to serve grapefruit broiled), and, on the other, to attempt reconstituting that same nature by an incongruous artifice (to arrange meringued mushrooms and holly leaves on a yule log cake, to replace shrimp heads around the adulterated béchamel hiding their bodies). A similar impulse is recognizable in the elaboration of petit bourgeois trinkets (ashtrays made in imitation of tiny saddles, cigarette lighters that closely resemble cigarettes, terrines in the shape of hares).

All this is because here, as in all petit bourgeois art, the irrepressible tendency toward extreme realism is countered—or balanced—by one of the constant imperatives of household journalism: what *L'Express* proudly calls *getting ideas*. Cooking in *Elle* is quite similarly a cuisine "of ideas." But here invention, confined to a magical reality, must apply only to *garnishing*, for the magazine's "distinguished" vocation precludes it from dealing with any real problems of alimentation (the real problem is not to stud a partridge with cherries, but to find the partridge, i.e., to pay for it).

This ornamental cuisine is in fact supported by an entirely mythical economy. It is openly a dream cuisine, as we can see in *Elle*'s photographs, which never show the dishes except from above, objects at once close up and inaccessible, whose consumption can readily be accomplished in a single glance. This is, in the full sense of the word, an advertisement cuisine, totally magical, especially if we remember that this magazine is read for the most part in low-income homes. The latter, moreover, explains the former: it is because *Elle* is addressed to a working-class public that it is very careful not to postulate an economical cuisine. Have a look at *L'Express*, for example, whose exclusively bourgeois public enjoys a comfortable purchasing power: its cuisine is real, not magical; *Elle* prints the recipe for fantasy partridges, *L'Express* for salade niçoise. *Elle*'s public is entitled only to fiction, the public of *L'Express* can be offered real dishes, with every assurance that it can prepare them.

THE *BATORY* CRUISE

Since there are now to be bourgeois trips taken in Soviet Russia, the French press has begun to elaborate certain myths of comprehension with regard to the Communist reality. Messieurs Sennep and Macaigne, of *Le Figaro*, having embarked on the *Batory*, have written for their paper the sketch of a new alibi, the impossibility of judging a country like Russia in a few days. Hasty conclusions are no good, Monsieur Macaigne declares gravely, ridiculing his traveling companions and their generalizing mania.

It is quite entertaining to see a paper which promulgates anti-Sovietism year after year on the basis of gossip a thousand times more improbable than an authentic stay, however short, in the USSR, here suffering a fit of agnosticism and wrapping itself in the noble cloak of an insistence on scientific objectivity, at the very moment when its envoys can at last approach what they used to speak of so readily and so decisively from a distance. This is because, for the requirements of his cause, the journalist divides up his functions, like Maître Jacques his garments. To whom do you want to speak? To Monsieur Macaigne the professional journalist who informs

Eight hundred French tourists—a few journalists among them—embarked on the Batory *cruise to travel to Russia in late August 1955. In September and October of that same year, war veterans refused to take service in the Algerian War, hence causing disruption in France's engagement in the early stages of the conflict.*

and who judges, in a word who *knows*, or to Monsieur Macaigne the innocent tourist who out of pure probity wants to draw no conclusions from what he sees? This *tourist* is a wonderful alibi here: thanks to him, one can look without understanding, travel without taking any interest in political realities; the tourist belongs to a subhumanity deprived of judgment and who ridiculously exceeds his condition when he claims to have any. And Monsieur Macaigne mocks those of his fellow travelers who seem to have had the absurd notion of adding to the sights of the street a few figures, a few general facts, the rudiments of a possible depth in the knowledge of an unknown country: the crime of *lèse-tourisme*, i.e., of *lèse-obscurisme*, which, at *Le Figaro*, is not forgiven.

Hence for the general theme of the USSR as a permanent object of criticism has been substituted the seasonal theme of the street, the only reality granted to the tourist. The street has suddenly become a neutral terrain, where one can observe without claiming to conclude. But we discover what observations are involved. For this honest reserve never prevents tourist Macaigne from pointing out in the immediate life before him several awkward accidents likely to recall Soviet Russia's barbarous vocation: the Russian locomotives emit a long moan quite unrelated to the whistle of ours; the station platforms are wooden; the hotels are badly run; there are Chinese characters written on certain trucks (theme of the yellow peril); finally, a fact which reveals a truly retarded civilization, there are no bistros in Russia—nothing but pear juice!

But above all, the myth of the street allows him to develop the major theme of all political mystifications: the divorce between the people and the regime. Even if the Russian people are saved, it is as the reflection of French liberties. That an old woman should burst into tears, that a dockworker (*Le Figaro* is social) should offer flowers to the visitors from Paris, have less to do with an emotion of hospitality than with the expres-

1. The actor Gérard Philipe in 1951.
(© Ministère de la Culture/Médiathèque du Patrimoine,
Dist. RMN/Art Resource NY)

2. Miss Europe, *Paris-Match*, issue #287, September 25, 1954. (© Paris-Match/Scoop)

3. Marlon Brando, *Paris-Match*, issue #293, November 6, 1954. (© Paris-Match/Scoop)

4. Abbé Pierre, *Paris-Match* cover, issue #255, February 13, 1954. (© Hubert de Segonzac/Paris-Match/Scoop)

5. Floods, *Paris-Match*, issue #305, January 29, 1955. (© Paris-Match/Scoop)

Face à Bichon, soi cannibale de la tribu des « nègres rouges ». Il a failli être mangé. Les mangeurs d'hommes se sont laissé fléchir par son sourire d'enfant. Il est devenu leur idole.

6. The child Bichon in Africa, *Paris-Match*, issue #305, January 29, 1955.
(© Paris-Match/Scoop)

7. Greta Garbo in the movie *Queen Christina* (1933). (© Everett Collection)

8. Malki's fiancée, *Paris-Match*, issue #319, May 7, 1955. (© Paris-Match/Scoop)

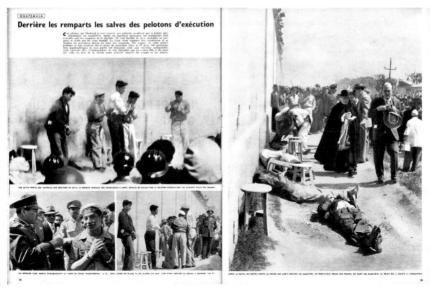

9. Execution of Guatemalan Communists, *Paris-Match*, issue #276, July 10, 1954. (© Paris-Match/Scoop)

10. Louison Bobet cycling up Mont Ventoux, stage 11 in 1955 Tour de France.
(© Presse Sports)

11. Cyclists in Saint-Gaudens-Pau, stage 18 in 1955 Tour de France.
(© Presse Sports)

12. "The Pink Dinner," *Elle* magazine, issue #477, January 31, 1955. (© Elle/Scoop)

13. The new Citroën car, *Paris-Match* cover, issue #340, October 15, 1955. (© Paris-Match/Scoop)

14. Minou Drouet at home playing and writing, *Paris-Match*, issue #348, December 10, 1955. (© Paris-Match/Scoop)

sion of a political nostalgia: the French bourgeoisie *en voyage* is the symbol of French freedom, French happiness.

Hence it is only when it has been illumined by the sun of capitalist civilization that the Russian people can be recognized as spontaneous, affable, generous. Then there will be nothing but advantages in revealing their overflowing kindness: which always signifies a deficiency of the Soviet regime, a plenitude of Western happiness: The "indescribable" gratitude the young Intourist guide expresses to the doctor (from Passy) who offers her nylons certainly indicates the economic backwardness of the Communist regime and the enviable prosperity of Western democracy. As always (and I have remarked on the phenomenon apropos of the *Blue Guide*), we pretend to treat as comparable terms privileged luxury and popular standing; we ascribe to the credit of all of France the inimitable chic of our Parisian toilette, as if all Frenchwomen dressed themselves chez Dior or Balenciaga; and we photograph the young Soviet women dazed by French fashions as if we were dealing with a primitive tribe stopped cold by the fork or the phonograph. In a general way, the trip to the USSR serves chiefly to establish the bourgeois honors of Western civilization. Parisian gowns, locomotives which whistle rather than moan, the bistros, pear juice abandoned, and above all, the French privilege par excellence: Paris, i.e., a combination of grand couturiers and the Folies-Bergère: it is this inaccessible treasure which apparently stimulates the Russians' dreams, according to the *Batory* tourists.

In the face of which the regime can remain faithful to its caricature, that of an oppressive order which maintains everything in the uniformity of machines. The waiter in the sleeping car having asked Monsieur Macaigne to return the spoon with his glass of tea, Monsieur Macaigne deduces (always in a great gesture of political agnosticism) the existence of a gigantic paperwork bureaucracy whose sole concern is to keep up the exact inventory of teaspoons. A new pasture for national vanity, quite proud of the disorder of the French. The anarchy of customs and of superficial behavior is an excellent alibi for order: individualism is a bourgeois myth which allows us to vaccinate the order and tyranny of class with a harmless freedom: the *Batory* brought the flabbergasted Russians the spectacle of a glamorous freedom, that of chattering during museum visits and "being funny" in the metro.

No question but that "individualism" is a luxury product for export only. In France, and applied to an object of quite different importance, it has, at least for *Le Figaro*, another name. When four hundred Air Force veterans, called up for North African service, refused to serve one Sunday, *Le Figaro* no longer spoke of the sympathetic anarchy and enviable individualism of the French: no longer any question here of museum or metro, but rather of colonial investments and big money; whereupon "disorder" was no longer the phenomenon of a glorious Gallic virtue, but the artificial product of a few "agents"; it was no longer glamorous but *lamentable*, and the *monumental lack of discipline* of the French, formerly praised with so many waggish and self-satisfied winks, has become, on the road to Algeria, a shameful treason. *Le Figaro* knows its bourgeoisie: freedom out front, on display, but Order back home, a constitutive necessity.

THE MAN IN THE STREET ON STRIKE

There are still people for whom a strike is a scandal: i.e., not only a mistake, a disorder, or a misdemeanor, but a moral crime, an intolerable action which in their eyes is an offense to Nature. *Inadmissible, scandalous, revolting* are the words used by certain readers of *Le Figaro* about a recent strike. This is a language which dates, in fact, from the Restoration and which expresses its profound mentality; that was the period when the bourgeoisie, only recently in power, operated a kind of crasis between Morality and Nature, giving the one the protection of the other: fearing they would have to naturalize Morality, they moralized Nature, pretended to identify the political and the natural order, and ended by declaring immoral everything which contested the structural laws of the society they were determined to defend. To Charles X's prefects as to *Le Figaro*'s readers today, a strike seemed first of all a challenge to the prescriptions of moralized reason: to strike is "to defy the world," i.e., to infringe less a civic than a "natural legality," to attack the philosophic basis of bourgeois society, that mixture of morality and logic which is *common sense*.

For the scandal proceeds from an inconsistency: a strike is scandalous because it affects precisely those whom it does not concern. It is reason which suffers and rebels: direct, mechanical, one might say computable causality, which has already appeared to us as the basis of petit bourgeois logic in Monsieur Poujade's speeches—this causality is disturbed: a strike's effect is incomprehensibly remote from its cause, quite escapes it, and it is this which is intolerable, shocking. Contrary to what we might suppose about petit bourgeois dreams, this class has a tyrannical, infinitely sensitive notion of causality: the basis of its morality is not magical at all, but rational. Only, it is a linear, narrow rationality based on a virtually numerical correspondence of causes and effects. What this rationality lacks is obviously the notion of complex functions, the imagination of a remote operation of determinisms, of a solidarity of events which the materialist tradition has systematized under the name of *totality*.

Such a restriction of effects requires a division of functions. We might readily imagine that "men" are united: therefore, we oppose not man to man, but the striker to the ordinary man. The ordinary man (also called the man in the street, whose conglomeration received the innocent name of *population*: we have already seen all this in Monsieur Macaigne's vocabulary)— the ordinary man is an imaginary, even algebraic character thanks to whom it becomes possible to break up the contagious dispersion of effects and to retain a reduced causality about which we will be able to reason calmly and virtuously. By arguing a special status in the worker's general condition, bourgeois reason breaks the social circuit and demands for its own profit a solitude which it is the strike's very function to deny: the strike protests against what is expressly addressed to it. The man in the street and the taxpayer (that other alias) are literally characters, i.e., actors promoted according to the needs of the cause to surface roles, their mission is to preserve the essentialist separation of social cells, which we know was the first ideological principle of the bourgeois revolution.

So that in effect we rediscover here a constitutive feature of the reactionary mentality, which is to disperse the collectivity into individuals and the individual into essences. What the entire bourgeois theater does to psychological man, setting

Old against Young, Cuckold against Lover, Priest against Man of the World, the readers of *Le Figaro* do to the social being: to set striker against taxpayer is to constitute the world into a theater, to derive from the total man a special actor, and to oppose these arbitrary actors to each other in the lie of a symbolic structure which pretends to believe that the part is merely a perfect reduction of the whole.

This constitutes an example of a general technique of mystification which consists in formalizing the social disorder as much as possible. For example, the bourgeoisie is not concerned, it says, to know which side in a strike is right or wrong: having divided the effects the better to isolate the only one which concerns it, the bourgeoisie claims to have no interest in the cause: the strike is reduced to a solitary incident, to a phenomenon we avoid explaining the better to manifest its scandal. Similarly, the public services worker, the civil servant will be abstracted from the working mass, as if the entire salaried status of these workers were somehow drawn to, fixed at, and subsequently sublimated in the very surface of their functions. This prejudiced reduction of the social conditions makes it possible to dodge reality without abandoning the euphoric illusion of a direct causality which begins just where it is convenient for the bourgeoisie that it should: as the citizen suddenly finds himself reduced to the pure concept of the man in the street, so young draft-age Frenchmen wake up one morning sublimated into a pure military essence which will be virtuously taken for the *natural* point of departure of universal logic: military status thus becomes the unconditional origin of a new causality, which it will henceforth be monstrous to question: to contest this status can therefore in no case be the effect of a general and previous causality (the citizen's political consciousness) but only the product of accidents posterior to the operation of the new causal series: from the bourgeois point of view, a soldier's refusal to serve can only be the result of agents or alcohol, as if there existed no other good reason for this action: a belief whose stupidity is exceeded only by its bad faith, since it is obvious that the contestation of a status can find its root and nourishment only in a consciousness which takes its distance with regard to that status.

We are dealing here with a new outbreak of essentialism. Hence it is logical that, in the face of the lies of essence and of party, the strike should posit the being and the truth of a totality. The strike signifies that man is total, that all his functions are connected with one another, that the roles of man in the street, taxpayer, and soldier are much too fragile to oppose the contagion of facts, and that in society all are concerned by all. By protesting that a strike is a disturbance to those it does not concern, the bourgeoisie testifies to a cohesion of social functions which it is the very goal of the strike to manifest: the paradox is that the petit bourgeois invokes the *naturalness* of his isolation at the very moment when the strike overwhelms him with the obviousness of his subordination.

AFRICAN GRAMMAR

The official vocabulary of African affairs is, as we might suspect, purely axiomatic. Which is to say that it has no value as communication, but only as intimidation. It therefore constitutes a *writing*, i.e., a language intended to bring about a coincidence between norms and facts, and to give a cynical reality the guarantee of a noble morality. In a general way it is a language which functions essentially as a code, i.e., the words have no relation to their content, or else a contrary one. It is a writing we might call cosmetic, because it aims at covering the facts with a sound of language or, if we prefer, with the sufficient sign of language. I should like to indicate briefly the way in which a lexicon and a grammar can be politically committed.

BAND (of outlaws, rebels, or civil criminals). This is the very example of an axiomatic language. The disparagement of the vocabulary here serves in a precise way to deny the state of war, which permits annihilating the notion of an interlocutor. "No arguments with outlaws." The moralization of language thus permits referring the problem of peace to an arbitrary change of vocabulary.

In 1955, Morocco, then a French protectorate, was the scene of violent uprisings sparked by France's exile of Sultan Muhammad V and his replacement by the unpopular Muhammad Ben Arafa, whose reign was perceived as illegitimate. Violence in the Algerian War escalated that same year.

When the "band" is French, it is sublimated under the name of *community*.

LACERATION (cruel, painful). This term helps accredit the notion of History's *irresponsibility*. The state of war is masked under the noble garment of tragedy, as if the conflict were essentially Evil, and not a (remediable) evil. Colonization evaporates, engulfed in the halo of an impotent lament, which *recognizes* the misfortune in order to establish it only the more successfully.

Phraseology: "The government of the Republic is resolved to make all possible efforts to bring to an end the cruel lacerations Morocco is suffering." (Letter from Monsieur Coty to Ben Arafa.)

". . . The Moroccan people, painfully divided against itself . . ." (Declaration by Ben Arafa.)

DISHONOR. We know that in ethnology, at least according to Lévi-Strauss's very suggestive hypothesis, *mana* is a kind of algebraic symbol, intended to represent "an indeterminate value of signification, in itself without meaning and therefore capable of receiving any meaning, whose unique function is to fill a gap between signifier and signified." *Honor* is quite specifically our *mana*, something like a blank place in which we arrange the entire collection of inadmissible meanings and which we make sacred in the manner of a taboo.

Phraseology: "It would be to dishonor the Muslim populations to let it be supposed that these men could be considered in France as their representatives. It would also be to dishonor France." (Communiqué of the Ministry of the Interior.)

DESTINY. It is at the very moment when, History testifying once again to its freedom, colonized peoples begin to deny the fatality of their condition that the bourgeois vocabulary makes the greatest use of the word *destiny*. Like honor, destiny is a *mana* in which are modestly collected colonization's most sinister determinisms.

Naturally, Destiny exists only in a linked form. It is not military conquest which has subjected Algeria to France, it is a conjunction performed by Providence which has united two destinies. The link is declared indissoluble in the very period when it is dissolving with an explosiveness which cannot be concealed.

Phraseology: "We intend, as for ourselves, to give the peoples whose destiny is linked to ours a true independence within voluntary association." (Monsieur Pinay to the UN.)

GOD. Sublimated form of the French government.

Phraseology: "When the Omnipotent designated us to wield supreme power." (Declaration by Ben Arafa.)

". . . With the abnegation and the sovereign dignity of which you have always given the example . . . Your Majesty thus intends to obey the will of the Almighty." (Letter from Monsieur Coty to Ben Arafa, dismissed by the government.)

WAR. The goal is to deny the thing. For this, two means are available: either to name it as little as possible (most frequent procedure); or else to give it the meaning of its contrary (more cunning procedure, which is at the basis of almost all the mystifications of bourgeois discourse). *War* is then used in the sense of *peace*, and *pacification* in the sense of *war*.

Phraseology: "War does not keep measures of pacification from being taken." (General de Monsabert.) By which we are to understand that (official) peace does not, fortunately, prevent (real) war.

MISSION. This is the third *mana* word. Into it we can put whatever is wanted: schools, electricity, Coca-Cola, police operations,

raids, death sentences, concentration camps, freedom, civilization, and the "presence" of France.

Phraseology: "You know, however, that France has a mission in Africa which she alone can fulfill." (Monsieur Pinay to
the UN.)

POLITICS. Assigned to a limited domain: on the one hand,
there is France; and on the other, politics. North African affairs, when they concern France, are not within the domain of
politics. When things become serious, abandon Politics for the
Nation. For men of the Right, Politics is the Left: *they* are
France.

Phraseology: "To seek to protect the French community and
the virtues of·France is not to engage in politics." (General
Tricon-Dunois.)

In a contrary sense and bracketed with the word *conscience*
(*politics of conscience*), the word *politics* becomes euphemistic;
it then signifies a practical sense of spiritual realities, the nuance which permits a Christian to set out in good conscience
to "pacify" Africa.

Phraseology: ". . . To refuse service a priori in an army im-
minently to serve in Africa, in order to avoid such a situation
(to contradict an inhuman order), this abstract Tolstoyism
cannot be identified with a politics of conscience, for it is no
politics at all." (Dominican editorial in *La Vie intellectuelle*.)

POPULATION. This is a favorite word of the bourgeois vocabulary. It serves as an antidote to the excessively brutal *classes*,
which, moreover, is "without reality." *Population* is meant to
depoliticize the plurality of groups and minorities by pushing
individuals back into a neutral, passive collection which is entitled to the bourgeois pantheon only on the level of a politically unconscious existence. The term is generally ennobled by
its plural: *the Muslim populations,* which does not fail to sug-

gest a difference in maturity between the Metropolitan unity
and the pluralism of the colonized, France *gathering* beneath
her what is by nature diverse and numerous.

When it is necessary to make a disparaging judgment (war
occasionally compels such severities), we readily fraction the
population into elements. Elements are generally fanatic or
manipulated. (For only fanaticism or unconsciousness can im-
pel anyone to try to abandon colonized status.)

Phraseology: "The elements of the population which have
been able to join the rebels under circumstances . . ." (Communiqué from the Ministry of the Interior.)

SOCIAL. *Social* is always bracketed with *economic.* This duo
uniformly functions as an alibi, i.e., it announces or justifies
on each occasion certain repressive operations, to the point
where we might say that it signifies them. The social is essentially schools (France's civilizing mission, education of over-
seas peoples, gradually led to maturity); the economic is
interests, always *obvious* and *reciprocal,* which *indissolubly* link
Africa and Metropolitan France. These "progressive" terms,
once suitably drained, can function with impunity as magical
units.

Phraseology: "Social and economic domain, social and economic installations."

The predominance of substantives in the whole vocabulary of which we have just provided a few samples derives obviously from the huge consumption of concepts necessary to the
cover-up of reality. Though general and advanced to the last
degree of decomposition, the exhaustion of this language
does not attack verbs and substantives in the same way: it destroys the verb and inflates the noun. Here moral inflation
bears on neither objects nor actions, but always on ideas, "notions," whose assemblage obeys less a communication pur-

pose than the necessity of a petrified code. Codification of the official language and its substantivation thus go hand in hand, for the myth is fundamentally nominal, insofar as nomination is the first procedure of distraction.

The verb undergoes a curious legerdemain: if it is a main verb, we find it reduced to the state of a simple copula, meant simply to posit the existence or the quality of the myth. (Monseiur Pinay to the UN: "*There would be* an illusory détente . . . *it would be* inconceivable . . . *What would be* a nominal independence?" . . . etc.) The verb arduously attains full semantic status only on the level of the future, the possible, or the unintentional, in a remote distance where the myth runs less risk of being contradicted. (A Moroccan government *will be constituted . . . called upon to negotiate* reforms . . . the effort undertaken by France *with a view to constructing* a free association . . . etc.)

In this presentation, the substantive generally requires what two excellent grammarians, Damourette and Pichon, who lack neither rigor nor humor in their terminology, used to call the notorious plate, which means that the noun's substance is always presented to us as known. We are here at the very heart of the myth's formation: it is because France's *mission*, the *laceration* of the Moroccan people, or Algeria's *destiny* is given grammatically as a postulate (a quality generally conferred upon each by the use of the definite article) that we cannot contest them discursively. Notoriety is the first form of naturalization.

I have already observed the quite banal emphasis put on certain plural forms (*populations*). It must be added that this emphasis overvalues or depreciates at will certain intentions: *populations* installs a euphoric sentiment of pacifically subjugated multitudes; but when we speak of *elementary nationalisms*, the plural aims at degrading further, if it is possible, the notion of (enemy) nationalism by reducing it to a collection of mediocre units. This is what our two grammarians, experts *avant la lettre* in African affairs, had further foreseen by distinguishing the *massive plural* from the *numerative plural*: in the first expression, the plural flatters an idea of mass; in the second, it insinuates an ideal of division. Thus grammar inflects the myth: it delegates its plurals to different moral tasks.

The adjective (or the adverb) often plays a curiously ambiguous role: it seems to proceed from an anxiety, from the sentiment that the substantives used, despite their notorious character, have undergone a wear and tear which cannot be entirely concealed; hence the necessity to reinvigorate them: independence becomes *true*, aspirations become *authentic*, destinies *indissolubly* linked. Here the adjective aims at clearing the noun of its past disappointments, presenting it in a new, innocent, credible state. As in the case of main verbs, the adjective confers a future value upon discourse. Past and present are the business of the substantives, great concepts in which the idea alone dispenses us from proof (Mission, Independence, Friendship, Cooperation, etc.); action and predicate, in order to be irrefutable, must take shelter behind some unreal form: finality, promise, or adjuration.

Unfortunately these adjectives of reinvigoration are worn out almost as fast as they are used, so that it is finally the adjectival relaunching of the myth which most certainly designates its inflation. It suffices to read *true, authentic, indissoluble*, or *unanimous* to get wind of the emptiness of the rhetoric. This is because at bottom these adjectives, which we might call adjectives of essence because they develop under a modal form the substance of the name they accompany—these adjectives cannot modify anything: independence cannot be anything but independent, friendship friendly, and cooperation unanimous. By the impotence of their effort, these wretched adjectives here come to manifest the ultimate health of language. Try as the official rhetoric will to reinforce the facades of reality, there is a moment when the words resist it and oblige it to reveal beneath the myth the alternative of lie or truth: independence is or is not, and all the adjectival designs which strive to give nothingness the qualities of being are the very signature of culpability.

NEITHER/NOR CRITICISM

In one of the first issues of the daily edition of *L'Express* can be read a profession of faith by an (anonymous) critic who produced a fine piece of balanced rhetoric asserting that criticism must be "neither a parlor game nor a municipal service"— i.e., neither reactionary nor Communist, neither gratuitous nor political.

Here is a mechanism of double exclusion largely deriving from that numerical frenzy which we have already encountered several times and which I thought might be broadly defined as a petit bourgeois feature: various methods would be reckoned as if on a scale, heaped in one pan or the other as one thought best, so as to appear, oneself, an unpersuadable arbiter endowed with an ideal, and thereby *just*, spirituality— like the beam which judges the scale's weighing process.

The tares necessary to such an accountancy are formed by the morality of the terms employed. According to an old terrorist procedure (there is no escaping terrorism), one judges with the same breath with which one names, and the word, ballasted by a prior culpability, comes quite naturally to weigh down one of the pans of the scale. For instance, say *culture* were to be opposed to *ideologies*. Culture is a noble, universal good, situated beyond social prejudices: culture has no weight. Ideologies, though, are partisan inventions: so, let the scales judge! One sets them back to back under culture's severe gaze (without realizing that culture too, after all, is an ideology). Everything happens as if in one pan there were certain heavy, prejudicial, dubious words (*ideology, catechism, militant*) meant to play a scale's defamatory game; and in the other pan there were certain light, pure, immaterial words ennobled by some divine right, sublime to the point of escaping the crude law of numbers (*adventure, passion, grandeur, virtue, honor*), words located above the sorry computation of lies; the latter group is charged with passing judgment on the former: in one pan, criminal words and in the other, arbitrating words. It goes without saying that the fine morality of the Middle Party ends up with a new dichotomy quite as simplistic as the one we sought to expose in the very name of complexity. True, our world may be subject to certain alternations, but you can be sure that for this scission there is no Tribunal: no salvation for the Judges, they too are thoroughly committed.

Moreover, it is enough to see which other myths appear in this *Neither/Nor* criticism, to understand in which pan such criticism is located. Without effusing about the myth of time-lessness implicit in any appeal to eternal "culture" ("an art for all time"), I also find in our *Neither/Nor* doctrine two current expedients of bourgeois mythology. The first consists in a certain notion of freedom, conceived as "the rejection of a priori judgment." Now, a literary judgment is always determined by the tonality in which it is couched, and the very *absence* of system—especially carried to the state of a profession of faith—derives from a very well-defined system, which in this case is an extremely common type of bourgeois ideology (or of culture, as our anonymous writer might say). One might even say that it is precisely when a man proclaims his total freedom (as from any a priori judgment) that his subordination is least debatable. We may quite safely challenge anyone's ever exercising an *innocent* criticism, pure of all systematic determination: the *Neither/Nor* critics are indeed committed to a system, which is not necessarily the one to which they proclaim allegiance. Literature cannot be judged without a certain prior notion of Man and of History, of Good, of Evil, of Society, etc.: even in that "harmless" word *adventure*, so eagerly moralized by our *Neither/Nor* critics in opposition to the nasty systems by which they are "not surprised," what an inheritance, what fatality, what routine! All freedom invariably ends by resuming possession of a certain known coherence, which is nothing but a certain a priori. Hence the critic's freedom is not to reject the choice (impossible!), it is to make clear what choice of freedom he is making, or not making.

The second bourgeois symptom of our text is the euphoric reference to a writer's "style" as one of Literature's eternal values. And yet nothing can escape History's interrogation, not even *good writing*. Style is a carefully dated critical value, and to make claims in the name of "style" at the very moment when a number of important writers have attacked this last bastion of the mythology of classicism is to give evidence of a certain archaism: no, to revert to "style" once again hardly suggests "adventure"! Better advised in its ulterior issuers, *L'Express* lately published a pertinent protest by Alain Robbe-Grillet against the magical recourse to Stendhal ("it reads just like Stendhal"). An alliance of a certain style and a certain humanity (Anatole France, for instance) may no longer suffice as a basis for Literature. It is even to be feared that "style," compromised by so many fraudulently human works, has finally become an a priori suspect object: in any case it is a value which must not be consigned to a writer's credit without proper appraisal. This does not mean, of course, that Literature can exist in the absence of a certain formal artifice. But, with all respect to our *Neither/Nor* critics, ever the adepts of a bipartite universe of which they would constitute the divine transcendance, the opposite of *good writing* is not necessarily *bad writing*: nowadays it is perhaps just *writing*. Literature has entered a difficult, restricted, mortal state. It is no longer its ornaments that it is defending, but its skin: I rather fear that the new *Neither/Nor* criticism has fallen a season behind.

STRIPTEASE

Striptease—at least Parisian striptease—is based on a contradiction: to desexualize a woman at the very moment she is denuded. So that it could be said that we are dealing in a sense with a spectacle of fear, or rather of "scare me," as if the eroticism here remained a sort of delicious terror, for which it suffices to announce the ritual signs in order to provoke at once the idea of sex and its conjuration.

Only the undressing's duration makes voyeurs of the public; but here, as in any mystifying spectacle, decor, accessories, and stereotypes combine to contradict the activity's initial provocation and ultimately engulf it in insignificance: evil is *advertised* the better to embarrass and to exorcise it. French striptease appears to rely on what I have previously called Operation Astra, a mystifying procedure which consists of vaccinating the public with a touch of evil, the better to immerse it in a henceforth immunized Morality: a few atoms of eroticism, designated by the situation of the spectacle itself, are actually absorbed into a reassuring ritual which effaces the flesh as surely as a vaccine or a taboo paralyze and contain sickness or sin.

There will therefore be in striptease a whole series of coverings affixed to the woman's body, even as she pretends to denude it. Exoticism is the first of these distancings, for it is inevitably a petrified eroticism that displaces the body to realms of legend or romance: a Chinese girl wielding an opium pipe (obligatory symbol of sinity), an undulating vamp with a gigantic cigarette holder; a Venetian setting with gondola, paniered dress, and somebody singing a serenade, all this aims at constituting the woman *from the start* as a disguised object; the striptease's purpose is then no longer to bring to light a secret depth, but to signify, through the shedding of a baroque and artificial costume, nakedness as a woman's *natural* vesture, which means, finally, regaining a perfectly chaste state of the flesh.

The classical accessories of the music hall, here mobilized without exception, also constantly alienate the revealed body, push it back into the enveloping comfort of a familiar rite: furs, fans, gloves, feathers, fishnet stockings, in a word, the whole closetful of adornment, ceaselessly reintegrate the living body with the category of luxurious objects which surround man with a magical decor. Beplumed or gloved, woman here advertises herself as the frozen music hall element; and to strip herself of such ritual objects no longer participates in a new denudation: furs, feathers, and gloves continue to impregnate woman with their magical virtues even once they are taken off, providing a sort of enveloping memory of a luxurious carapace, for it is an obvious law that the entirety of striptease is given in the very nature of the forsaken garment: if the latter is improbable, as in the case of the Chinese girl or the woman in furs, the nude who follows remains herself quite unreal, smooth, and closed up like a lovely slippery object, withdrawn by her very extravagance from human usages: this is the profound signification of the diamond- or sequin-covered G-string which is the very end of the striptease: this ultimate triangle, by its pure and geometric form, by its hard and glittering substance, defends her sex like a sword of chastity and definitively repels the woman into a mineral universe, the (precious) stone here being the irrefutable theme of the total and useless object.

Contrary to popular prejudice, the dance accompanying striptease from beginning to end is in no way an erotic factor. It is even, most likely, quite the contrary: here the faintly rhythmic undulation exorcises the fear of immobility; not only does it afford the spectacle the alibi of art (the music hall dances are always "artistic"), but it especially constitutes the last, most effective barrier: the dance, composed of ritual gestures seen a thousand times, acts as a cosmetic of movements, conceals nudity, smothers the spectacle under a layer of meaningless and yet principal gestures, for the nakedness is here relegated to the status of parasitical operations, performed in an improbable distance. Here we see the professionals of striptease wrap themselves in a miraculous ease which constantly clothes them, affords them the icy indifference of skillful practitioners haughtily taking refuge in the certitude of their technique: their knowledge clothes them like a garment.

All this scrupulous exorcism of sex can be verified a contrario in the "popular contests" of amateur striptease events: here "debutantes" undress in front of several hundred spectators without resorting, or resorting very crudely, to magic which incontestably reestablishes the spectacle's erotic power: here, initially, we find many fewer Chinese girls and Spanish senoritas, not much in the way of furs and feathers (instead strict suits and sensible coats), rarely an original disguise; clumsy steps, inadequate choreography, girls constantly threatened by immobility, above all "technical" embarrassments (resistance of panties, a slip, a brassiere) which give the gestures of undressing an unexpected importance, denying the woman the alibi of art and the refuge of the object, imprisoning her in a condition of weakness and timidity.

Yet at the Moulin-Rouge, a different kind of conjuration appears, probably typically French, an exorcism which aims, moreover, less to abolish eroticism than to domesticate it: the master of ceremonies tries to give striptease a reassuring petit bourgeois status. First of all, striptease is a *sport*: there is a Striptease Club which organizes "healthy" competitions whose laureates emerge crowned, rewarded by edifying prizes (a sub-scription to physical-culture lessons), a novel (which has to be Robbe-Grillet's *Le Voyeur*), or useful ones (a pair of nylons, five thousand francs). And then, striptease is connected to a *career* (debutantes, semiprofessionals, professionals), i.e., to the honorable exercise of a specialization (striptease performers are qualified workers); they can even be given the magical alibi of work, the *vocation:* one girl is "on the right track" or "likely to fulfill her promise" or, on the contrary, "taking her first steps" on the arduous road to a career in striptease. Finally and above all, the contestants are situated socially: one is a salesgirl, another a secretary (there are many secretaries in the Striptease Club). Striptease rejoins the audience, makes itself familiar, bourgeois, as if the French, contrary to the American public (at least so we are told), and following an irrepressible tendency of their social status, could conceive of eroticism only as a household propriety, protected by the alibi of a weekly sport, much more than by that of the magical spectacle: that is how, in France, striptease is nationalized.

THE NEW CITROËN

I believe that the automobile is, today, the almost exact equivalent of the great Gothic cathedrals: I mean, a great creation of the period, passionately conceived by unknown artists, consumed in its image, if not in its use, by an entire populace which appropriates in it an entirely magical object.

The new Citroën manifestly falls from heaven insofar as it presents itself first of all as a superlative *object*. It must not be forgotten that the object is the supernatural's best messenger: in this object there is easily a perfection and an absence of origin, a completion and a brilliance, a transformation of life into matter (matter being much more magical than life), and all in all a *silence* which belongs to the order of the marvelous. The DS (the Déesse, or Goddess) has all the characteristics (at least the public begins by unanimously attributing them to it) of one of those objects from another world that nourished the neomania of the eighteenth century and that of our science fiction: the Déesse is *first of all* a new *Nautilus*.

This is why it rouses interest less in its substance than in the joints of that substance. We know that smoothness is always an attribute of perfection because its contrary betrays a technical and entirely human operation of adjustment: Christ's tunic was seamless, just as the spaceships of science fiction are of unbroken metal. The DS 19 makes no claim to being

See illustration 13.

totally smooth, though its general shape is nicely rounded; however, it is the encasing of its sections which most interests the public: the edges of its windows are furiously tested, people run their hands along the wide rubber grooves which connect the rear window to its nickel surrounds. The DS has the beginnings of a new phenomenology of assembly, as if we were leaving a world of welded elements for a world of juxtaposed elements held together by the sole virtue of their marvelous shape, which, of course, is intended to introduce the notion of a more readily cooperative nature.

As for the material itself, there is no question that it promotes a taste for lightness in a magical sense. There is a return to a certain aerodynamism, new insofar as it is less massive, less incisive, more relaxed than in earlier periods of this fashion. Here speed is expressed in less aggressive, less sportif signs, as if it were shifting from a heroic form to a classical one. Such spiritualization can be discerned in the importance, the quality, and the actual substance of the glazed surfaces. The Déesse is visibly an exaltation of glass, and the cast metal is only a base. Here the sheets of glass are not windows, openings pierced in the dark shell, they are large spaces of empty air, having the smooth curvature and brilliance of soap bubbles, the hard thinness of a substance more entomological than mineral (the Citroën emblem, with its arrows, has now become a wingèd emblem, as if a change had occurred from an order of propulsion to an order of independent movement, from an order of the engine to that of the organism).

We are now confronted with a humanized art, and it may be that the DS marks a change in automobile mythology. Hitherto the superlative car belonged, one might say, to the bestiary of power; here it becomes at once more spiritual and more objective, and despite certain neomaniacal concessions (the empty steering wheel, for instance), it is now more *domestic*, more in accord with that sublimation of utensility we recognize in our contemporary household arts: the dashboard looks more like the worktable of a modern kitchen than a factory control room: the slender panes of matte rippled metal, the little levers with their white ball finials, the simplified dials, the very discreteness of the chromium, everything indicates a sort of control exerted over movement, henceforth conceived as comfort rather than performance. We evidently are shifting from an alchemy of speed to an appetite for driving.

It seems that the public has admirably divined the novelty of the themes proposed: initially responsive to neologism (an entire press campaign kept people on the alert for years), it made every effort to adopt an attitude of adaptation and utensility ("You've got to get used to it"). In the exhibition halls, the sample cars are visited with an intense, affectionate care: this is the great tactile phase of discovery, the moment when the visual marvelous will submit to the reasoned assault of touching (for touch is the most demystifying of all the senses, unlike sight, which is the most magical): sheet metal stroked, upholstery punched, seats tested, doors caressed, cushions fondled; behind the steering wheel driving is mimed with the whole body. Here the object is totally prostituted, appropriated: upon leaving Metropolis heaven, the Déesse is mediatized in fifteen minutes, accomplishing in this exorcism the entire dumb show of petit bourgeois annexation.

LITERATURE ACCORDING TO MINOU DROUET

L'Affaire Minou Drouet has for some time come to look like a detective story: Did she do it or didn't she? To this mystery have been applied the habitual police methods (minus torture—and even that?): interrogation, sequestration, graphology, psychotechniques, and of course internal analysis of the documents. If society has mobilized a quasi-judiciary machinery in order to solve a "poetic" riddle, we suspect it has not done so out of a simple love of poetry; it is because the image of a child poet is both surprising and necessary: this is an image which must be authenticated in as scientific a manner as possible insofar as it governs the central myth of bourgeois art: the myth of irresponsibility (of which the genius, the child, and the poet are merely the sublimated figures).

Until the discovery of objective documents, all those who have taken part in the police investigation (and they are indeed numerous) have had to rely solely on a certain normative notion of childhood and of poetry, the idea which they have within themselves. The arguments made about the case of Minou Drouet are by nature tautological, they have no demonstrative value: I cannot prove that the verses shown to me

---

Marie-Noëlle Drouet, known as Minou Drouet, gained fame at the age of eight, when the French publisher Julliard issued some of her poems and letters, quickly hailed as genius by the critics. The writings later generated fierce controversy over their true author. See illustration 14.

are really a child's if I do not first know what childhood is and what poetry is: which comes down to closing the trial over itself. This is a new example of that illusory detective science which functioned so furiously in the case of old Dominici: completely based on a certain tyranny of *likelihood*, it constructs a circular truth which carefully leaves out the reality of the accused or of the problem: every police inquiry of this kind consists in uniting postulates we ourselves have posited from the start: to be guilty, for old Dominici, was to coincide with the "psychology" which the chief prosecutor carried within himself; it was to assume, in the fashion of a magical transference, the guilty part who is inside the magistrates; it was to constitute oneself as a scapegoat, the *likelihood* never being anything but the accused's disposition to resemble his judges. Similarly, to question oneself (furiously, as has been done in the press) as to the authenticity of Drouetist poetry is to start with a prejudice as to childhood and as to poetry, and, whatever we find on the way, inevitably to return to it; it is to postulate both a poetic and a childhood normality, by virtue of which we shall judge Minou Drouet; it is, whatever we decide, to enjoin Minou Drouet to take the burden upon herself, at once as prodigy and as victim, as mystery and as product, i.e., ultimately as pure magical object, with the entire poetic myth and the entire childhood myth of our moment.

Moreover, it is the variable combination of these two myths which produces the difference in our reactions and our judgments. Three mythological ages are represented here: a few belated classics, hostile by tradition to poetry-as-disorder, condemn Minou Drouet in any case: if her poetry is authentic, it is the poetry of a child, hence suspect, not being "reasonable"; and if it is the poetry of an adult, it is condemned because then it is false. Closer to our own moment, a group of venerable neophytes, proud to accede to an irrational poetry, are agog at having discovered (in 1955) the poetic power of childhood, calling "a miracle" a banal literary phenomenon, long since familiar; others, finally, old militants of childhood poetry, those who were at the myth's root tip when it was avant-garde, wearied by the heavy memory of a heroic campaign, of a knowledge which nothing can any longer intimidate, look skeptically askance at the poetry of Minou Drouet (Cocteau: "All children nine years old have genius, except Minou Drouet"). The fourth age, that of today's poets, seems not to have been consulted: virtually unknown to the public at large, it has been decided that their judgment would have no demonstrative value, insofar as they represent no myth: I doubt, moreover, that they recognize anything of themselves in the poetry of Minou Drouet.

But whether Minou Drouet's poetry is declared innocent or adult (i.e., whether it is praised or suspect) is in either case to acknowledge it to be based on a profound alterity posited by nature itself between childhood and maturity, it is to postulate the child as an asocial being, or at the very least as one capable of spontaneously applying its own criticism to itself and of forbidding itself the use of accepted words, with the sole purpose of manifesting itself fully as an ideal child: to believe in the poetic "genius" of childhood is to believe in a kind of literary parthenogenesis, to posit literature once again as a gift of the gods. Here all trace of "culture" is attributed to lying, as if the use of vocabularies were strictly governed by nature, as if the child did not live in a constant osmosis with an adult milieu; and metaphor, image, figures of speech are attributed to childhood as signs of pure spontaneity, whereas, consciously or not, they are the seat of a powerful elaboration, they suppose a "depth" in which individual maturity has a decisive part to play.

Whatever the results of the inquiry, the riddle is therefore of little interest, it enlightens us neither as to childhood nor as to poetry. What conclusively renders this mystery indifferent

to us is that, whether childish or adult, this poetry has a perfectly historical reality: we can date it, and the least we can say
is that it is a little older than eight, which is Minou Drouet's
age. There were, as a matter of fact, around 1914, a certain
number of minor poets whom the histories of our literature,
deeply embarrassed to classify a vacuum, generally group under
the chaste names of Isolated, Retarded, Whimsical, Intimist,
etc. It is incontestably here that we must put young Drouet—or
her muse—alongside poets as glamorous as Madame Burnat-
Provins, Roger Allard, or Tristan Klingsor. Minou Drouet's
poetry is of their puissance; it is a docile, sugary poetry, entirely based on the belief that poetry is a matter of metaphor,
its content nothing more than a kind of elegiac, bourgeois
sentiment. That this homely preciosity can pass for poetry,
and that the very name, in this regard, of Rimbaud, the inevitable child poet, should be advanced is a pure derivation of the
myth. Moreover, a very clear myth, for the function of these
poets is obvious: they furnish the public the *signs* of poetry,
not poetry itself; they are economical and reassuring. One
woman has nicely expressed this superficially emancipated
and profoundly prudent function of intimist "sensibility":
Madame de Noailles, who (coincidentally) prefaced the poems of another child of "genius," one Sabine Sicaud, dead at
fourteen.

Authentic or not, this poetry is therefore dated—markedly
so. But warranted today by a press campaign and the faith of
several personalities, it gives us precisely what society believes
to be childhood *and* poetry. Quoted, vaunted, opposed, the
texts of the Drouet family are precious mythological raw
material.

First of all, there is the myth of the genius, which we are
certainly never done with. The classics had decreed that this
was all a matter of patience. Today genius is a way of gaining
time, of doing at eight what we normally do at twenty-five. A

simple question of temporal quantity: a matter of going a little faster than everyone else. Childhood therefore becomes the privileged site of genius. In Pascal's time, childhood was regarded as a waste of time; the point was to get out of it as fast as possible. Since the romantic era (i.e., since the triumph of the bourgeoisie), it has been a matter of remaining in childhood as long as possible; any adult action imputable to childhood (even a retarded childhood) participates in its atemporality, appears glamorous because produced *in advance*. The *displaced* overvaluation of this age presumes that we regard it as private, closed over itself, possessing a special status, a kind of ineffable and intransmissible essence.

But precisely when childhood is defined as a miracle, we protest that this miracle is nothing other than a premature accession to the adult's powers. Therefore the specialty of childhood remains ambiguous, tainted with that same ambiguity which affects all the objects of the classical universe: like the green peas in Sartre's comparison, childhood and maturity are different ages, closed, incommunicable, yet identical: the miracle of Minou Drouet is to have produced an adult's though a child's poetry, to have brought the poetic essence into the childhood essence. The astonishment here does not derive from a true destruction of essences (which would be quite healthy), but simply from their hurried amalgam. Which is nicely accounted for by the entirely bourgeois notion of the *child prodigy* (Mozart, Rimbaud, Roberto Benzi); an admirable object insofar as it fulfills the ideal function of all capitalist activity: to gain time, to reduce human duration to a numerative problem of precious moments.

No doubt this childhood "essence" takes different forms according to the age of its exemplars: for "modernists," childhood receives its dignity from its very irrationality (at *L'Express*, psychopedagogy has not been overlooked): whence the farcical confusion with Surrealism! But for Monseiur Henriot, who refuses to glorify any source of disorder, childhood must produce nothing except what is charming and distinguished: the child can be neither trivial nor vulgar, which is still to imagine a kind of ideal childhood nature, descending from heaven outside of any and all social determinism; which is also to leave outside the gates of childhood a great many children, and to recognize as such only the pleasing scions of the bourgeoisie. The age at which man precisely *becomes himself,* i.e., impregnates himself with society and with artifice, is paradoxically for Monsieur Henriot the age of "naturalness"; and the age when a child can quite readily kill another child (a news story contemporary with the Minou Drouet case) is, again for Monsieur Henriot, the age when one cannot be lucid and parodic, but only "sincere," "charming," and "distinguished."

Where our commentators do find themselves in agreement is with regard to a certain adequate character of Poetry: for all of them, Poetry is an uninterrupted series of *trouvailles* (finds), which is the ingenuous name for metaphor. The more a poem is stuffed with "formulas," the more it passes for successful. Yet it is only bad poets who make "good" images, or at least who do only that: they naïvely conceive poetic language as a series of verbal lucky finds added one to the next, convinced no doubt that since poetry is a vehicle of unreality, the object must be *translated* at all costs, turning from Larousse to metaphor, as if it were enough to misname things in order to poeticize them. The result is that this purely metaphoric poetry is entirely constructed out of a sort of poetical dictionary, of which Molière produced several pages for his own day and in which the poet pursues his poem as if he had to translate "prose" into "verse." Drouet poetry is, with much application, this uninterrupted metaphor, in which its zealots of both sexes delightedly recognize the bright imperative countenance of Poetry, of *their* poetry (nothing is more reassuring than a dictionary).

This surplus of "finds" produces its own series of additive admirations; adherences to the poem is no longer a total action, determined slowly and patiently throughout a period of rests (as in music), but an accumulation of ecstasies, of bravos, of salutations addressed to a successful verbal acrobatics: here again, it is quantity which establishes value. Minou Drouet's texts in this sense appear as the antiphrasis of all poetry insofar as they flee that solitary weapon of writers, literality: yet it is this weapon alone which can strip the poetic metaphor of its artifice, reveal it as the fulguration of a truth, won over a continuous nausea of language. To speak only of modern Poetry (for I doubt that there is an essence of poetry outside of its History)—the poetry of Apollinaire, of course, and not that of Madame Burnat-Provins—it is certain that its beauty, its truth proceed from a profound dialectic between the life and death of language, between density of the word and the ennui of syntax. Now the poetry of Minou Drouet chatters endlessly like those creatures terrified of silence: it visibly dreads the letter and lives on an accumulation of expedients: it identifies life with the fidgets. Which is what reassures us about this poetry. Though some persons attempt to accuse it of strangeness, though some others pretend to receive it with amazement and in a contagion of dithyrambic images, its very garrulity, its procession of "finds," that calculating order of a cheap profusion— all this only establishes a showy and economic Poetry: here again the *simili* reigns, one of the most precious discoveries of the bourgeois world, since it permits making money without diminishing the appearance of the merchandise. It is no accident that *L'Express* has taken up Minou Drouet: hers is the ideal poetry of a universe in which *seeming* is scrupulously calculated; Minou too tries things out for others: all it costs is a little girl to accede to the luxury of Poetry.

Such Poetry has of course its corresponding Novel, which will be, in its genre, a language equally neat and practical, as decorative and domestic, whose function will be paraded for a reasonable price, a "healthy" novel which will carry in itself the spectacular signs of the fictional, a novel both solid and cheap: the Prix Goncourt, for instance, which was awarded in 1955 as a triumph of healthy tradition (here Stendhal, Balzac, and Zola take over from Mozart and Rimbaud) over the decadence of the avant-garde. The important thing, as on the women's pages of our popular newspapers, is to be dealing with literary objects whose form, use, and price are quite familiar before we buy them, and that nothing within them should disturb us: for there is no danger in calling Minou Drouet's poetry strange if we recognize it from the first as poetry. Literature, however, only begins out in front of the unnamable, facing the perception of an *elsewhere* alien to the very language which seeks it out. It is this creative doubt, this fecund death which our society condemns in its "good literature" and exorcises in its bad. To insist at the top of our lungs that the Novel be a novel, that Poetry be poetry and the Theater theater, this sterile tautology is of the same order as the denominative laws which govern, in the Civil Code, the ownership of property: here everything cooperates in the great bourgeois task, which is finally to reduce Being to Having, the object to a thing.

There remains, after all of this, the case of the little girl herself. But let Society not lament over her too hypocritically: it is society which is devouring Minou Drouet, it is of society and society alone that she is the victim. A propitiatory victim sacrificed so that the world will be bright, so that poetry, genius, and childhood, in a word, *disorder*, will be cheaply tamed, and so that real rebellion, when it appears, will find its place already taken in the newspapers. Minou Drouet is the child martyr of adults suffering from poetic luxury, she is the kidnap victim of a conformist order which reduces freedom to prodigy status. She is the little girl the beggar pushes onto the sidewalk when back home the mattress is stuffed with money. A little tear for Minou Drouet, a little thrill for poetry, and we are rid of literature.

ELECTORAL PHOTOGENY

Certain *candidat-députés* embellish their electoral prospectus with a portrait. This hypothesis that photography has a power of conversion calls for some analysis. First of all, the candidate's effigy establishes a personal link between electors and the candidate, who not only offers a platform but proposes a physical climate, an array of everyday choices expressed in a morphology, a wardrobe, a pose. Photography thus tends to restore elections' paternalistic basis, their "representative" nature somewhat unsettled by proportional representation and party rule (such support seems of greater use to the Right than to the Left). To the degree that photography is an ellipsis of language and the condensation of an ineffable social reality, it constitutes an anti-intellectual weapon and tends to dodge "politics" (i.e., a body of problems and solutions) for the sake of a "lifestyle"—a sociomoral status. We know that this opposition between effigy and political engagement is one\of the major myths of Poujadism (Poujade on television: "Look at me: I am like you").

Electoral photography is therefore the recognition of a certain depth, an irrational enterprise coextensive with politics. What is transmitted in the candidate's photograph is not his projects but his motives, certain family circumstances as well as mental, even erotic characteristics, an entire style of being of which he is simultaneously the product, the example, and the appeal. It is manifest that what most of our candidates offer in their effigy is a social position, the spectacular comfort of familial, juridical, religious norms, the innate possession of such bourgeois virtues as Sunday mass, xenophobia, steak-frites, and jokes about cheating on your wife—in short, what is called an ideology. Naturally, the use of electoral photography presupposes a certain complicity: the campaign photo is a mirror that reflects the familiar, the known, it proposes to the elector his own effigy clarified, magnified, proudly elevated into a type. Moreover, it is this glorification which quite precisely defines *photogeny*: the elector finds himself simultaneously expressed and heroized, he is invited to elect himself, to weigh the mandate he is about to give with a veritable physical transference: he is delegating his "race."

The types of delegation are not very varied. First there is that of social status, of respectability, either full-blooded and well fed (the "National" party lists) or genteel and distinguished (the Christian Democrat lists). Another type is that of the intellectual (I want to emphasize that we are dealing with signified, not natural types: intellectuality can be sanctimonious for parties like the Rassemblement National or "searching" for the Communist candidate). In both cases, the iconography seeks to signify the rare conjunction of will and thought, of action and reflection: slightly lowered eyelids indicate a piercing gaze which seems to gather its strength in a fine dream, though without ceasing to take in real obstacles, as if the exemplary candidate were here uniting a magnificent social idealism with a certain bourgeois empiricism. The latter type is quite simply that of the "handsome fellow," indicated to the public by his health and virility. Moreover, certain candidates proudly draw on both types at once: on one side of the handout, here is a handsome young hero (in uniform), and on the other, a mature and virile citizen surrounded by his little family. For most often the morphological type is aided by clear and distinct attributes: the candidate "among" his kids (dolled up

like all children photographed in France), the young para-
chutist with rolled-up sleeves, the officer covered with decorations. Photography here constitutes a veritable blackmail by
moral values: country, army, family, honor, fighting trim.

Photography's conventions themselves are replete with
signs. The full-face shot accentuates the candidate's realist
outlook, especially if he is furnished with "focalizing" spectacles. Here everything expresses penetration, gravity, frankness: the future *député* grills the enemy, the obstacle, the
"problem." A three-quarter pose, more common, suggests the
tyranny of an ideal: the gaze dissolves nobly into the future,
not confrontational yet dominating and fecundating a modestly indefinite elsewhere. Almost all the three-quarter shots
are ascensional, the countenance raised toward a supernatural
light which lures it upward, elevating it to regions of a superior humanity, where the candidate attains the Olympus of
lofty sentiments, where all political contradiction is resolved:
Algerian war and peace, social progress and executive benefits,
"free" education and subsidies to the sugar beet farmers, the
Right and the Left (an opposition always "transcended!"), all
this coexists peacefully in that pensive gaze, nobly fixed on
the occult interests of Order.

LOST CONTINENT

A film, *Lost Continent*, nicely illuminates the current myth of
exoticism. It is a full-length documentary on "the East,"
whose pretext is some vague ethnographic expedition, an obviously false one, moreover, led by three or four bearded Ital-
ians in the Malay Archipelago. The film is euphoric, everything
in it is easy, innocent. Our explorers are fine fellows, occupy-
ing their leisure with childish diversions: playing with a mascot bear cub (mascots are indispensable on any expedition: no
polar film without a tame seal, no tropical reportage without
its monkey) or comically spilling a dish of spaghetti on the
boat-deck. Which is to say that these good ethnologists are
hardly troubled by historical or sociological problems. Penetration of the East is never anything for them but a little boat
trip on an azure sea under an essential sun. And this East, the
very place which has today become the political center of the
world, is shown here all smoothed out and gaily colored like an
old-fashioned postcard.

The method of irresponsibility is clear: to color the world
is always a way of denying it (and perhaps we should begin
here with an inquiry into the use of color in films generally).
Deprived of all substance, forced into the expedient of color,
disembodied by the very luxuriance of the "images," the East
is ready for the disappearing act our film has in readiness for
it. Between the bear cub mascot and the comical spaghetti
incident, our studio ethnologists will have no difficulty postu-

lating an East formally exotic, in reality deeply resembling the West, at least the spiritualist West. Orientals have religions of their own? No problem, the differences are insignificant compared to the deep unity of idealism. Each rite is thereby at once specialized and eternalized, simultaneously promoted to the level of a fascinating spectacle and a para-Christian symbol. And if Buddhism is not literally Christian, that matters little enough since Buddhism too has nuns who shave their heads (a major theme in the pathos of all ceremonies of taking the veil), since it has monks who kneel and confess to their superior, and finally since, as in Seville, the faithful come and cover the god's statue with gold.* It is true that it is always the "forms" which emphasize the identity of all religions; but this identity, far from betraying them, exalts them, all to the credit of a superior catholicity.

We know that syncretism has always been one of the Church's major techniques of assimilation. In the seventeenth century, in this very East whose Christian predispositions *Lost Continent* has shown us, the Jesuits went very far in the ecumenicity of forms: it was the Malabar rites which the pope in fact ended by condemning. It is this very "all things are alike" which our ethnologists have hinted at: Orient and Occident, it is all the same, there are only differences in color, the essential is identical, which is the eternal postulation of man toward God, the absurd and contingent character of geographies in relation to this human nature, of which Christianity alone possesses the key. The legends themselves, all this "primitive" folklore whose foreignness seems to be constantly pointed out to us, has as its mission nothing but to illustrate "Nature": the rites, the accidents of culture are never related to any specific

---

*A good example here of the mystifying power of music: all the "Buddhist" scenes are accompanied by a vague musical syrup, part American crooning and part Gregorian chant; in any case it is monodic (the sign of monocalism).

historical order with an explicit social or economic status, but only with the great neutral forms of cosmic commonplaces (seasons, storms, death, etc.). If we are dealing with fishermen, it is never the mode of fishing that we are shown, but rather, drowned in the eternity of a chromatic sunset, a romantic essence of fisherman, described not as a worker dependent by his technique and his profits on a specific society, but rather as a theme of an eternal condition, that of a man far away and exposed to the dangers of the sea, the wife weeping and praying at home. It is the same for the refugees, a long procession of whom is shown at the start of the film making their way down a mountain; futile, of course, to locate them: they are eternal essences of refugees, it is in the *nature* of the East to produce them.

All told, exoticism clearly shows here its true justification, which is to deny any and all situation to History. By affecting the Oriental reality of several good native signs, we carefully vaccinate the Oriental reality against any responsible content. A bit of "situation," as superficial as possible, provides the necessary alibi and disposes of any deeper experience. Confronting anything foreign, Order knows only two behaviors which are both forms of mutilation: either to acknowledge the Other as another Punch and Judy show or to render it harmless as a pure reflection of the West. In any case the essential thing is to deprive it of its history. We see that the "beautiful images" of *Lost Continent* cannot be innocent: it cannot be innocent to *lose* the continent which has been found again at Bandung.

ASTROLOGY

It appears that in France the annual budget for "sorcery" is approximately three billion francs. Which warrants a glance at a weekly magazine, *Elle*, for instance. Contrary to what one might expect, nothing like a dreamworld is to be found here, but instead a strictly realistic description of a specific social milieu, that of the magazine's female readers. In other words, astrology is definitely not—at least not here—the prolegomenon to a dream, but only a mirror, the mere institution of reality.

The chief rubrics of destiny (*Chance, Outside, At Home, Your Heart*) scrupulously produce the complete rhythm of a working life; its unit is the week, in which "chance" marks one or two days. *Chance* is here the portion reserved for interiority, for moods: it is the experiential sign for duration, the only category by which subjective time is expressed and released. For the other days, the stars know nothing but a schedule: *Outside* is the professional timetable, the six days of the week, the seven hours a day of office or store. *At Home* is the evening meal, the rest of the evening before bedtime. *Your Heart* is the date after work or the Sunday adventure. But between these "realms," no communication: nothing which, from one agenda to another, might suggest the notion of a total alienation; the prisons are contiguous, they adjoin but don't contaminate one another. The stars never postulate a reversal of order, they influence on short terms, *à la petite semaine*, respectful of social status and the boss's calendar.

Here, "work" is that of employees, of secretaries or sales-girls; the microgroup surrounding the magazine's readers is al-most inevitably that of the office or the shop. The variations imposed, or rather proposed by the stars (for this astrology is a prudent theologian, it doesn't exclude free will) are mild, they never seek to upset your life: the weight of destiny affects only your appetite for work, your assiduity or reluctance, the likelihood of promotions, the acrimony or complicity of your relations with your fellow workers, and above all your fatigue— the stars insistently and wisely prescribe more sleep, always more.

Home is dominated by problems of mood, an atmosphere of confidence or hostility; quite often this depends on a fe-male population, where the most important relations will be those of mother and daughter. The petit bourgeois household is faithfully present here, with its "family visits," quite distinct from "in-laws," whom the stars seem not to hold in very high esteem. This entourage appears to be almost exclusively "fa-milial," there are few allusions to friends, the petit bourgeois world is essentially constituted of parents and colleagues, it does not involve veritable relational crises, only minor confrontations of temper or vanity. Love is of the Agony Column variety, another realm altogether, that of sentimental "affairs." But as with any commercial transaction, love here knows "promising starts," "miscalculations," and "bad choices." Disasters are of minor scope: one week fewer admirers, an indiscretion, a groundless jealousy. The sentimental heavens open wide only for the "longed-for solution," marriage: and even this must be "well matched."

A single feature idealizes this whole little astral world, on another side quite concrete, which is that there is never, here, a question of money. Astrological humanity runs on its monthly salary: it is what it is, no one ever speaks of it, since it permits "life." A life which the stars describe much more than they predict: the future is rarely risked, and prediction is always neutralized by the balancing of possibles: if there are failures, they will be unimportant: if faces are darkened, your good humor will brighten them; if there are tiresome relatives, they will turn out to be useful, etc.: and if your general mood must improve, it will be the consequence of some procedure you will have followed, or perhaps thanks to the absence of any procedure (I'm quoting).

The stars are moral, they let themselves be moved by virtue: courage, patience, good humor, self-control are always required when one faces timidly announced mishaps. And the paradox is that this universe of pure determinism is immediately conquered by freedom of character: astrology is above all a school of will. Yet even if its issues are pure mystification, even if it merely dodges problems of behavior, in the consciousness of its readers it remains an institution of reality: it is not a route of evasion but a realistic evidence of the salesgirl's, of the employee's life conditions.

Then what purpose can it serve, this pure description, since it seems to offer no oneiric compensation? It serves to exorcise reality by naming it. By doing so, it joins the ranks of all the enterprises of semialienation (or of semiliberation) which make it their duty to objectify reality, though without going so far as to demystify it. We all know well at least one other of these nominalist attempts: Literature, which in its degraded forms can go no further than to name the experience of our lives; astrology and Literature have the same mission of a "retarded" institution of reality: astrology *is* the Literature of the petit bourgeois world.

THE BOURGEOIS ART OF SONG

It will appear impertinent to lecture an excellent baritone, Gérard Souzay, but a release on which this singer has recorded several of Fauré's songs seems to me an ideal illustration of a whole musical mythology in which we can find the principal signs of bourgeois art. This art is essentially *descriptive*, it constantly imposes not emotion but the signs of emotion. Which is precisely what Gérard Souzay does: having to sing, for instance, the words *tristesse affreuse* (horrible sadness), he is not content with the simple semantic content of these words or with the musical line which supports them: he must further dramatize the phonetics of the *affreuse,* must suspend and then explode the double fricative, releasing misery in the very density of the letters; no one can ignore the fact that it is a question of particularly terrible pangs. Unfortunately, this pleonasm of intentions muffles both word and music, and chiefly their junction, which is the very object of the vocal art. It is true of music as of the other arts, including literature: the highest form of artistic expression is on the side of literality, i.e., ultimately of a certain algebra: all form must tend toward abstraction, which, as we know, is not at all contrary to sensuality.

And this is precisely what bourgeois art rejects; it always wants to treat its consumers as naïve customers for whom it must chew up the work and overindicate the intention lest they be insufficiently gripped (but art is also an ambiguity, it always contradicts, in a sense, its own message, and especially music, which is never, literally, either sad or gay). To underline the word by the abusive contour of phonetics, to make the guttural of the word *creuse* (hollow) into the spade digging a grave, and the dental of the word *sein* (breast) into a penetrating sweetness, is to practice a literality of intention, not of description, it is to establish abusive correspondences. We must remark here, moreover, that the melodramatic spirit from which Gérard Souzay's interpretations derive is precisely one of the historic acquisitions of the bourgeoisie: we rediscover this same overload of intention in the art of our traditional actors, who are, as we know, actors formed by and for the bourgeoisie.

This kind of phonetic pointillism, which gives each letter an incongruous importance, sometimes touches on the absurd: it is a comical solemnity that insists on the double *n* of our *solennel* (solemn), and it is a somewhat nauseating happiness, this *bonheur*, that signified by an initial emphasis, expelling happiness out of the mouth like a plum pit. This comes back to a mythological constant, of which we have already spoken apropos of poetry: to conceive of art as an additive series of accumulated, i.e., fully signifying details: the pointillist perfection of Gérard Souzay is exactly equivalent to Minou Drouet's taste for the metaphor of detail, or to the poultry costumes of *Chantecler* made (in 1910) of thousands of real feathers sewn one over the other. In this art there is an intimidation by detail which is obviously the opposite of realism, since realism supposes a typification, i.e., a presence of structure, hence of duration.

This analytic art is doomed to failure particularly in music, whose truth can never be anything but of a respiratory order, prosodic and not phonetic. Hence Gérard Souzay's phrasings are constantly destroyed by the excessive expression of a word, clumsily meant to inject a parasitical intellectual order into the song's seamless fabric. It seems that we are touching here on a major difficulty of musical execution: to produce the nuance from an internal zone of the music and never impose it from outside as a purely intellective sign: there is a sensual truth of music, a sufficient truth which does not tolerate the constraint of *expression*. This is why the interpretation of excellent virtuosos so often leaves us unsatisfied: their overspectacular rubato, product of a visible effort toward signification, destroys an organism which scrupulously contains its own message within itself. Certain amateurs, or better still, certain professionals who have rediscovered what we might call the letter of the musical text, like Panzéra for song or Lipatti for the piano, manage to add *no intention* to the music: they do not fuss over each detail, contrary to bourgeois art, which is always indiscreet. They trust in music's immediately definitive substance.

PLASTIC

In spite of its having Greek shepherds' names (Polystyrene, Phenoplast, Polyvinyl, Polyethylene), plastic, of which the products have just been concentrated in an exhibition, is an essentially alchemical substance. At the entrance to the stall, the public waits in a long line to see accomplished the magical operation par excellence: the conversion of substance. An ideally shaped machine, tubulated and oblong (the right shape to manifest the secret of an itinerary), effortlessly draws from a heap of greenish crystals a series of gleaming fluted pin trays. At one end the raw telluric substance, and at the other the perfect human object; and between these two extremes, nothing; nothing but a trajectory, scarcely watched over by a helmeted employee, half god, half robot.

Thus, more than a substance, plastic is the very idea of its infinite transformation. As its vulgar name indicates, it is ubiquity made visible; moreover, this is the reason why it is a miraculous substance: a miracle is always a sudden conversion of nature. Plastic remains completely impregnated by this astonishment: it is less an object than the trace of a movement.

And since this movement is here virtually infinite, transforming the original crystals into a multitude of increasingly surprising objects, plastic is, ultimately, a spectacle to be deciphered: the very spectacle of its end products. In front of each final shape (valise, brush, automobile body, toy, fabric, tube, basin, or paper), the mind unceasingly takes the primitive substance for an enigma. This is because plastic's quick-change talent is total: it can form pails as well as jewels. Whence a perpetual astonishment, the reverie of man at the sight of the proliferations of substance, detecting the connections between the singular of its origin and the plural of its effects. Moreover, this astonishment is a source of pleasure, since it is by the scope of transformations that man measures his power, and since it is precisely plastic's itinerary which gives him the euphoria of a prestigious slide through Nature.

But the price to be paid for this success is that plastic, sublimated as a movement, almost fails to exist as a substance. Its constitution is negative: neither hard nor deep, it must content itself with a neutral substantial quality despite its utilitarian advantages: *resistance*, a state which signifies no more than the simple suspension of yielding. In the poetic order of major substances, plastic is a disgraced material, lost between the effusion of rubber and the flat hardness of metal: it achieves none of the true productions of the mineral order: foam, fibers, strata. It is a *shaped* substance: whatever its final state, plastic retains a flocculant appearance, something opaque, creamy, and coagulated, an impotence ever to attain the triumphant sleekness of Nature. But what most betrays it is the sound it makes, at once hollow and flat; its noise is its undoing, as are its colors, for it seems able to preserve only the most chemical versions: of yellow, red, and green it keeps nothing but the most aggressive state, using them as mere names, capable of displaying only the concepts of colors.

The fashion for plastic highlights an evolution in the myth of the simili. It is commonly acknowledged that the simili is a historically bourgeois usage (the earliest vestimentary "imitation" materials date from the dawn of capitalism); but till now the simili has always meant pretension, being part of a world of appearance, not of usage; it was intended to reproduce cheaply the rarest substances, diamonds, silks, feathers, silver, all the luxurious brilliance of the world. Plastic is in decline, it is a household material. It is the first magical material that consents to be prosaic; but it is precisely because of its prosaic nature that it triumphs. For the first time, artifice aims for the common, not for the rare. And thereby nature's ancestral function has been modified: it is no longer the Idea, the pure Substance which is to be regained or imitated; an artificial substance, more fecund than all the world's deposits, will replace it, will command the very invention of shapes. A luxury object always derives from the earth, always recalls in a precious way its mineral or animal origin, the natural theme of which it is merely an actuality. Plastic is entirely engulfed in its usage: one of these days objects will be invented merely for the pleasure of using them. The hierarchy of substances is forthwith abolished, a single one will replace them all: the whole world, even life itself, *can* be plasticized since, we are told, plastic aortas are beginning to be manufactured.

THE GREAT FAMILY OF MAN

A major exhibition of photographs, whose purpose is to show the universality of human actions in the daily lives of all the countries around the world, has opened in Paris: birth, death, work, games, and knowledge everywhere impose the same behavior: there is a family of Man.

The Family of Man, at least that was the original title of this exhibition, came to us from the United States. The French translated it as *La Grande famille des hommes*. Thus what might initially have passed for an expression of a zoological order, merely retaining the similitude of behaviors, the unity of a species, was here largely moralized, sentimentalized. We are at once returned to that ambiguous myth of the human "community," whose alibi nourishes a large swath of our humanism.

This myth functions in two stages: first the difference in human morphologies is affirmed, exoticism is stressed, the many variations of the species are manifested, the diversity of skins, skulls, and customs and notions of Babel are extended over the image of the world. And then, from this pluralism, magically enough, a unity is derived: man is born, works, laughs, and dies in the same fashion everywhere; and if in these actions some ethnic particularity still subsists, there is now some under-

---

The Family of Man, *a photography exhibition curated by Edward Steichen, was shown in Paris at the Musée d'Art Moderne in 1956.*

standing that there is deep inside each one of us an identical "nature," that their diversity is merely formal and does not belie the existence of a common matrix. This evidently comes down to postulating a human essence, whereupon God is reintroduced into our Exhibition: the diversity of mankind proclaims his richness, his power; the unity of its actions demonstrates his will. All this is confided to us by the prospectus which affirms, under the pen of Monsieur André Chamson, that "this view of the human condition must somewhat resemble God's benevolent gaze on our absurd and sublime anthill."

This pietistic intention is accentuated by the quotations accompanying each chapter of the Exhibition: these quotations are frequently "primitive" sayings, verses of the Old Testament; all define an eternal wisdom, an order of affirmations which escape History: "The Earth is a mother who never dies. Eat bread and salt and speak the truth," etc.: this is the realm of gnomic truths, the junction of all the ages of humanity at the most neutral degree of their identity, here where the evidence of the truism has no more value than at the heart of a purely "poetic" language. Everything here, the content and appeal of the pictures, the discourse justifying them, aims at suppressing the determining weight of History: we are kept at the surface of an identity, prevented by sentimentality itself from penetrating in that further zone of human conduct, where historical alienation introduces those "differences" which we shall here call quite simply injustices.

This myth of the human "condition" relies on a very old mystification, which consists in always placing Nature at the bottom of History. Any classical humanism postulates that if we scratch the surface of human history, the relativity of men's institutions, or the superficial diversity of their skins (but why not ask the parents of Emmett Till, the young black murdered by white men, what *they* think of *the great family of men?*), we soon reach the bedrock of a universal human nature. A progressive humanism, to the contrary, must always consider inverting the terms of this old imposture, constantly scouring nature, its "laws" and its "limits," to discover History there and finally to posit Nature as itself historical.

Examples? But those in our exhibition. Birth, death? Yes, they are facts of nature, universal facts. But if we take History away from them, there is nothing more to say about them, any commentary about them becomes purely tautological; photography's failure here seems flagrant to me: to *repeat* birth or death teaches literally nothing. For such natural facts to accede to a true language, they must be inserted into an order of knowledge, i.e., we must postulate that they can be transformed, indeed submit their "naturality" to our human criticism. For universal as they are, they are signs of a historic writing. Doubtless the child is *always* born, but in the general volume of the human problem, what does the "essence" of that action mean to us compared to the child's modes of being, which indeed are perfectly historical? Whether the child is born with ease or difficulty, whether or not he causes his mother suffering at birth, whether the child lives or dies, and, if he lives, whether he accedes to some sort of future—this, and not the eternal lyric of birth, should be the subject of our Exhibitions. And the same applies to death: Are we really to sing its essence once again and thereby risk forgetting that we can still do so much against it? It is this capacity still so new, too new, which we must enlarge, and not the sterile identity of "natural" death.

And what are we to say of work, which the Exhibition locates among the great universal facts, aligning it with birth and death, as if it were so obviously of the same order of fatality? That work is an ancestral fact does not in the least prevent it from remaining an entirely historical one. First of all, quite obviously, in its modes, its motives, its purposes and profits, to the point that it will never fail to confuse, in a purely gestural identity, the colonial worker and the Western worker (let us also ask the North African laborers of the Goutte d'Or district of Paris what they think of *the great family of men*). And secondly, in its very fatality: we know of course that work is "natural" insofar as it is "profitable," and that by modifying the fatality of profit we may someday modify the fatality of work. It is of this work, entirely historified, that we will have to speak, and not of an eternal aesthetic of laborious gestures.

Hence, I very much fear that the final justification of all this Adamism is merely to give the world's immobility the alibi of a certain "wisdom" and of a certain "lyrical" nature which will eternalize the actions of man only the better to render them harmless.

AT THE MUSIC HALL

Whatever the theater, we experience time there as continuous. In the music hall, time is by definition interrupted; it is an immediate time. And this is the meaning of *variété*, or entertainment: that stage time be a just, real, sidereal time, the time of the thing itself and not that of its anticipation (tragedy) or of its reconsideration (epic). The advantage of this literal time is that it can serve gesture best, for it is quite obvious that gesture exists as spectacle only from the moment when time is severed (we see this clearly in historical painting, where the character's caught gesture, what I have elsewhere called the numen, suspends duration). Ultimately, entertainment is not a simple technique of distraction, but a condition of artifice (in the Baudelairean sense of the word). To remove gesture from its sweetish pulp of duration, to present it in a superlative, definitive state, to give it the character of pure visuality, to disengage it from any cause, to exhaust it as spectacle and not as signification, such is the original aesthetic of the music hall. Objects (of jugglers) and gestures (of acrobats) cleansed of time (i.e., of both a pathos and a Logos) gleam like pure artifices, which cannot fail to suggest the cold precision of Baudelaire's visions of hashish, of a world absolutely purified of all spirituality because it has, precisely, renounced time.

Hence everything is done, in the music hall, to prepare a veritable promotion of object and gesture (which in the modern West can be done only *against* psychological spectacles, and notably against the theater). A music hall turn is almost always constituted by the confrontation of a gesture and a substance: skaters and their lacquered springboard, body exchanges of acrobats, dancers, and balancing acts (I confess a great predilection for balancing acts, for in them the body is objectivized *gently*: it is not a hard object catapulted through the air as in pure acrobatics, but rather a soft, dense substance, responsive to very slight movements), comic sculptors and their many-colored clays, prestidigitators gobbling up paper, silk, and cigarettes, pickpockets and their lifted watches, wallets, etc. Now the gesture and its object are the natural raw materials of a value which has had access to the stage only in the music hall (and the circus), and this value is Work. The music hall, at least in its variety aspect (for singing, which has become the star of the American version, relates to a different mythology), the music hall is the aesthetic form of work. Here each number is presented either as the exercise or as the product of labor: sometimes the action (that of the juggler, the acrobat, the mime) appears as the summa of a long apprenticeship, sometimes the work (artists, sculptors, humorists) is re-created altogether before the public *ab origine*. In any case, it is a new event which is produced, and this event is constituted by the fragile perfection of an effort. Or rather, a more subtle artifice, the effort is perceived at its apogee, at that almost impossible moment when it is about to be engulfed in the perfection of its achievement, without nonetheless having quite abandoned the risk of its failure. At the music hall, everything is *almost* attained, but it is precisely this *almost* which constitutes the spectacle and retains for it, despite its preparation, its virtue as work. Hence what the music hall spectacle makes visible is not the action's result but its mode of being, the tenuousness of its successful surface. What we have here is a way of making possible a contradictory state of human history: that the artist's gesture should set forth at one and the same time the crude musculature of an arduous labor, standing for the past, and the aerial smoothness of an easy action issuing from a magical heaven: the music hall is human work memorialized and sublimated; danger and effort are signified at the same time that they are subsumed by laughter or by grace.

Naturally the music hall requires a profound enchantment whereby it erases all rugosity from labor and leaves only its finished design. Here reign the gleaming balls, the light wands, the tubular furniture, the chemical silks, the grating chalks, and the glittering clubs; here visual luxury parades *facility*, disposed in the brightness of substances and the continuity of gestures: sometimes man is a support planted in the center, a tree along which slides a woman branch; sometimes the entire hall shares in the coenesthesia of energy, of weight not vanquished but sublimated by rebounds. In this metallized world, old myths of germination appear and give this representation of labor the guarantee of primordial natural movements, nature always being the image of the continuous, i.e., in the long run, of the easy.

All this muscular magic of the music hall is essentially urban; it is no accident that the music hall is an Anglo-Saxon phenomenon, born in the world of abrupt urban concentrations and the great Protestant myths of labor: the promotion of objects, of metals, and of dreamed gestures, the sublimation of labor by its magical effacement and not by its consecration, as in rural folklore—all this has to do with the artifice of cities. The city rejects the notion of a formless nature, it reduces space to a continuation of solid, shiny objects, *products* to which the artist's action gives the glamorous status of a quite human thought: work, especially when mythified, makes matter euphoric because it seems to *think* matter in a spectacular fashion; metallized, flung away, caught up again, manipulated, quite luminous with movements in perpetual dialogue with gesture, objects lose the sinister stubbornness of their absurdity: artificial and utensils, they cease for a moment to *bore*.

THE LADY OF THE CAMELLIAS

They still perform, somewhere in the world, *The Lady of the Camellias* (and it had another run in Paris some time ago). Such success must alert us to a mythology of Love which probably still subsists, for Marguerite Gautier's alienation by the class of her masters is not fundamentally different from that of today's petites bourgeoises in a world just as classified.

Yet in fact the central myth of *The Lady of the Camellias* is not love, it is Recognition. Marguerite loves in order to be recognized, and this is why her passion (in the etymological, not the libidinal, sense) derives entirely from other people. Armand, on the other hand (the son of a District Tax-Collector), presents an example of classical, bourgeois love, descended from essentialist culture and living on in Proust's analysis: his is a segregative love, the love of the owner who carries off his prey; an interiorized love which acknowledges the world only intermittently and always with a feeling of frustration, as if the world were never anything but the threat of a theft (jealousies, quarrels, mistakes, anxieties, irritations, moods). Marguerite's love is the perfect opposite of this. She was first touched by feeling herself *recognized* by Armand, and passion was subsequently, for her, only the permanent solicitation of that recognition; this is why the sacrifice she granted to Monsieur Duval by renouncing Armand is not at all moral (despite the phraseology employed), it is existential; it is only the logical consequence of the postulate of recognition, a superior means (much superior to love) of getting herself recognized by the world of her masters. And if Marguerite conceals her sacrifice and gives it the mask of cynicism, this can only be at the moment when the argument truly becomes Literature: the recognizing and grateful gaze of the bourgeois is here delegated to the reader, who, in his turn, *recognizes* Marguerite through her lover's very misjudgment.

Which is to say that the misunderstandings which move the plot forward are here not of a psychological order (even if the language is abusively so): Armand and Marguerite are not of the same social world, and between them there can be neither Racinian tragedy nor Marivaudage. The conflict is external: we are not dealing with a single passion divided against itself, but with two passions of different nature, because they come from different locations in society. Armand's passion, the bourgeois and appropriative type, is by definition the murder of the other participant; and that of Marguerite can only crown her effort to be recognized by a sacrifice which will constitute in its turn the indirect murder of Armand's passion. The simple social disparity, relayed and amplified by the opposition of two amorous ideologies, can therefore produce here an impossible love, an impossibility of which Marguerite's death (however syrupy it is onstage) is in some sense the algebraic symbol.

The difference of loves evidently results from a difference of lucidities: Armand lives in an essence and an eternity of love, Marguerite lives in the consciousness of her alienation, she lives only within it: she knows herself, and in a sense *wills* herself to be a courtesan. And her own adaptive behaviors are also behaviors of recognition: now she excessively assumes her own legend, plunges into the classical whirlwind of the courtesan's life (similar to those pederasts who assume themselves by advertising the facts of their sexuality), now she announces a power of transcendence which aims to cause recognition less of a "natural" virtue than of a devotion suited to her station, as if the function of her sacrifice were to manifest not the murder of the courtesan that she is, but to advertise, on the contrary, a superlative courtesan, enhanced, without losing anything of herself, by an elevated bourgeois sentiment.

So we see more clearly the mythic content of this love, archetype of petit bourgeois sentimentality. It is a special state of the myth, defined by a semilucidity or, more precisely, a parasitical lucidity (the very one we've brought to attention in astrological reality). Marguerite *knows* her alienation, which is to say that she sees reality as an alienation. But she prolongs this knowledge by behaviors of pure servility: either she plays the personage her masters expect of her, or else she tries to connect with a *value* properly interior to that same world of those masters. In both cases, Marguerite is never anything more than an alienated lucidity: she sees that she is suffering but imagines no other remedy than one parasitical on her own suffering: she knows herself to be an "object" but cannot think any other destination for herself than to adorn the masters' museum. Despite the grotesquerie of the *affabulation*, such a personage does not lack a certain dramatic richness: doubtless it is neither tragic (the fatality which hangs over Marguerite is social, not metaphysical), nor comic (Marguerite's behavior derives from her condition, not from her essence), nor even, of course, revolutionary (Marguerite attempts no criticism of her alienation). But it would require, actually, little enough to attain the status of the Brechtian personage, an alienated object though a source of criticism. What keeps her from it—irremediably—is her positivity: Marguerite Gautier, "touching" for her tuberculosis and her fine phrases, spreads to the whole of her public the contagion of her blindness: patently stupid, she would have opened their petit bourgeois eyes. Phrase-mongering and noble, in a word, "serious," she only puts them to sleep.

POUJADE AND THE INTELLECTUALS

Who are the intellectuals, for Poujade? Essentially "professors" ("Sorbonnards, worthy pedagogues, county capital intellectuals") and technicians ("technocrats, polytechnicians, polyvalents, or polyvillains"). It is possible that Poujade's severity with regard to intellectuals is based on a simple fiscal rancor: the "professor" is a profiteer; first of all because he is on salary ("Poor Old Pierrot, you didn't know how lucky you were when you were on a salary"*), and then because he doesn't have to declare what he earns from private lessons (for which he is paid in cash). As for the technician, he is a sadist: under the loathed form of the controller, he tortures the taxpayer. But since Poujadism has sought to construct its major archetypes right away, the intellectual has quickly been transferred from the fiscal category into that of the myths.

Like any mythic being, the intellectual participates in a general theme, a substance: *air*, i.e. (though this is anything but a scientific identity), *the void*. Superior, the intellectual soars, he does not "stick" to reality (reality is of course the ground, an ambiguous myth which signifies at one and the same time race, rurality, province, common sense, the numberless obscure, etc.). A restaurant owner who caters regularly to intellectuals calls them "helicopters," a disparaging image which subtracts from flight the airplane's virile power: the intellectual

*Most quotations come from Poujade's book *J'ai choisi le combat.*

is detached from reality but remains up in the air, in place, circling around and around; his ascent is cowardly, equally remote from the heavens of religion and from the solid ground of common sense. What he lacks are "roots" in the nation's heart. The intellectuals are neither idealists nor realists, they are murky creatures, "dopes." Their exact altitude is that of *clouds*, an old Aristophanic refrain (the intellectual, in those days, was Socrates). Suspended in the upper void, the intellectuals are filled by it, they are "the drum that resounds emptily": here we perceive the inevitable basis of all anti-intellectualism: the suspicion of language, the reduction of all adverse speech to a noise, in accord with the constant procedure of petit bourgeois polemics, which consists in unmasking in others an infirmity to the one we do not see in ourselves, accusing the adversary of the effects of our own faults, calling obscurity our own blindness and verbal derangement our own deafness.

The altitude of "superior" minds is here again identified with abstraction, doubtless by the intermediary of a state common to height and conceptualization of *rarefaction*. We are dealing here with a mechanical abstraction, the intellectuals being thinking machines (what they lack is not "heart," as the sentimentalist philosophers would say, but "shrewdness," a kind of tactic nourished by intuition). This theme of machine-made thought is of course furnished with picturesque attributes which reinforce its malevolence: first of all, derision (the intellectuals are skeptical about Poujade), then malignity, for the machine, in its abstraction, is sadistic: the officials of the rue de Rivoli are "vicious types" who take pleasure in making the taxpayer suffer: tools of the System, they have its cold complexity, that kind of sterile invention, of negative proliferation which already, apropos of the Jesuits, wrung such loud cries from Michelet. Moreover, the polytechnicians have, for Poujade, virtually the same role as that the Jesuits held for the old liberals: source of all fiscal evils (by the intermediary of the rue de Rivoli, euphemistic designation of Hell), builders of the System which they subsequently serve like corpses, *perinde ac cadaver*, according to the Jesuit slogan.

This is because science and knowledge, for Poujade, are curiously capable of excess. Since every human phenomenon, even every mental one, exists only in terms of quantity, it suffices to compare its volume to the capacity of the average Poujadist in order to declare it excessive: it is probable that the *excesses* of science are precisely its virtues and that it begins exactly where Poujade finds it to be useless. But this quantification is precious to Poujadist rhetoric, since it engenders monsters, i.e., those polytechnicians who support a pure, abstract science which applies to reality only in a punitive form.

Not that Poujade's judgment of the polytechnicians (and the intellectuals) is hopeless: it will doubtless be possible to "reform" the "French intellectual." What the intellectual suffers from is a hypertrophy (hence he can be operated on); he has added to the small businessman's normal quantity of intelligence an appendage of excessive weight: this appendage is curiously constituted by science itself, at once objectivized and conceptualized, a kind of ponderous substance which sticks to man or is removed from him exactly like the apple the grocer adds or subtracts in order to obtain an exact weight. That the polytechnician is *besotted by mathematics* means that once past a certain degree of knowledge we approach a qualitative world of poisons. Having grown beyond the healthy limits of quantification, knowledge is discredited insofar as it can no longer be defined as work. The intellectuals—polytechnicians, professors, Sorbonnards, and officials—do nothing: they are aesthetes, they frequent not the good country bistro but the *chic bars of the Left Bank*. Here appears a theme dear to all strong regimes: the identification of intellectuality with idleness; the intellectual is by definition lazy,

he will have to be put to work once and for all, it will be necessary to convert an activity which can be measured only by its
harmful excess into a *concrete* labor, i.e., accessible to Poujadist measurement. We find that ultimately there can be no
labor more quantified—and hence more beneficial—than to
dig holes or to pile stones: that is labor in the pure state, and
in fact it is the labor all post-Poujadist regimes logically end by
reserving for the *idle intellectual.*

This quantification of labor involves, naturally, a promotion of physical strength, that of the muscles, the chest, the
arms; conversely, the head is a suspect site insofar as its products are qualitative, not quantitative. Here we return to the
usual discredit cast on the brain ("fish rot from the head
down," as Poujade often says), whose fatal disgrace is of course
the very eccentricity of its position, right at the top of the
body, near the *cloud*, far from the *roots*. We exploit the very
ambiguity of *superior* here; a whole cosmogony is constructed
which keeps playing on vague similitudes among the physical,
the moral, and the social: that the body should struggle
against the head is the whole struggle of the *little guys*, of the
vital darkness against the up there.

Poujade himself very rapidly developed the legend of his
own physical strength. Furnished with a physical education
instructor's diploma, a former RAF flier, a rugby player, his
antecedents warrant his *value*: the chief bestows on his troops,
in exchange for their adherence, an essentially measurable
strength—after all, it is the *body's* strength. Hence Poujade's
first power (by which we are to understand the basis of the
commercial confidence we can place in him) is his resistance
("Poujade is the devil himself, he is unbeatable"). His first
campaigns were, above all, physical performances which
touched on the superhuman ("He's the devil in person"). This
steely strength equals ubiquity (Poujade is everywhere at

once), it affects matter itself (Poujade cracks up all the cars he uses). Yet there is another value in Poujade besides resistance: a kind of physical *charm*, lavished over and above his strength-as-merchandise, like one of those superfluous objects by which, in archaic law, the acquirer bound the vendor of real estate: this "tip," which establishes the leader and appears as Poujade's genius, the share set aside for quality in this economy of pure computation, is *his voice*. Doubtless it is issued from a privileged site of the body, a site at once median and muscular, the thorax, which is in all this corporeal mythology the antihead par excellence; but the voice, vehicle of the correcting word, escapes the harsh law of quantities: for the process of wear and tear, the fate of ordinary objects, it substitutes its fragility, a glorious risk of deluxe objects; for it, we invoke not the heroic scorn of fatigue, not implacable endurance, but rather the delicate caress of the vaporizer, the velvety support of the microphone; Poujade's voice receives by transference the imponderable and glamorous value devolved, in other mythologies, upon the intellectual's brain.

Naturally, Poujade's lieutenants must participate in the same image, cruder, less diabolic, of course—that of the "stalwart." "Virile Launay, former rugby player . . . doesn't look like an *enfant de Marie*." Cantalou, "tall, powerful, muscular, has a clear gaze, and a frank, virile handshake." For, according to a familiar crasis, physical plenitude establishes a kind of moral clarity: only the strong can be frank. As we can imagine, the essence common to all these powers is virility, for which the moral substitute is "character," a rival of the intelligence, which is not admitted into the Poujadist heaven: it is replaced by a special intellectual virtue: shrewdness; the hero, for Poujade, is a being endowed with both aggressiveness and cunning. This perspicuity, however intellective it may be, does not reintroduce reason, abhorred in the Poujadist pantheon: the petit bourgeois gods grant or withdraw it at will, according to a pure order of chance: it is, moreover, all things considered, a virtually physical gift, comparable to an animal's sense of smell; merely a rare flower of strength, an entirely nervous power of sensing what is in the wind ("Me, I walk by radar").

Conversely, it is through his corporeal mediocrity that the intellectual is condemned: Mendès-France looks like "a bottle of Vichy water" (double scorn addressed to water and to dyspepsia). Sheltering in the hypertrophy of a fragile and useless head, the entire intellectual being is stricken by the gravest of physical flaws, fatigue (corporeal substitute for decadence): though idle, he is congenitally exhausted, just as the Poujadist, though hardworking, is always fresh and ready. We touch here upon the profound idea of any morality of the human body: the idea of race. The intellectuals are one race, the Poujadists are another.

Yet Poujade has a conception of race that at first glance is paradoxical. Remarking that the average Frenchman is the product of many mixtures (the familiar refrain: France, the racial melting pot), Poujade contrasts proudly this variety of origins with the narrow sect of those who have never mixed their blood with any but each other (by which is meant, of course, the Jews). He exclaims, pointing to Mendès-France: "You're the racist!"; then he explains: "Of the two of us, he's the one who can be a racist, he's the one who has a race." Poujade practices what we might call the racism of crossbreeding, without danger, moreover, since the vaunted "crossbreeding" has never mixed, according to Poujade himself, anything but Duponts, Durands, and Poujades, i.e., the same with the same. Obviously the notion of a synthetic "race" is a precious one, for it permits playing sometimes on syncretism, sometimes on race. In the first case, Poujade uses the old, once-revolutionary notion of the Nation, which has nourished all the French liberalisms (Michelet vs. Augustin Thierry, Gide vs. Barrès, etc.): "My ancestors, Celts, Gauls, all mixed with others. I am the fruit of the melting pot of invasions and exo-duses." In the second case, he rediscovers with no difficulty at all the fundamental racist object, Blood (here it is chiefly Celtic blood, that of Le Pen, *solid Breton*, separated by a racial abyss from the *aesthetes of the New Left*, or Gallic blood, in which Mendès is lacking). As for the intelligence, we are deal-ing here with an arbitrary distribution of values: the addition of certain bloods (that of the Duponts, the Durands, and the Poujades) produces only pure blood, and we may remain within the reassuring order of a summation of homogeneous quantities; but other bloods (that, notably, of the *technocrats without a country*) are purely qualificational phenomena, thereby discredited in the Poujadist universe; they cannot in-terbreed, accede to the salvation of the large French quantity, to that "vulgar" whose numerical triumph is opposed to the fatigue of "distinguished" intellectuals.

This racial opposition between the strong and the ex-hausted, the Gauls and the men without a country, the vulgar and the distinguished, is, moreover, quite simply the opposi-tion between the provinces and Paris. Paris summarizes all the French vices: System, sadism, intellectuality, fatigue: "Paris is a monster, for life there is unbalanced: life shakes you up, dazzles and overwhelms you from morning to night, etc." Paris participates in that same poison, an essentially qualitative sub-stance (what Poujade elsewhere calls, not realizing how well he is putting it: dialectics), which, as we have seen, is opposed to the quantitative world of common sense. To confront qual-ity was for Poujade the decisive test, his Rubicon: *to go up to Paris*, to collect there the moderate provincial deputies cor-rupted by the capital, veritable renegades of their race, waited for back home in the village with pitchforks—this expedition has defined a great racial migration even more than a political extension.

Confronting so constant a suspicion, could Poujade rescue

some form of the intellectual, give him an ideal image, in a word, postulate a *Poujadist intellectual*? Poujade merely tells us that only "intellectuals worthy of the name" will enter his Olympus. Thus we are back to one of those famous definitions by identity (A=A), which I have on several occasions called tautologies, i.e., nothingness. All anti-intellectualism ends this way in the death of language, i.e., in the destruction of sociability.

Most of these Poujadist themes, paradoxical as it may appear, are corruptions of romantic themes. When Poujade wants to define the People, it is the preface to *Ruy Blas* that he quotes at length: and the intellectual seen by Poujade is more or less Michelet's jurist and Jesuit, dry, empty, sterile, and sneering. This is because today's petite bourgeoisie is reaping the heritage of yesterday's liberal bourgeoisie, precisely the one which assisted its social promotion: Michelet's sentimentalism contained many reactionary seeds. As Barrès knew. If it were not for all the discrepancies of talent, Poujade could still sign many pages of Michelet's *Le Peuple* (1846).

Which is why, precisely on this matter of the intellectuals, Poujadism goes much further than Poujade; the anti-intellectualist ideology affects various political milieus, and it is not necessary to be a Poujadist to nourish a hatred of ideas. For what is inculpated here is any form of explicative, committed culture, and what is saved is an "innocent" culture, the culture whose naïveté leaves the tyrant's hands free. This is why writers in the literal sense of the word are not excluded by the Poujadist family (some, extremely well known, have sent their works to Poujade embellished with flattering dedications). What is condemned is the intellectual, i.e., a consciousness, or better still: an Observation (Poujade recalls somewhere how much as a lycée student, he suffered from being looked at by his fellow students). *That no one look at us* is the principle of Poujadist anti-intellectualism. Only, from the ethnologist's point of view, the practices of integration and of exclusion are obviously complementary, and in a sense which is not the one he supposes, Poujade needs intellectuals, for if he condemns them it is on account of a magical evil: in the Poujadist society the intellectual has the accursed and necessary role of a lapsed witch doctor.

II

MYTH TODAY

TRANSLATED BY ANNETTE LAVERS

What is a myth today? I shall give at the outset a first, very simple answer, which is perfectly consistent with etymology: *myth is a type of speech.**

MYTH IS A TYPE OF SPEECH

Of course, it is not *any* type: language needs special conditions in order to become myth: we shall see them in a minute. But what must be firmly established at the start is that myth is a system of communication, that it is a message. This allows one to perceive that myth cannot possibly be an object, a concept, or an idea; it is a mode of signification, a form. Later, we shall have to assign to this form historical limits, conditions of use, and reintroduce society into it: we must nevertheless first describe it as a form.

It can be seen that to purport to discriminate among mythical objects according to their substance would be entirely illusory: since myth is a type of speech, everything can be a myth, provided it is conveyed by a discourse. Myth is not defined by the object of its message, but by the way in which it utters this message: there are formal limits to myth, there are no "substantial" ones. Everything, then, can be a myth?

*Innumerable other meanings of the word *myth* can be cited against this. But I have tried to define things, not words.

Yes, I believe this, for the universe is infinitely fertile in suggestions. Every object in the world can pass from a closed, silent existence to an oral state, open to appropriation by society, for there is no law, whether natural or not, which forbids talking about things. A tree is a tree. Yes, of course. But a tree as expressed by Minou Drouet is no longer quite a tree, it is a tree which is decorated, adapted to a certain type of consumption, laden with literary self-indulgence, revolt, images, in short with a type of social *usage* which is added to pure matter.

Naturally, everything is not expressed at the same time: some objects become the prey of mythical speech for a while, then they disappear, others take their place and attain the status of myth. Are there objects which are *inevitably* a source of suggestiveness, as Baudelaire suggested about Woman? Certainly not: one can conceive of very ancient myths, but there are no eternal ones; for it is human history which converts reality into speech, and it alone rules the life and death of mythical language. Ancient or not, mythology can only have a historical foundation, for myth is a type of speech chosen by history: it cannot possibly evolve from the "nature" of things.

Speech of this kind is a message. It is therefore by no means confined to oral speech. It can consist of modes of writing or of representations; not only written discourse but also photography, cinema, reporting, sport, shows, publicity, all of these can serve as a support to mythical speech. Myth can be defined neither by its object nor by its material, for any material can arbitrarily be endowed with meaning: the arrow which is brought in order to signify a challenge is also a kind of speech. True, as far as perception is concerned, writing and pictures, for instance, do not call upon the same types of consciousness; and even with pictures, one can use many kinds of reading: a diagram lends itself to signification more than a drawing, a copy more than an original, and a caricature more than a portrait. But this is the point: we are no longer dealing here with a theoretical mode of representation: we are dealing with *this* particular image, which is given for *this* particular signification. Mythical speech is made of a material which has *already* been worked on so as to make it suitable for communication: it is because all the materials of myth (whether pictorial or written) presuppose a signifying consciousness that one can reason about them while discounting their substance. This substance is not unimportant: pictures, to be sure, are more imperative than writing, they impose meaning at one stroke, without analyzing or diluting it. But this is no longer a constitutive difference. Pictures become like writing as soon as they are meaningful: like writing, they call for a lexis.

We shall therefore take *language*, *discourse*, *speech*, etc., to mean any significant unit or synthesis, whether verbal or visual; a photograph will be a kind of speech for us in the same way as a newspaper article; even objects will become speech, if they mean something. This generic way of conceiving language is in fact justified by the very history of writing: long before the invention of our alphabet, objects like the Inca quipu, or drawings, as in pictographs, have been accepted as speech. This does not mean that one must treat mythical speech like language; myth in fact belongs to the province of a general science, coextensive with linguistics, which is *semiology*.

MYTH AS A SEMIOLOGICAL SYSTEM

For mythology, since it is the study of a type of speech, is but one fragment of this vast science of signs which Saussure postulated some forty years ago under the name of *semiology*. Semiology has not yet come into being. But since Saussure himself, and sometimes independently of him, a whole section of contemporary research has constantly been referred to the problem of meaning: psychoanalysis, structuralism, eidetic psychology, some new types of literary criticism of which Bachelard has given the first examples, are no longer concerned with facts except inasmuch as they are endowed with significance. Now to postulate a signification is to have recourse to semiology. I do not mean that semiology would account for all these aspects of research equally well: they have different contents. But they have a common status: they all are sciences dealing with values. They are not content with meeting the facts: they define and explore them as tokens for something else.

Semiology is a science of forms, since it studies significations apart from their content. I should like to say one word about the necessity and the limits of such a formal science. The necessity is that which applies in the case of any exact language. Zhdanov made fun of Alexandrov the philosopher, who spoke of *"the spherical structure of our planet." "[I]t was thought until now,"* Zhdanov said, *"that form alone could be spherical."* Zhdanov was right: one cannot speak about structures in terms of forms, and vice versa. It may well be that on the plane of "life" there is but a totality where structures and forms cannot be separated. But science has no use for the ineffable: it must speak about "life" if it wanted to transform it. Against a certain quixotism of synthesis, quite platonic incidentally, all criticism must consent to the ascesis, to the artifice of analysis; and in analysis, it must match method and language. Less terrorized by the spectre of "formalism," historical criticism might have been less sterile; it would have understood that the specific study of forms does not in any way contradict the necessary principles of totality and History. On the contrary: the more a system is specifically defined in its forms, the more amenable it is to historical criticism. To parody a well-known saying, I shall say that a little formalism turns one away from History, but that a lot brings one back to it. Is there a better example of total criticism than the description of saintliness, at once formal and historical, semiological and ideological, in Sartre's *Saint Genet?* The danger, on the contrary, is to consider forms ambiguous objects, half form and half substance, to endow form with a substance of form, as was done, for instance, by Zhdanovian realism. Semiology, once its limits are settled, is not a metaphysical trap: it is a science among others, necessary but not sufficient. The important thing is to see that the unity of an explanation cannot be based on the amputation of one or another of its approaches but, as Engels said, on the dialectical coordination of the particular sciences it makes use of. This is the case with mythology: it is a part both of semiology, inasmuch as it is a formal science, and of ideology, inasmuch as it is a historical science: it studies ideas-in-form.*

Let me therefore restate that any semiology postulates a relation between two terms, a *signifier* and a *signified*. This relation concerns objects which belong to different categories, and this is why it is not one of equality but one of equivalence. We must here be on our guard, for despite common parlance, which simply says that the signifier *expresses* the signified, we are dealing, in any semiological system, not with two but with three different terms. For what we grasp is not at all one term after the other, but the correlation which unites them: there are, therefore, the signifier, the signified, and the sign, which is the associative total of the first two terms. Take a bunch of roses: I use it to *signify* my passion. Do we have here, then, only a signifier and a signified, the roses and my passion? Not even that; to put it accurately, there are here only "passionified" roses. But on the plane of analysis, we do have three terms; for these roses weighted with passion perfectly and correctly allow themselves to be decomposed into roses and passion: the former

*The development of publicity, of a national press, of radio, of illustrated news, not to speak of the survival of a myriad rites of communication which rule social appearances, makes the development of a semiological science more urgent than ever. In a single day, how many really nonsignifying fields do we cross? Very few, sometimes none. Here I am, before the sea; it is true that it bears no message. But on the beach, what material for semiology! Flags, slogans, signals, signboards, clothes, suntan even, which are so many messages to me.

and the latter existed before uniting and forming this third object, which is the sign. It is as true to say that on the plane of experience I cannot dissociate the roses from the message they carry, as to say that on the plane of analysis I cannot confuse the roses as signifier and the roses as sign: the signifier is empty, the sign is full, it is a meaning. Or take a black pebble: I can make it signify in several ways, it is a mere signifier; but if I weight it with a definite signified (a death sentence, for instance, in an anonymous vote), it will become a sign. Naturally, there are among the signifier, the signified, and the sign functional implications (such as that of the part to the whole) which are so close that to analyze them may seem futile; but we shall see in a moment that this distinction has a capital importance for the study of myth as semiological schema.

Naturally, these three terms are purely formal, and different contents can be given to them. Here are a few examples: for Saussure, who worked on a particular but methodologically exemplary semiological system—the language or *langue*—the signified is the concept, the signifier is the acoustic image (which is mental), and the relation between concept and image is the sign (the word, for instance), which is a concrete entity.* For Freud, as is well known, the human psyche is a stratification of tokens or representatives. One term (I refrain from giving it any precedence) is constituted by the manifest meaning of behavior, another, by its latent or real meaning (it is, for instance, the substratum of the dream); as for the third term, it is here also a correlation of the first two: it is the dream itself in its totality, the parapraxis (a mistake in speech or behavior) or the neurosis, conceived as compromises, as economies effected thanks to the joining of a form (the first term) and an intentional function (the second term). We can

---

*The notion of *word* is one of the most controversial in linguistics. I keep it here for the sake of simplicity.

see here how necessary it is to distinguish the sign from the signifier: a dream, to Freud, is no more its manifest datum than its latent content: it is the functional union of these two terms. In Sartrean criticism, finally (I shall keep to these three well-known examples), the signified is constituted by the original crisis in the subject (the separation from his mother to Baudelaire, the naming of the theft for Genet); Literature as discourse forms the signifier, and the relation between crisis and discourse defines the work, which is signification. Of course, this tridimensional pattern, however constant in its form, is actualized in three different ways: one cannot therefore say too often that semiology can have its unity only at the level of forms, not contents; its field is limited, it knows only one operation: reading, or deciphering.

In myth, we find again the tridimensional pattern which I have just described: the signifier, the signified, and the sign. But myth is a peculiar system, in that it is constructed from a semiological chain which existed before it: it *is a second-order semiological system*. That which is a sign (namely the associative total of a concept and an image) in the first system becomes a mere signifier in the second. We must here recall that the materials of mythical speech (the language itself, photography, painting, posters, rituals, objects, etc.), however different at the start, are reduced to a pure signifying function as soon as they are caught by myth. Myth sees in them only the same raw material; their unity is that they all come down to the status of a mere language. Whether it deals with alphabetical or pictorial writing, myth wants to see in them only a sum of signs, a global sign, the final term of a first semiological chain. And it is precisely this final term which will become the first term of the greater system which it builds and of which it is only a part. Everything happens as if myth had shifted the formal system of the first significations sideways. As this lateral shift is essential for the analysis of myth, I shall represent it in the following way, it being understood, of course, that the spatialization of the pattern is here only a metaphor:

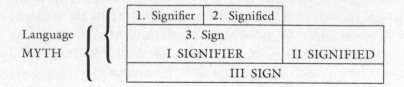

It can be seen that in myth there are two semiological systems, one of which is staggered in relation to the other: a linguistic system, the language (or the modes of representation which are assimilated to it), which I shall call the language object, because it is the language which myth gets hold of in order to build its own system; and myth itself, which I shall call the metalanguage, because it is a second language, in which one speaks about the first. When he reflects on a metalanguage, the semiologist no longer needs to ask himself questions about the composition of the language object, he no longer has to take into account the details of the linguistic schema; he will need only to know its total term, or global sign, and only inasmuch as this term lends itself to myth. This is why the semiologist is entitled to treat in the same way writing and pictures: what he retains from them is the fact that they both are signs, that they both reach the threshold of myth endowed with the same signifying function, that they constitute, one just as much as the other, a language object.

It is now time to give one or two examples of mythical speech. I shall borrow the first from an observation by Valéry.* I am a pupil in the second form in a French lycée. I open my Latin grammar, and I read a sentence, borrowed from Aesop or Phaedrus: *quia ego nominor leo.* I stop and think. There is something ambiguous about this statement: on the one hand,

* *Tel quel,* II, p. 191.

the words in it do have a simple meaning: *because my name is lion*. And on the other hand, the sentence is evidently there in order to signify something else to me. Inasmuch as it is addressed to me, a pupil in the second form, it tells me clearly: I am a grammatical example meant to illustrate the rule about the agreement of the predicate. I am even forced to realize that the sentence in no way *signifies* its meaning to me, that it tries very little to tell me something about the lion and what sort of name he has; its true and fundamental signification is to impose itself on me as the presence of a certain agreement of the predicate. I conclude that I am faced with a particular, greater semiological system, since it is coextensive with the language: there is, indeed, a signifier, but this signifier is itself formed by a sum of signs, it is in itself a first semiological system (*my name is lion*). Thereafter, the formal pattern is correctly unfolded: there is a signified (*I am a grammatical example*), and there is a global signification, which is none other than the correlation of the signifier and the signified; for neither the naming of the lion nor the grammatical example is given separately.

And here is now another example: I am at the barber's, and a copy of *Paris-Match* is offered to me. On the cover, a young Negro in French uniform is saluting, with his eyes uplifted, probably fixed on a fold of the tricolor. All this is the *meaning* of the picture. But, whether naïvely or not, I see very well what it signifies to me: that France is a great Empire, that all her sons, without any color discrimination, faithfully serve under her flag, and that there is no better answer to the detractors of an alleged colonialism than the zeal shown by this Negro in serving his so-called oppressors. I am therefore again faced with a greater semiological system: there is a signifier, itself already formed with a previous system (*a black soldier is giving the French salute*); there is a signified (it is here a purposeful mixture of Frenchness and militariness); finally, there is a presence of the signified through the signifier.

Before tackling the analysis of each term of the mythical system, one must agree on terminology. We now know that the signifier can be looked at, in myth, from two points of view: as the final term of the linguistic system, or as the first term of the mythical system. We therefore need two names. On the plane of language, that is, as the final term of the first system, I shall call the signifier meaning (*my name is lion, a Negro is giving the French salute*); on the plane of myth, I shall call it: form. In the case of the signified, no ambiguity is possible: we shall retain the name *concept*. The third term is the correlation of the first two: in the linguistic system, it is the *sign*; but it is not possible to use this word again without ambiguity, since in myth (and this is the chief peculiarity of the latter), the signifier is already formed by the *signs* of the language. I shall call the third term of the myth the signification. This word here is all the better justified since myth has in fact a double function: it points out and it notifies, it makes us understand something, and it imposes it on us.

THE FORM AND THE CONCEPT

The signifier of myth presents itself in an ambiguous way: it is at the same time meaning and form, full on one side and empty on the other. As meaning, the signifier already postulates a reading, I grasp it through my eyes, it has a sensory reality (unlike the linguistic signifier, which is purely mental), there is a richness in it: the naming of the lion, the Negro's salute are credible wholes, they have at their disposal a sufficient rationality. As a total of linguistic signs, the meaning of the myth has its own value, it belongs to history, that of the lion or that of the Negro: in the meaning, a signification is already built, and could not very well be self-sufficient if myth did not take hold of it and did not turn it suddenly into an empty, parasitical form. The meaning is *already* complete, it postulates a kind of knowledge, a past, a memory, a comparative order of facts, ideas, decisions.

When it becomes form, the meaning leaves its contingency behind; it empties itself, it becomes impoverished, history evaporates, only the letter remains. There is here a paradoxical permutation in the reading operations, an abnormal regression from meaning to form, from the linguistic sign to the mythical signifier. If one encloses *quia ego nominor leo* in a purely linguistic system, the clause finds again there a fullness, a richness, a history: I am an animal, a lion, I live in a certain country, I have just been hunting, they would have me share my prey with a heifer, a cow, and a goat; but being the stronger, I award myself all the shares for various reasons, the last of which is quite simply that *my name is lion*. But as the form of the myth, the clause hardly retains anything of this long story. The meaning contained a whole system of values: a history, a geography, a morality, a zoology, a Literature. The form has put all this richness at a distance: its newly acquired penury calls for a signification to fill it. The story of the lion must recede a great deal in order to make room for the grammatical example, one must put the biography of the Negro in parentheses if one wants to free the picture, and prepare it to receive its signified.

But the essential point in all this is that the form does not suppress the meaning, it only impoverishes it, it puts it at a distance, it holds it at one's disposal. One believes that the meaning is going to die, but it is a death with reprieve; the meaning loses its value, but keeps its life, from which the form of the myth will draw its nourishment. The meaning will be for the form like an instantaneous reserve of history, a timed richness, which it is possible to call and dismiss in a sort of rapid alternation: the form must constantly be able to be rooted again in the meaning and to get there what nature it needs for its nutriment; above all, it must be able to hide there. It is this constant game of hide-and-seek between the meaning and the form which defines myth. The form of myth is not a symbol: the Negro who salutes is not the symbol of the French Empire: he has too much presence, he appears as a rich, fully experienced, spontaneous, innocent, *indisputable* image. But at the same time this presence is tamed, put at a distance, made almost transparent; it recedes a little, it becomes the accomplice of a concept which comes to it fully armed, French imperiality: once made use of, it becomes artificial.

Let us now look at the signified: this history which drains out of the form will be wholly absorbed by the concept. As for the latter, it is determined, it is at once historical and intentional; it is the motivation which causes the myth to be uttered. Grammatical exemplarity, French imperiality are the very drives behind the myth. The concept reconstitutes a chain of causes and effects, motives and intentions. Unlike the form, the concept is in no way abstract: it is filled with a situation. Through the concept, it is a whole new history which is implanted in the myth. Into the naming of the lion, first drained of its contingency, the grammatical example will attract my whole existence: Time, which caused me to be born at a certain period when Latin grammar was taught; History, which sets me apart, through a whole mechanism of social segregation, from the children who do not learn Latin; pedagogic tradition, which caused this example to be chosen from Aesop or Phaedrus; my own linguistic habits, which see the agreement of the predicate as a fact worthy of notice and illustration. The same goes for the Negro-giving-the-salute: as form, its meaning is shallow, isolated, impoverished; as the concept of French imperiality, here it is again tied to the totality of the world: to the general History of France, to its colonial adventures, to its present difficulties. Truth to tell, what is invested in the concept is less reality than a certain knowledge of reality; in passing from the meaning to the form, the image loses some knowledge: the better to receive the knowledge in the concept. In actual fact, the knowledge contained in a mythical concept is confused, made of yielding, shapeless associations. One must fully stress this open character of the concept; it is not at all an abstract, purified essence; it is a formless, unstable, nebulous condensation, whose unity and coherence are above all due to its function.

In this sense, we can say that the fundamental character of the mythical concept is to be *appropriated*: grammatical exemplarity very precisely concerns a given form of pupils, French imperiality must appeal to such and such group of readers and not another. The concept closely corresponds to a function, and it is defined as a tendency. This cannot fail to recall the signified in another semiological system, Freudianism. In Freud, the second term of the system is the latent meaning (the content) of the dream, of the parapraxis, of the neurosis. Now Freud does remark that the second-order meaning of behavior is its real meaning, that which is appropriate to a complete situation, including its deeper level; it is, just like the mythical concept, the very intention of behavior.

A signified can also have several signifiers: this is indeed the case in linguistics and psychoanalysis. It is also the case in the mythical concept: it has at its disposal an unlimited mass of signifiers: I can find a thousand Latin sentences to actualize for me the agreement of the predicate, I can find a thousand images which signify to me French imperiality. This means that *quantitively*, the concept is much poorer than the signifier, it often does nothing but re-present itself. Poverty and richness are in reverse proportion in the form and the concept: to the qualitative poverty of the form, which is the repository of a rarefied meaning, there corresponds the richness of the concept which is open to the whole of History; and to the quantitative abundance of the forms there corresponds a small number of concepts. This repetition of the concept through different forms is precious to the mythologist, it allows him to decipher the myth: it is the insistence of a kind of behavior which reveals its intention. This confirms that there is no regular ratio between the volume of the signified and that of the signifier. In language, this ratio is proportionate, it hardly exceeds the word, or at least the concrete unit. In myth, on the contrary, the concept can spread over a very large expanse of signifier. For instance, a whole book may be the signifier of a single concept; and conversely, a minute form (a word, a gesture, even incidental, so long as it is noticed) can serve as signifier to a concept filled with a very rich history. Although unusual in language, this disproportion between signifier and signified is not specific to myth: in Freud, for instance, the parapraxis is a signifier whose thinness is out of proportion to the real meaning which it betrays.

As I said, there is no fixity in mythical concepts: they can come into being, alter, disintegrate, disappear completely. And it is precisely because they are historical that history can very easily suppress them. This instability forces the mythologist to use a terminology adapted to it, and about which I should now like to say a word, because it often is a cause for irony: I mean neologism. The concept is a constituting element of myth: if I want to decipher myths, I must somehow be able to name concepts. The dictionary supplies me with a few: Goodness, Kindness, Wholeness, Humaneness, etc. But by definition, since it is the dictionary which gives them to me, these particular concepts are not historical. Now what I need most often is ephemeral concepts, in connection with limited contingencies: neologism is then inevitable. China is one thing, the idea which a French petit bourgeois could have of it not so long ago is another: for this peculiar mixture of bells, rickshaws, and opium dens, no other word possible but *Siniess*.* Unlovely? One should at least get some consolation from the

*Or perhaps *Sinity*? Just as if Latin/Latinity = Basque/x, x = Basquity.

fact that conceptual neologisms are never arbitrary: they are built according to a highly sensible proportional rule.

THE SIGNIFICATION

In semiology, the third term is nothing but the association of the first two, as we saw. It is the only one which is allowed to be seen in a full and satisfactory way, the only one which is consumed in actual fact. I have called it: the signification. We can see that the signification is the myth itself, just as the Saussurean sign is the word (or more accurately the concrete unit). But before listing the characters of the signification, one must reflect a little on the way in which it is prepared, that is, on the modes of correlation of the mythical concept and the mythical form.

First we must note that in myth, the first two terms are perfectly manifest (unlike what happens in other semiological systems): one of them is not "hidden" behind the other, they both are given *here* (and not one here and the other there). However paradoxical it may seem, *myth hides nothing*: its function is to distort, not to make disappear. There is no latency of the concept in relation to the form: there is no need of an unconscious in order to explain myth. Of course, one is dealing with two different types of manifestation: form has a literal, immediate presence; moreover, it is extended. This stems—this cannot be repeated too often—from the nature of the mythical signifier, which is already linguistic: since it is constituted by a meaning which is already outlined, it can appear only through a given substance (whereas in language, the signifier remains mental). In the case of oral myth, this extension is linear (*because my name is lion*); in that of visual myth, it is multidimensional (in the center, the Negro's uniform, at the top, the blackness of his face, on the left, the military salute, etc.). The elements of the form therefore are related as to place and proximity: the mode of presence of the form is spatial. The concept, on the contrary, appears in global fashion, it is a kind of nebula, the condensation, more or less hazy, of a certain knowledge. Its elements are linked by associative relations: it is supported not by an extension but by a depth (although this metaphor is perhaps still too spatial): its mode of presence is memorial.

The relation which unites the concept of the myth to its meaning is essentially a relation of *deformation*. We find here again a certain formal analogy with a complex semiological system such as that of the various types of psychoanalysis. Just as for Freud the manifest meaning of behavior is distorted by its latent meaning, so in myth the meaning is distorted by the concept. Of course, this distortion is possible only because the form of the myth is already constituted by a linguistic meaning. In a simple system like language, the signified cannot distort anything at all because the signifier, being empty, arbitrary, offers no resistance to it. But here, everything is different: the signifier has, so to speak, two aspects: one full, which is the meaning (the history of the lion, of the Negro soldier), one empty, which is the form (*because my name is lion*; *Negro-French-soldier-saluting-the-tricolor*). What the concept distorts is of course what is full, the meaning: the lion and the Negro are deprived of their history, changed into gestures. What Latin exemplarity distorts is the naming of the lion, in all its contingency; and what French imperiality obscures is also a primary language, a factual discourse which was telling me about the salute of a Negro in uniform. But this distortion is not an obliteration: the lion and the Negro remain here, the concept needs them; they are half amputated, they are deprived of memory, not of existence: they are at once stubborn, silently rooted there, and garrulous, a speech wholly at the service of the concept. The concept, literally, deforms, but does not abolish the meaning; a word can perfectly render this contradiction: it alienates it.

What must always be remembered is that myth is a double system; there occurs in it a sort of ubiquity: its point of departure is constituted by the arrival of a meaning. To keep a spatial metaphor, the approximate character of which I have already stressed, I shall say that the signification of the myth is constituted by a sort of constantly moving turnstile which presents alternately the meaning of the signifier and its form, a language object and a metalanguage, a purely signifying and a purely imagining consciousness. This alternation is, so to speak, gathered up in the concept, which uses it like an ambiguous signifier, at once intellective and imaginary, arbitrary and natural.

I do not wish to prejudge the moral implications of such a mechanism, but I shall not exceed the limits of an objective analysis if I point out that the ubiquity of the signifier in myth exactly reproduces the physique of the *alibi* (which is, as one realizes, a spatial term): in the alibi too, there is a place which is full and one which is empty, linked by a relation of negative identity ("I am not where you think I am, I am where you think I am not"). But the ordinary alibi (for the police, for instance) has an end; reality stops the turnstile's revolving at a certain point. Myth is a *value*, truth is no guarantee for it; nothing prevents it from being a perpetual alibi: it is enough that its signifier has two sides for it always to have an "elsewhere" at its disposal. The meaning is always there to *present* the form; the form is always there to *outdistance* the meaning. And there never is any contradiction, conflict, or split between the meaning and the form: they are never at the same place. In the same way, if I am in a car and I look at the scenery through the window, I can at will focus on the scenery or on the windowpane. At one moment I grasp the presence of the glass and the distance of the landscape; at another, on the contrary, the transparence of the glass and the depth of the landscape; but the result of this alternation is constant: the glass is at once present and empty to me, and the landscape unreal and full. The same thing occurs in the mythical signifier: its form is empty but present, its meaning absent but full. To wonder at this contradiction I must voluntarily interrupt this turnstile of form and meaning, I must focus on each separately, and apply to myth a static method of deciphering, in short, I must go against its own dynamics: to sum up, I must pass from the state of the reader to that of mythologist.

And it is again in this duplicity of the signifier which determines the characters of the signification. We now know that a myth is a type of speech defined by its intention (*I am a grammatical example*) much more than by its literal sense (*my name is lion*); and that in spite of this, its intention is somehow frozen, purified, eternalized, *made absent* by this literal sense (*The French Empire? It's just a fact: look at this good Negro who salutes like one of our own boys*). This constituent ambiguity of mythical speech has two consequences for the signification, which henceforth appears both like a notification and like a statement of fact.

Myth has an imperative, buttonholing character, stemming from a historical concept, directly springing from contingency (a Latin class, a threatened Empire), it is *I* whom it has come to seek. It has turned toward me, I am subjected to its intentional force, it summons me to receive its expansive ambiguity. If, for instance, I take a walk in Spain, in the Basque country,* I may well notice in the houses an architectural unity, a common style, which leads me to acknowledge the Basque house as a definite ethnic product. However, I do not feel personally concerned or, so to speak, attacked by this unitary style: I see only too well that it was here before me, without me. It is a complex product which has its determinations at the level of a very wide history: it does not call out to me, it does not provoke me into naming it, except if I think of inserting it into a vast picture of rural habitat. But if I am in the Paris region and I

---

*I say "in Spain" because, in France, petit bourgeois advancement has caused a whole "mythical" architecture of the Basque chalet to flourish.

catch a glimpse, at the end of the rue Gambetta or the rue Jean-Jaurès, of a natty white chalet with red tiles, dark brown half-timbering, an asymmetrical roof, and a wattle-and-daub front, I feel as if I were personally receiving an imperious injunction to name this object a Basque chalet: or, even better, to see it as the very essence of *"Basquity."* This is because the concept appears to me in all its appropriative nature: it comes and seeks me out in order to oblige me to acknowledge the body of intentions which have motivated it and arranged it there as the signal of an individual history, as a confidence and a complicity: it is a real call, which the owners of the chalet send out to me. And this call, in order to be more imperious, has agreed to all manner of impoverishments: all that justified the Basque house on the plane of technology—the barn, the outside stairs, the dovecote, etc.—has been dropped; there remains only a brief order, not to be disputed. And the adhomination is so frank that I feel this chalet has just been created on the spot, *for me*, like a magical object springing up in my present life without any trace of the history which has caused it.

For this interpellant speech is at the same time a frozen speech: at the moment of reaching me, it suspends itself, turns away, and assumes the look of a generality: it stiffens, it makes itself look neutral and innocent. The appropriation of the concept is suddenly driven away once more by the literalness of the meaning. This is a kind of *arrest*, in both the physical and the legal sense of the term: French imperiality condemns the saluting Negro to be nothing more than an instrumental signifier, the Negro suddenly hails me in the name of French imperiality; but at the same moment the Negro's salute thickens, becomes vitrified, freezes into an eternal reference meant to *establish* French imperiality. On the surface of language something has stopped moving: the use of the signification is here, hiding behind the fact, and conferring on it a notifying look; but at the same time, the face paralyzes the intention, gives it something like a malaise producing immobility: in order to make it innocent, it freezes it. This is because myth is speech *stolen and restored*. Only, speech which is restored is no longer quite that which was stolen: when it was brought back, it was not put exactly in its place. It is this brief act of larceny, this moment taken for a surreptitious faking, which gives mythical speech its benumbed look.

One last element of the signification remains to be examined: its motivation. We know that in a language the sign is arbitrary: nothing compels the acoustic image *tree* "naturally" to mean the concept *tree*: the sign, here, is unmotivated. Yet this arbitrariness has limits, which come from the associative relations of the word: the language can produce a whole fragment of the sign by analogy with other signs (for instance, one says *amiable* in French, and not *amable*, by analogy with *aime*). The mythical signification, on the other hand, is never arbitrary; it is always in part motivated, and unavoidably contains some analogy. For Latin exemplarity to meet the naming of the lion, there must be an analogy, which is the agreement of the predicate; for French imperiality to get hold of the saluting Negro, there must be identity between the Negro's salute and that of the French soldier. Motivation is necessary to the very duplicity of myth: myth plays on the analogy between meaning and form, there is no myth without motivated form.* In order to grasp the power of motivation in myth, it is enough to reflect for a moment on an extreme case. I have here

---

*From the point of view of ethics, what is disturbing in myth is precisely that its form is motivated. For if there is a "health" of a language, it is the arbitrariness of the sign which is its grounding. What is sickening in myth is its resort to a false nature, its superabundance of significant forms, as in these objects which decorate their usefulness with a natural appearance. This will to weigh the signification with the full guarantee of nature causes a kind of nausea: myth is too rich, and what is in excess is precisely its motivation. This nausea is like the one I feel before the arts which refuse to choose between *physis* and *antiphysis*, using the first as an ideal and the second as an economy. Ethically, there is a kind of baseness in hedging one's bets.

before me a collection of objects so lacking in order that I can find no *meaning* in it; it would seem that here, deprived of any previous meaning, the form could not root its analogy in anything, and that myth is impossible. But what the form can always give one to read is disorder itself: it can give a signification to the absurd, make the absurd itself a myth. This is what happens when common sense mythifies surrealism, for instance. Even the absence of motivation does not embarrass myth; for this absence will itself be sufficiently objectified to become legible: and finally, the absence of motivation will become a second order motivation, and myth will be reestablished.

Motivation is unavoidable. It is nonetheless very fragmentary. To start with, it is not "natural": it is history which supplies its analogies to the form. Then the analogy between the meaning and the concept is never anything but partial: the form drops many analogous features and keeps only a few: it keeps the sloping roof, the visible beams in the Basque chalet, it abandons the stairs, the barn, the weathered look, etc. One must even go further: a *complete* image would exclude myth, or at least would compel it to seize only its very completeness. This is just what happens in the case of bad painting, which is wholly based on the myth of what is "filled out" and "finished" (it is the opposite and symmetrical case of the myth of the absurd: here the form mythifies an "absence," there, a surplus). But in general myth prefers to work with poor, incomplete images, where the meaning is already relieved of its fat, and ready for signification, such as caricatures, pastiches, symbols, etc. Finally, the motivation is chosen among other possible ones: I can very well give to French imperiality many other signifiers besides a Negro's salute: a French general pins a decoration on a one-armed Senegalese, a nun hands a cup of tea to a bedridden Arab, a white schoolmaster teaches attentive pickaninnies: the press undertakes every day to demonstrate that the store of mythical signifiers is inexhaustible. The nature of the mythical signification can in fact be well conveyed by one particular simile: it is neither more nor less arbitrary than an ideograph. Myth is a pure ideographic system, where the forms are still motivated by concepts which they represent while not yet, by a long way, covering the sum of its possibilities for representation. And just as historically, ideographs have gradually left the concept and have become associated with the sound, thus growing less and less motivated, so the worn-out state of a myth can be recognized by the arbitrariness of its signification: the whole of Molière is seen in a doctor's ruff.

READING AND DECIPHERING MYTH

How is a myth received? We must here once more come back to the duplicity of its signifier, which is at once meaning and form. I can produce three different types of reading by focusing on the one, or the other, or both at the same time.*

1. If I focus on an empty signifier, I let the concept fill the form of the myth without ambiguity, and I find myself before a simple system, where the signification becomes literal again: the Negro who salutes is an *example* of French imperiality, he is a *symbol* for it. This type of focusing is, for instance, that of the producer of myths, of the journalist who starts with a concept and seeks a form for it.†

2. If I focus on a full signifier, in which I clearly distinguish the meaning and the form, and consequently the distortion which the one imposes on

---

*The freedom in choosing what one focuses on is a problem which does not belong to the province of semiology; it depends on the concrete situation of the subject.
†We receive the naming of the lion as a pure *example* of Latin grammar because we are, *as grown-ups*, in a creative position in relation to it. I shall come back later to the value of the context in this mythical schema.

the other, I undo the signification of the myth, and I receive the latter as an imposture: the saluting Negro becomes the *alibi* of French imperiality. This type of focusing is that of the mythologist: he deciphers the myth, he understands a distortion.

3. Finally, if I focus on the mythical signifier as on an inextricable whole made of meaning and form, I receive an ambiguous signification: I respond to the constituting mechanism of myth, to its own dynamics, I become a reader of myths. The saluting Negro is no longer an example or symbol, still less an alibi: he is the very *presence* of French imperiality.

The first two types of focusing are static, analytical; they destroy the myth, either by making its intention obvious or by unmasking it: the former is cynical, the latter demystifying. The third type of focusing is dynamic, it consumes the myth according to the very ends built into its structure: the reader lives the myth as a story at once true and unreal.

If one wishes to connect a mystical schema to general history, to explain how it corresponds to the interests of a definite society, in short, to pass from semiology to ideology, it is obviously at the level of the third type of focusing that one must place oneself: it is the reader of myths himself who must reveal their essential function. How does he receive this particular myth *today*? If he receives it in an innocent fashion, what is the point of proposing it to him? And if he reads it using his powers of reflection, like the mythologist, does it matter which alibi is presented? If the reader does not see French imperiality in the saluting Negro, it was not worth weighing the latter with it; and if he sees it, the myth is nothing more than a political proposition, honestly expressed. In one word, either the intention of the myth is too obscure to be efficacious or it is too clear to be believed. In either case, where is the ambiguity?

This is but a false dilemma. Myth hides nothing and flaunts nothing: it distorts; myth is neither a lie nor a confession: it is an inflexion. Placed before the dilemma which I mentioned a moment ago, myth finds a third way out. Threatened with disappearance if it yields to either of the first two types of focusing, it gets out of this tight spot thanks to a compromise—it *is* this compromise. Entrusted with "glossing over" an intentional concept, myth encounters nothing but betrayal in language, for language can only obliterate the concept if it hides it, or unmask it if it formulates it. The elaboration of a second-order semiological system will enable myth to escape this dilemma: driven to having either to unveil or to liquidate the concept, it will *naturalize* it.

We reach here the very principle of myth: it transforms history into nature. We now understand why, *in the eyes of the myth consumer*, the intention, the adhomination of the concept can remain manifest without, however, appearing to have an interest in the matter: what causes mythical speech to be uttered is perfectly explicit, but it is immediately frozen into something natural; it is not read as a motive but as a reason. If I read the Negro saluting as symbol pure and simple of imperiality, I must renounce the reality of the picture, it discredits itself in my eyes when it becomes an instrument. Conversely, if I decipher the Negro's salute as an alibi of coloniality, I shatter the myth even more surely by the obviousness of its motivation. But for the myth reader, the outcome is quite different: everything happens as if the picture *naturally* conjured up the concept, as if the signifier *gave a foundation* to the signified: the myth exists from the precise moment when French imperiality achieves the natural state: myth is speech justified *in excess*.

Here is a new example which will help with understanding clearly how the myth reader is led to rationalize the signified by means of the signifier. We are in the month of July, I read a big headline in *France-Soir*: THE FALL IN PRICES: FIRST INDI-

CATIONS. VEGETABLES: PRICE DROP BEGINS. Let us quickly sketch the semiological schema: the example being a sentence, the first system is purely linguistic. The signifier of the second system is composed here of a certain number of accidents, some lexical (the words: *first*, *begins*, *the* [fall]), some typographical (enormous headlines where the reader usually sees news of world importance). The signified or concept is what must be called by a barbarous but unavoidable neologism: governmentality, the Government presented by the national press as the Essence of efficacy. The signification of the myth follows clearly from this: fruit and vegetable prices are falling *because* the government has so decided. Now it so happens in this case (and this is on the whole fairly rare) that the newspaper itself has, two lines below, allowed one to see through the myth which it had just elaborated—whether this is due to self-assurance or honesty. It adds (in small type, it is true): 'The fall in prices is helped by the return of seasonal abundance." This example is instructive for two reasons. Firstly, it conspicuously shows that myth essentially aims at causing an immediate impression—it does not matter if one is later allowed to see through the myth, its action is assumed to be stronger than the rational explanations which may later belie it. This means that the reading of a myth is exhausted at one stroke. I cast a quick glance at my neighbor's *France-Soir*: I cull only a *meaning* there, but I read a true signification; I *receive* the presence of governmental action in the fall of fruit and vegetable prices. That is all, and that is enough. A more attentive reading of the myth will in no way increase its power or its ineffectiveness: a myth is at the same time imperfectible and unquestionable; time or knowledge will not make it better or worse.

Secondly, the naturalization of the concept, which I have just identified as the essential function of myth, is here exemplary. In a first (exclusively linguistics) system, causality would be, literally, natural: fruit and vegetable prices fall because they are in season. In the second (mythical) system, causality is artificial, false; but it creeps, so to speak, through the back door of Nature. This is why myth is experienced as innocent speech: not because its intentions are hidden—if they were hidden, they could not be efficacious—but because they are so naturalized.

In fact, what allows the reader to consume myth innocently is that he does not see it as a semiological system but as an inductive one. Where there is only an equivalence, he seems a kind of causal process: the signifier and the signified have, in his eyes, a natural relationship. This confusion can be expressed otherwise: any semiological system is a system of values; now the myth consumer takes the signification for a system of facts: myth is read as a factual system, whereas it is but a semiological system.

MYTH AS STOLEN LANGUAGE

What is characteristic of myth? To transform a meaning into form. In other words, myth is always a language robbery. I rob the Negro who is saluting, the white and brown chalet, the seasonal fall in fruit prices, not to make them into examples or symbols, but to naturalize through them the Empire, my taste for Basque things, the Government. Are all primary languages a prey for myth? Is there no meaning which can resist this capture with which form threatens it? In fact, nothing can be safe from myth, myth can develop its second-order schema from any meaning and, as we saw, start from the very lack of meaning. But all languages do not resist equally well.

Articulated language, which is most often robbed by myth, offers little resistance. It contains in itself some mythical dispositions, the outline of a sign structure meant to manifest the intention which led to its being used: it is what could be called the *expressiveness* of language. The imperative or the subjunctive mode, for instance, is the form of a particular signified, different from the meaning: the signified is here my will or my request. This is why some linguists have defined the indicative, for instance, as a zero state or degree, compared to the subjunctive or the imperative. Now, in a fully constituted myth, the meaning is never at zero degree, and this is why the concept can distort it, naturalize it. We must remember once again that the privation of meaning is in no way a zero degree: this is why myth can perfectly well get hold of it, give it, for instance, the signification of the absurd, of surrealism, etc. At bottom it would only be the zero degree which could resist myth.

Language lends itself to myth in another way: it is very rare that it imposes at the outset a full meaning which it is impossible to distort. This comes from the abstractness of its concept: the concept of tree is vague, it lends itself to multiple contingencies. True, a language always has at its disposal a whole appropriating organization (*this* tree, *the* tree *which*, etc.). But there always remains, around the final meaning, a halo of virtualities where other possible meanings are floating: the meaning can almost always be *interpreted*. One could say that a language offers to myth an openwork meaning. Myth can easily insinuate itself into it, and swell there: it is a robbery by colonization (for instance: *the* fall in prices has started. But what fall? That caused by the season or that caused by the government? The signification becomes here a parasite of the article, in spite of the latter's being definite).

When meaning is too full for myth to be able to invade it, myth goes around it, and carries it away bodily. This is what happens to mathematical language. In itself, it cannot be distorted, it has taken all possible precautions against interpretation: no parasitical signification can worm itself into it. And this is why, precisely, myth takes it away en bloc; it takes a certain mathematical formula ($E = mc^2$) and makes of this unalterable meaning the pure signifier of mathematicity. We can see that what is here robbed by myth is something which resists, something pure. Myth can reach everything, corrupt everything, and even the very act of refusing oneself to it. So that the more the language object resists at first, the greater its final prostitution; whoever here resists completely yields completely: Einstein on one side, *Paris-Match* on the other. One can give a temporal image of this conflict: mathematical language is a *finished* language which derives its very perfection from this acceptance of death. Myth, on the contrary, is a language which does not want to die: it wrests from the meanings which give it its sustenance an insidious, degraded survival, it provokes in them an artificial reprieve in which it settles comfortably, it turns them into speaking corpses.

Here is another language which resists myth as much as it can: our poetic language. Contemporary poetry* is *a regressive semiological system*. Whereas myth aims at an ultrasignification, at the amplification of a first system, poetry, on the contrary, attempts to regain an infrasignification, a presemiological state of language; in short, it tries to transform the sign back into meaning: its ideal, ultimately, would be to reach not the meaning of words but the meaning of things themselves.† This is why it clouds the language, increases as much as it can the abstractness of the concept and the arbitrariness of the sign, and stretches to the limit the link between signifier and

---

*Classical poetry, on the contrary, would be, according to such norms, a strongly mythical system, since it imposes on the meaning one extra signified, which is *regularity*. The alexandrine, for instance, has value both as meaning of a discourse and as signifier of a new whole, which is its poetic signification. Success, when it occurs, comes from the degree of apparent fusion of the two systems. It can be seen that we deal in no way with a harmony between content and form, but with an *elegant* absorption of one form into another. By *elegance* I mean the most economical use of the means employed. It is because of an age-old abuse that critics confuse *meaning* and *content*. The language is never anything but a system of forms, and the meaning is a form.

†We are again dealing here with the *meaning*, in Sartre's use of the term, as a natural quality of things, situated outside a semiological system (*Saint Genet*, p. 283).

signified. The openwork structure of the concept is here maximally exploited: unlike what happens in prose, it is all the potential of the signified that the poetic sign tries to actualize, in the hope of at least reaching something like the transcendent quality of the thing, its natural (not human) meaning. Hence the essentialist ambitions of poetry, the conviction that it alone catches *the thing in itself,* inasmuch, precisely, as it wants to be an antilanguage. All told, of all those who use speech, poets are the least formalist, for they are the only ones who believe that the meaning of the words is only a form, with which they, being realists, cannot be content. This is why our modern poetry always asserts itself as a murder of language, a kind of spatial, tangible analogue of silence. Poetry occupies a position which is the reverse of that myth: myth is a semiological system which has the pretension of transcending itself into a factual system; poetry is a semiological system which has the pretension of contracting into an essential system.

But here again, as in the case of mathematical language, the very resistance offered by poetry makes it an ideal prey for myth: the apparent lack of order of signs, which is the poetic facet of an essential order, is captured by myth, and transformed into an empty signifier, which will serve to *signify* poetry. This explains the *improbable* character of modern poetry: by fiercely refusing myth, poetry surrenders to it bound hand and foot. Conversely, the *rules* in classical poetry constituted an accepted myth, the conspicuous arbitrariness of which amounted to perfection of a kind, since the equilibrium of a semiological system comes from the arbitrariness of its signs.

A voluntary acceptance of myth can in fact define the whole of our traditional Literature. According to our norms, this Literature is an undoubted mythical system: there is a meaning, that of the discourse; there is a signifier, which is this same discourse as form or writing; there is a signified, which is the concept of literature; there is signification, which is the literary discourse. I began to discuss this problem in *Writing Degree Zero*, which was, all told, nothing but a mythology of literary language. There I defined writing as the signifier of the literary myth, that is, as a form which is already filled with meaning and which receives from the concept of Literature a new signification.* I suggested that history, in modifying the writer's consciousness, had provoked, a hundred years or so ago, a moral crisis of literary language: writing was revealed as a signifier, Literature as signification; rejecting the false nature of traditional literary language, the writer violently shifted his position in the direction of an antinature of language. The subversion of writing was the radical act by which a number of writers have attempted to reject Literature as a mythical system. Every revolt of this kind has been a murder of Literature as signification: all have postulated the reduction of literary discourse to a simple semiological system, or even, in the case of poetry, to a pre-semiological system. This is an immense task, which required radical types of behavior: it is well known that some went as far as the pure and simple scuttling of the discourse, silence—whether real or transposed—appearing as the only possible weapon against the major power of myth: its recurrence.

It thus appears that it is very difficult to vanquish myth from the inside: for the very effort one makes in order to escape its stranglehold becomes in its turn the prey of myth: myth can always, as a last resort, signify the resistance which is brought to bear against it. Truth to tell, the best weapon

---

*Style, at least as I defined it then, is not a form, it does not belong to the province of a semiological analysis of Literature. In fact, style is a substance constantly threatened with formalization. To start with, it can perfectly well become degraded into a mode of writing: there is a "Malraux-type" writing, and even in Malraux himself. Then, style can also become a particular language, that used by the writer *for himself and for himself alone.* Style then becomes a sort of solipsistic myth, the language which the writer speaks *to himself.* It is easy to understand that at such a degree of solidification, style calls for a deciphering. The works of J. P. Richard are an example of this necessary critique of styles.

against myth is perhaps to mythify it in its turn, and to produce an *artificial myth*: and this reconstituted myth will in
fact be a mythology. Since myth robs language of something,
why not rob myth? All that is needed is to use it as the departure point for a third semiological chain, to take its signification
as the first term of a second myth. Literature offers some great
examples of such artificial mythologies. I shall evoke here only
Flaubert's *Bouvard and Pécuchet*. It is what could be called an
experimental myth, a second-order myth. Bouvard and his
friend Pécuchet represent a certain kind of bourgeoisie (which
is incidentally in conflict with other bourgeois strata): their
discourse *already* constitutes a mythical type of speech; its
language does have a meaning, but this meaning is the empty
form of a conceptual signified, which here is a kind of technological unsatedness. The meeting of meaning and concept
forms, in this first mythical system, a signification which is the
rhetoric of Bouvard and Pécuchet. It is at this point (I am
breaking the process into its components for the sake of analysis) that Flaubert intervenes: to this first mythical system, which
already is a second semiological system, he superimposes a
third chain, in which the first link is the signification, or the
final term, of the first myth. The rhetoric of Bouvard and Pécuchet becomes the form of the new system; the concept here
is due to Flaubert himself, to Flaubert's gaze on the myth
which Bouvard and Pécuchet have built for themselves: it consists of their natively ineffectual inclinations, their inability to
feel satisfied, the panic succession of their apprenticeships, in
short what I would very much like to call (but I see storm
clouds on the horizon): bouvard-and-pécuchet-ity. As for the
final signification, it is the book, it is *Bouvard and Pécuchet* for
us. The power of the second myth is that it gives the first its
basis as a naïveté which is looked at. Flaubert has undertaken
a real archaeological restoration of a given mythical speech: he
is the Viollet-le-Duc of a certain bourgeois ideology. But less

naïve than Viollet-le-Duc, he has strewn his reconstitution with supplementary ornaments which demystify it. These ornaments (which are the form of the second myth) are subjective in kind: there is a semiological equivalence between the subjunctive restitution of the discourse of Bouvard and Pécuchet and their ineffectualness.*

Flaubert's great merit (and that of all artificial mythologies: there are remarkable ones in Sartre's work) is that he gave to the problem of realism a frankly semiological solution. True, it is a somewhat incomplete merit, for Flaubert's ideology, since the bourgeois was for him only an aesthetic eyesore, was not at all realistic. But at least he avoided the major sin in literary matters, which is to confuse ideological with semiological reality. As ideology, literary realism does not depend at all on the language spoken by the writer. Language is a form, it cannot possibly be either realistic or unrealistic. All it can do is either to be mythical or not, or perhaps, as in *Bouvard et Pécuchet*, countermythical. Now, unfortunately, there is no antipathy between realism and myth. It is well known how often our "realistic" literature is mythical (if only as a crude myth of realism) and how our "literature of the unreal" has at least the merit of being only slightly so. The wise thing would of course be to define the writer's realism as an essentially ideological problem. This certainly does not mean that there is no responsibility of form toward reality. But this responsibility can be measured only in semiological terms. A form can be judged (since forms are on trial) only as signification, not as expression. The writer's language is not expected to *represent* reality but to signify it. This should impose on critics the duty of using two rigorously distinct methods: one must deal with the writer's realism either as an ideological

---

*A subjunctive form because it is in the subjunctive mode that Latin expressed "indirect style or discourse," which is an admirable instrument for demystification.

substance (Marxist themes in Brecht's work, for instance) or as a semiological value (the props, the actors, the music, the colors in Brechtian dramaturgy). The ideal of course would be to combine these two types of criticism; the mistake which is constantly made is to confuse them: ideology has its methods, and so has semiology.

THE BOURGEOISIE AS A JOINT-STOCK COMPANY

Myth lends itself to history in two ways: by its form, which is only relatively motivated; by its concept, the nature of which is historical. One can therefore imagine a diachronic study of myths, whether one submits them to a retrospection (which means founding a historical mythology) or whether one follows some of yesterday's myths down to their present forms (which means founding prospective history). If I keep here to a synchronic sketch of contemporary myths, it is for an objective reason: our society is the privileged field of mythical signification. We must now say why.

Whatever the accidents, the compromises, the concessions, and the political adventures, whatever the technical, economic, or even social changes which history brings us, our society is still a bourgeois society. I am not forgetting that since 1789, in France, several types of bourgeoisie have succeeded one another in power; but the same status—a certain regime of ownership, a certain order, a certain ideology—remains at a deeper level. Now a remarkable phenomenon occurs in the matter of naming this regime: as an economic fact, the bourgeoisie is *named* without any difficulty; capitalism is openly professed.* As a political fact, the bourgeoisie has some difficulty in acknowledging itself: there are no "bourgeois" parties in the Chamber of Deputies. As an ideological fact, it completely

---

*"The fate of capitalism is to make the worker wealthy," *Paris-Match* tells us.

disappears: the bourgeoisie has obliterated its name in passing from reality to representation, from economic man to mental man. It comes to an agreement with the facts, but does not compromise about values, it makes its status undergo a real *exnominating* operation: the bourgeoisie is defined as *the social class which does not want to be named. Bourgeois, petit bourgeois, capitalism,** *proletariat*† are the locus of an unceasing hemorrhage: meaning flows out of them until their very name becomes unnecessary.

This exnominating phenomenon is important; let us examine it a little more closely. Politically, the hemorrhage of the name *bourgeois* is effected through the idea of *nation*. This was once a progressive idea, which has served to get rid of the aristocracy; today, the bourgeoisie merges into the nation, even if it has, in order to do so, to exclude from it the elements which it decides are allogenous (the Communists). This planned syncretism allows the bourgeoisie to attract the numerical support of its temporary allies, all the intermediate, therefore "shapeless" classes. A long-continued use of the word *nation* has failed to depoliticize it in depth; the political substratum is there, very near the surface, and some circumstances make it suddenly manifest. There are in the Chamber some "national" parties, and nominal syncretism here makes conspicuous what it had the ambition of hiding: an essential disparity. Thus the political vocabulary of the bourgeoisie already postulates that the universal exists: for it, politics is already a representation, a fragment of ideology.

Politically, in spite of the universalistic effort of its vocabu-

---

*The word *capitalism* is taboo, not economically but ideologically; it cannot possibly enter the vocabulary of bourgeois representations. Only in Farouk's Egypt could a prisoner be condemned by a tribunal for "anticapitalist plotting" in so many words.

†The bourgeoisie never uses the word *proletariat*, which is supposed to be a Left-wing myth, except when it is in its interest to imagine the proletariat's being led astray by the Communist Party.

lary, the bourgeoisie eventually strikes against a resisting core which is, by definition, the revolutionary party. But this party can constitute only a political richness: in a bourgeois culture, there is neither proletarian culture nor proletarian morality, there is no proletarian art; ideologically, all that is not bourgeois is obliged to *borrow* from the bourgeoisie. Bourgeois ideology can therefore spread over everything and in doing so lose its name without risk: no one here will throw this name of *bourgeois* back at it. It can without resistance subsume bourgeois theater, art, and humanity under their eternal analogues; in a word, it can exnominate itself without restraint when there is only one single human nature left: the defection from the name *bourgeois* is here complete.

True, there are revolts against bourgeois ideology. This is what one generally calls the avant-garde. But these revolts are socially limited, they remain open to salvage. First, because they come from a small section of the bourgeoisie itself, from a minority group of artists and intellectuals, without a public other than the class which they contest, and who remain dependent on its money in order to express themselves. Then these revolts always get their inspiration from a very strongly made distinction between the ethically and the politically bourgeois: what the avant-garde contests is the bourgeois in art or morals—the shopkeeper, the Philistine, as in the heyday of Romanticism; but as for political contestation, there is none.* What the avant-garde does not tolerate about the bourgeoisie is its language, not its status. This does not necessarily mean that it approves of this status; simply, it leaves it

*It is remarkable that the adversaries of the bourgeoisie on matters of ethics or aesthetics remain for the most part indifferent, or even attached, to its political determinations. Conversely, its political adversaries neglect to issue a basic condemnation of its representations: they often go so far as to share them. This diversity of attacks benefits the bourgeoisie, it allows it to camouflage its name. For the bourgeoisie should be understood only as a synthesis of its determinations and its representations.

aside. Whatever the violence of the provocation, the nature it finally endorses is that of "derelict" man, not alienated man; and derelict man is still Eternal Man.* This anonymity of the bourgeoisie becomes even more marked when one passes from bourgeois culture proper to its derived, vulgarized, and applied forms, to what one could call public philosophy, that which sustains everyday life, civil ceremonials, secular rites, in short the unwritten norms of interrelationships in a bourgeois society. It is an illusion to reduce the dominant culture to its inventive core: there is also a bourgeois culture which consists of consumption alone. The whole of France is steeped in this anonymous ideology: our press, our films, our theater, our pulp literature, our rituals, our Justice, our diplomacy, our conversations, our remarks about the weather, a murder trial, a touching wedding, the cooking we dream of, the garments we wear, everything, in everyday life, is dependent on the representation which the bourgeoisie *has and makes us have* of the relations between the man and the world. These "normalized" forms attract little attention, by the very fact of their extension, in which their origin is easily lost. They enjoy an intermediate position: being neither directly political nor directly ideological, they live peacefully between the action of the militants and the quarrels of the intellectuals; more or less abandoned by the former and the latter, they gravitate toward the enormous mass of the undifferentiated, of the insignificant, in short, of nature. Yet it is through its ethic that the bourgeoisie pervades France: practiced on a national scale, bourgeois norms are experienced as the evident laws of a natural order—the further the bourgeois class propagates its representations, the more naturalized it becomes. The fact of bourgeoisie becomes absorbed into an amorphous universe,

*There can be figures of derelict man which lack all order (Ionesco, for example). This does not affect in any way the security of the Essences.

whose sole inhabitant is Eternal Man, who is neither proletarian nor bourgeois.

It is therefore by penetrating the intermediate classes that the bourgeois ideology can most surely lose its name. Petit bourgeois norms are the residue of bourgeois culture, they are bourgeois truths which have become degraded, impoverished, commercialized, slightly archaic, or, shall we say, out of date? The political alliance of the bourgeoisie and the petite bourgeoisie has for more than a century determined the history of France; it has rarely been broken, and each time only temporarily (1848, 1871, 1936). This alliance got closer as time passed, it gradually became a symbiosis; transient awakenings might happen, but the common ideology was never questioned again. The same "natural" varnish covers up all "national" representations: the big wedding of the bourgeoisie, which originates in a class ritual (the display and consumption of wealth), can bear no relation to the economic status of the lower middle class: but through the press, the news, and literature, it slowly becomes the very norm as dreamed, though not actually lived, of the petit bourgeois couple. The bourgeoisie is constantly absorbing into its ideology a whole section of humanity which does not have its basic status and cannot live up to except in imagination, that is, at the cost of an immobilization and an impoverishment of consciousness.* By spreading its representations over a whole catalog of collective images for petit bourgeois use, the bourgeoisie countenances the illusory lack of differentiation of the social classes: it is as from the moment when a typist earning twenty pounds a month *recognizes herself* in the big wedding of the bourgeoisie that bourgeois exnomination achieves its full effect.

---

*To induce a collective content for the imagination is always an inhuman undertaking, not only because dreaming essentializes life into destiny, but also because dreams are impoverished, and the alibi of an absence.

The flight from the name *bourgeois* is not therefore an illusory, accidental, secondary, natural, or insignificant phenomenon: it is the bourgeois ideology itself, the process through which the bourgeoisie transforms the reality of the world into an image of the world, History into Nature. And this image has a remarkable feature: it is upside down.* The status of the bourgeoisie is particular, historical: man as represented by it is universal, eternal. The bourgeois class has precisely built its power on technical, scientific progress, on an unlimited transformation of nature: bourgeois ideology yields in return an unchangable nature. The first bourgeois philosophers pervaded the world with significations, subjected all things to an idea of the rational, and decreed that they were meant for man: bourgeois ideology is of the scientist or the intuitive kind, it records facts or perceives values, but refuses explanations; the order of the world can be seen as sufficient or ineffable, it is never seen as significant. Finally, the basic idea of a perfectible mobile world produces the inverted image of an unchanging humanity, characterized by an indefinite repetition of its identity. In a word, in the contemporary bourgeois society, the passage from the real to the ideological is defined as that from an *antiphysis* to a *pseudophysis*.

MYTH IS DEPOLITICIZED SPEECH

And this is where we come back to myth. Semiology has taught us that myth has the task of giving a historical intention a natural justification, and making contingency appear eternal. Now this process is exactly that of bourgeois ideology. If our society is objectively the privileged field of mythical

* "If men and their conditions appear throughout ideology inverted as in a camera obscura, this phenomenon follows from their historical vital progress . . ." (Marx, *The German Ideology*).

significations, it is because formally myth is the most appropriate instrument for the ideological inversion which defines this society: at all the levels of human communication, myth operates the inversion of *antiphysis* into *pseudophysis*.

What the world supplies to myth is a historical reality, defined, even if this goes back quite awhile, by the way in which men have produced or used it; and what myth gives in return is a *natural* image of this reality. And just as bourgeois ideology is defined by the abandonment of the name *bourgeois*, so myth is constituted by the loss of the historical quality of things: in it, things lose the memory that they once were made. The world enters languages as a dialectical relation between activities, between human actions; it comes out of myth as a harmonious display of essences. A conjuring trick has taken place; it has turned reality inside out, it has emptied it of history and has filled it with nature, it has removed from things their human meaning so as to make them signify a human insignificance. The function of a myth is to empty reality: it is, literally, a ceaseless flowing out, a hemorrhage, or perhaps an evaporation, in short, a perceptible absence.

It is now possible to complete the semiological definition of myth in a bourgeois society: *myth is depoliticized speech*. One must naturally understand *political* in its deeper meaning, as describing the whole of human relations in their real, social structure, in their power of making the world; one must above all give an active value to the prefix *de-*: here it represents an operational movement, it permanently embodies a defaulting. In the case of the soldier Negro, for instance, what is got rid of is certainly not French imperiality (on the contrary, since what must be actualized is its presence); it is the contingent, historical, in one word, *fabricated*, quality of colonialism. Myth does not deny things, on the contrary, its function is to talk about them; simply, it purifies them, it makes them innocent, it gives them a natural and eternal justification, it gives them a clarity which is not that of an explanation but that of a statement of fact. If I *state the fact* of French imperiality without explaining it, I am very near to finding that it is natural and *goes without saying*: I am reassured. In passing from history to nature, myth acts economically: it abolishes the complexity of human acts, it gives them the simplicity of essences, it does away with all dialectics, with any going back beyond what is immediately visible, it organizes a world which is without contradictions because it is without depth, a world wide open and wallowing in the evident, it establishes a blissful clarity: things appear to mean something by themselves.*

However, is myth always depoliticized speech? In other words, is reality always political? Is it enough to speak about a thing naturally for it to become mythical? One could answer with Marx that the most natural object contains a political trace, however faint and diluted, the more or less memorable presence of the human act which has produced, fitted up, used, subjected, or rejected it.[†] The language object, which *speaks things*, can easily exhibit this trace; the metalanguage, which *speaks of things*, much less easily. Now myth always comes under the heading of metalanguage: the depolitization which it carries out often supervenes against a background which is already naturalized, depoliticized by a general metalanguage, which is trained to *celebrate* things and no longer "*act* them." It goes without saying that the force needed by myth to distort its object is much less in the case of a tree than in the case of a Sudanese: in the latter case, the political load is very near the surface, a large quantity of artificial nature is needed in order to disperse it; in the former case, it is remote, purified by a whole century-old layer of metalanguage. There

*To the pleasure principle of Freudian man could be added the clarity principle of mythological humanity. All the ambiguity of myth is there: its clarity is euphoric.
[†]Cf. Marx and the example of the cherry tree, *The German Ideology*.

are, therefore, strong myths and weak myths; in the former, the political quantum is immediate, the depolitization is abrupt; in the latter, the political quality of the object has *faded* like a color, but the slightest thing can bring back its strength brutally: What is more *natural* than the sea? and what is more "political" than the sea celebrated by the makers of the film *Lost Continent*?*

In fact, metalanguage constitutes a kind of preserve for myth. Men do not have with myth a relationship based on truth but on use: they depoliticize according to their needs. Some mythical objects are left dormant for a time; they are then no more than vague mythical schemata whose political load seems almost neutral. But this indicates only that their situation has brought this about, not that their structure is different. This is the case with our Latin-grammar example. We just note that here mythical speech works on a material which has long been transformed: the sentence by Aesop belongs to literature, it is at the very start mythified (therefore made innocent) by its being fiction. But it is enough to replace the initial term of the chain for an instant into its nature as language object, to gauge the emptying of reality operated by myth: one can imagine the feelings of a *real* society of animals on finding itself transformed into a grammar example, into a predicative nature! In order to gauge the political load of an object and the mythical hollow which espouses it, one must never look at things from the point of view of the significa-tion, but from that of the signifier, of the thing which has been robbed; and within the signifier, from the point of view of the language object, that is, of the meaning. There is no doubt that if we consulted a *real* lion, he would maintain that the grammar example is a *strongly* depoliticized state, he would qualify as fully *political* the jurisprudence which leads him to

*Cf p. 184.

claim a prey because he is the strongest, unless we deal with a bourgeois lion who would not fail to mythify his strength by giving it the form of a duty.

One can clearly see that in this case the political insignificance of the myth comes from its situation. Myth, as we know, is a value: it is enough to modify its circumstances, the general (and precarious) system in which it occurs, in order to regulate its scope with great accuracy. The field of the myth is in this case reduced to a seventh-grade class of a French school. But I suppose that a child *enthralled* by the story of the lion, the heifer, and the cow, and recovering through the life of the imagination the actual reality of these animals, would appreciate with much less unconcern than we do that the disappearance of this lion changed into a predicate. In fact, we hold this myth to be politically insignificant only because it is not meant for us.

MYTH ON THE LEFT

If myth is depoliticized speech, there is at least one type of speech which is the opposite of myth: that which *remains* political. Here we must go back to the distinction between language object and metalanguage. If I am a woodcutter and I am led to name the tree which I am felling, whatever the form of my sentence, I "speak the tree," I do not speak about it. This means that my language is operational, transitively linked to its object; between the tree and myself, there is nothing but my labor, that is to say, an action. This is a political language: it represents nature for me only inasmuch as I am going to transform it, it is a language thanks to which I *act the object*; the tree is not an image for me, it is simply the meaning of my action. But if I am not a woodcutter, I can no longer "speak the tree," I can only speak *about* it, *on* it. My language is no longer the instrument of an "acted-upon tree," it is the "tree celebrated" which becomes the instrument of my language. I no longer have anything more than an intransitive relationship with the tree; the tree is no longer the meaning of reality as a human action, it is an *image-at-one's-disposal*. Compared to the real language of the woodcutter, the language I create is a second-order language, a metalanguage in which I shall henceforth not "act the things" but "act their names," and which is to the primary language what the gesture is to the act. This second-order language is not entirely mythical, but it is the very locus where myth settles; for myth can work only on objects which have already received the mediation of a first language.

There is therefore one language which is not mythical, it is the language of man as a producer: wherever man speaks in order to transform reality and no longer to preserve it as an image, wherever he links his language to the making of things, metalanguage is referred to a language object, and myth is impossible. This is why revolutionary language proper cannot be mythical. Revolution is defined as the cathartic act meant to reveal the political load of the world: it *makes* the world; and its language, all of it, is functionally absorbed in this making. It is because it generates speech which is *fully*—that is to say, initially and finally—political, and not, like myth, speech which is initially political and finally natural, that Revolution excludes myth. Just as bourgeois exnomination characterizes at once bourgeois ideology and myth itself, revolutionary denomination identifies revolution and the absence of myth. The bourgeoisie hides the fact that it is the bourgeoisie and thereby produces myth; Revolution announces itself openly as Revolution and thereby abolishes myth.

I have been asked whether there are myths "on the Left." Of course, inasmuch, precisely, as the Left is not a revolution. Left-wing myth supervenes precisely at the moment when revolution changes itself into "the Left"—that is, when it agrees to wear a mask, to hide its name, to generate an innocent metalanguage, and to distort itself into "nature." This revolutionary exnomination may or may not be tactical, this is no place to discuss it. At any rate, it is sooner or later experienced as a process contrary to revolution, and it is always more or less in relation to myth that revolutionary history defines its "deviations." There came a day, for instance, when it was socialism itself which defined the Stalin myth. Stalin, as a spoken object, has exhibited for years, in their pure state, the constituent characters of mythical speech: a meaning, which was the real Stalin, that of history; a signifier, which was the ritual invocation to Stalin and the *inevitable* character of the "natural" epithets with which his name was surrounded; a signified, which was the intention to respect orthodoxy, discipline, and unity, *appropriated* by the Communist parties to a definite situation; and a signification, which was a sanctified Stalin, whose historical determinants found themselves grounded in nature, sublimated under the name of *genius*— that is, something irrational and inexpressible: here depolitization is evident, it fully reveals the presence of a myth.*

Yes, myth exists on the Left, but it does not at all have there the same qualities as the bourgeois myth. *Left-wing myth is inessential.* To start with, the objects which it takes hold of are rare—only a few political notions—unless it has itself recourse to the whole repertoire of the bourgeois myths. Left-wing myth never reaches the immense field of human relationships, the very vast surface of "insignificant" ideology. Everyday life is inaccessible to it: in a bourgeois society, there are no "Left-wing" myths concerning marriage, cooking, the home, the theater, the law, morality, etc. Then it is an inciden-

---

*It is remarkable that Khrushchevism presented itself not as a political change, but essentially and only as a *linguistic conversion*. An incomplete conversion, incidentally, for Khrushchev devalued Stalin but did not explain him—did not repoliticize him.

tal myth, its use is not part of a strategy, as is the case with the bourgeois myth, but only of a tactic or, at the worst, of a deviation; if it occurs, it is as a myth suited to a convenience, not a necessity.

Finally, and above all, this myth is, in essence, poverty-stricken. It does not know how to proliferate; being produced on order and for a temporally limited prospect, it is invented with difficulty. It lacks a major faculty, that of fabulizing. Whatever it does, there remains about it something stiff and literal, a suggestion of something done to order. As it is expressively put, it remains barren. In fact, what can be more meager than the Stalin myth? No inventiveness here, and only a clumsy appropriation: the signifier of the myth (this form whose infinite wealth in bourgeois myth we have just seen) is not varied in the least: it is reduced to a litany.

This imperfection, if that is the word for it, comes from the nature of the "Left": whatever the imprecision of the term, the Left always defines itself in relation to the oppressed, whether proletarian or colonized.* Now the speech of the oppressed can only be poor, monotonous, immediate: his destitution is the very yardstick of his language: he has only one, always the same, that of his actions; metalanguage is a luxury, he cannot yet have access to it. The speech of the oppressed is real, like that of the woodcutter; it is a transitive type of speech: it is quasi-unable to lie; lying is a richness, a lie presupposes property, truths, and forms to spare. This essential barrenness produces rare, threadbare myths: either transient or clumsily indiscreet; by their very being, they label themselves as myths, and point to their masks. And this mask is hardly that of a pseudophysis: for that type of physis is also a richness of a sort, the oppressed can only borrow it; he is unable to throw out the

---

*Today it is the colonized peoples who assume to the full and ethical and political condition described by Marx as being that of the proletariat.

real meaning of things, to give them the luxury of an empty form, open to the innocence of a false Nature. One can say that in a sense, Left-wing myth is always an artificial myth, a reconstituted myth: hence its clumsiness.

MYTH ON THE RIGHT

Statistically, myth is on the right. There, it is essential; well fed, sleek, expansive, garrulous, it invents itself ceaselessly. It takes hold of everything, all aspects of the law, of morality, of aesthetics, of diplomacy, of household equipment, of Literature, of entertainment. Its expansion has the very dimensions of bourgeois exnomination. The bourgeoisie wants to keep reality without keeping the appearances: it is therefore the very negativity of bourgeois appearance, infinite like every negativity, which solicits myth infinitely. The oppressed is nothing, he has only one language, that of his emancipation; the oppressor is everything, his language is rich, multiform, supple, with all the possible degrees of dignity at its disposal: he has an exclusive right to metalanguage. The oppressed *makes* the world, he has only an active, transitive (political) language; the oppressor conserves it, his language is plenary, intransitive, gestural, theatrical: it is the Myth. The language of the former aims at transforming, of the latter at eternalizing.

Does this completeness of the myths of Order (this is the name the bourgeoisie gives to itself) include inner differences? Are there, for instance, bourgeois myths and petit bourgeois myths? There cannot be any fundamental differences, for whatever the public which consumes it, myth always postulates the immobility of Nature. But there can be degrees of fulfillment for expansion: some myths ripen better in some social strata: for myth also, there are microclimates.

The myth of Childhood-as-Poet, for instance, is an *advanced* bourgeois myth: it has hardly come out of inventive culture (Cocteau, for example) and is just reaching consumer culture (*L'Express*). Part of the bourgeoisie can still find it too obviously invented, not mythical enough to feel entitled to countenance it (a whole part of bourgeois criticism works only with duly mythical materials). It is a myth which is not yet well run in, it does not contain enough *nature*: in order to make the Child-Poet part of a cosmogony, one must renounce the prodigy (Mozart, Rimbaud, etc.) and accept new norms, those of psychopedagogy, Freudianism, etc.: as a myth, it is still unripe.

Thus every myth can have its history and its geography; each is in fact the sign of the other: a myth ripens because it spreads. I have not been able to carry out any real study of the social geography of myths. But it is perfectly possible to draw what linguists would call the isoglosses of a myth, the lines which limit the social region where it is spoken. As this region is shifting, it would be better to speak of the waves of implantation of the myth. The Minou Drouet myth has thus had at least three waves of amplification: (1) *L'Express*; (2) *Paris-Match*, *Elle*; (3) *France-Soir*. Some myths hesitate: Will they pass into tabloids, the home of the suburbanite of private means, the hairdresser's salon, the metro? The social geography of myths will remain difficult to trace as long as we lack an analytical sociology of the press.* But we can say that its place already exists.

Since we cannot yet draw up the list of the dialectal forms of bourgeois myth, we can always sketch its rhetorical forms. One must understand here by *rhetoric* a set of fixed, regulated,

*The circulation of newspapers is an insufficient datum. Other information comes only by accident. *Paris-Match* has given—significantly, as publicity—the composition of its public in terms of standard of living (*Le Figaro*, July 12, 1955): out of each one hundred readers living in town, fifty-three have a car, forty-nine a bathroom, etc., whereas the average standard of living in France is reckoned as follows: car, 22 percent; bathroom, 13 percent. That the purchasing power of the *Paris-Match* reader is high could have been predicted from the mythology of this publication.

insistent figures, according to which the varied forms of the mythical signifier arrange themselves. These figures are transparent inasmuch as they do not affect the plasticity of the signifier; but they are already sufficiently conceptualized to adapt to a historical representation of the world (just as classical rhetoric can account for a representation of the Aristotelian type). It is through their rhetoric that bourgeois myths outline the general prospect of the pseudophysis which defines the dream of the contemporary bourgeois world. Here are its principal figures:

1. *The inoculation.* I have already given examples of this very general figure, which consists in admitting the accidental evil of a class-bound institution the better to conceal its principal evil. One immunizes the contents of the collective imagination by means of a small inoculation of acknowledged evil; one thus protects it against the risk of a generalized subversion. This *liberal* treatment would not have been possible only a hundred years ago. Then the bourgeois Good did not compromise with anything, it was quite stiff. It has become much more supple since: the bourgeoisie no longer hesitates to acknowledge some localized subversions: the avant-garde, the irrational in childhood, etc. It now lives in a balanced economy: as in any sound joint-stock company, the smaller shares—in law but not in fact—compensate the big ones.

2. *The privation of History.* Myth deprives the object of which it speaks of all History.* In it, history

*Marx: ". . . we must pay attention to this history, since ideology boils down to either an erroneous conception of this history, *or to a complete abstraction from it*" (*The German Ideology*).

evaporates. It is a kind of ideal servant: it prepares all things, brings them, lays them out, the master arrives, it silently disappears: all that is left for one to do is enjoy this beautiful object without wondering where it comes from. Or even better: it can come only from eternity: the Spain of the *Blue Guide* has been made for the tourist, and "primitives" have prepared their dances with a view to an exotic festivity. We can see all the disturbing things which this felicitous figure removes from sight: both determinism and freedom. Nothing is produced, nothing is chosen: all one has to do is to possess these new objects from which all soiling trace of origin or choice has been removed. This miraculous evaporation of history is another form of a concept common to most bourgeois myths: the irresponsibility of man.

3. *Identification.* The petit bourgeois is a man unable to imagine the Other.* If he comes face-to-face with him, he blinds himself, ignores and denies him, or else transforms him into himself. In the petit bourgeois universe, all the experiences of confrontation are reverberating, any otherness is reduced to sameness. The spectacle and the tribunal, which are both places where the Other threatens to appear in full view, become mirrors. This is because the Other is a scandal which threatens the petit bourgeois's essence. Dominici cannot have access to social existence unless he is previously reduced to the state of a small simulacrum of the President

---

*Marx: ". . . what makes them representative of the petit bourgeois class, is that their minds, their consciousness do not extend beyond the limits which this class has set to its activities" (*The Eighteenth Brumaire of Louis Napoleon*). And Gorky: "the petit bourgeois is the man who has preferred himself to all else."

of the Assizes or the Public Prosecutor: this is the price one must pay in order to condemn him justly, since Justice is a weighing operation and since scales can only weigh like against like. There are, in any petit bourgeois consciousness, small simulacra of the hooligan, the parricide, the homosexual, etc., which periodically the judiciary extracts from its brain, puts in the dock, admonishes, and condemns: one never tries anybody but analogues *who have gone astray*: it is a question of direction, not of nature, for *that's how men are*. Sometimes—rarely—the Other is revealed as irreducible: not because of a sudden scruple, but because *common sense* rebels: a man does not have white skin, but a black one, another drinks pear juice, not Pernod. How can one assimilate the Negro, the Russian?

There is here a figure for emergencies: exoticism. The Other becomes a pure object, a spectacle, a clown. Relegated to the confines of humanity, he no longer threatens the security of the home. This figure is chiefly petit bourgeois. For, even if he is able to experience the Other in himself, the bourgeois can at least imagine the place where he fits in: this is what is known as liberalism, which is a sort of intellectual equilibrium based on recognized places. The petit bourgeois class is not liberal (it produces Fascism, whereas the bourgeoisie uses it): it follows the same route as the bourgeoisie, but lags behind.

4. *Tautology.* Yes, I know, it's an ugly word. But so is the thing. Tautology is this verbal device which consists in defining like by like ("Drama is drama"). We can view it as one of those types of magical behavior dealt with by Sartre in his *Emotions: Outline of a*

Theory: one takes refuge in tautology as one does in fear, or anger, or sadness, when one is at a loss for an explanation: the accidental failure of language is magically identified with what one decides is a natural resistance of the object. In tautology, there is a double murder: one kills rationality because it resists one, one kills language because it betrays one.

Tautology is a faint at the right moment, a saving aphasia, it is a death, or perhaps a comedy, the indignant "representation" of the *rights* of reality over and above language. Since it is magical, it can of course only take refuge behind the argument of authority: thus do parents at the end of their tether reply to the child who keeps on asking for explanations: "because that's how it is" or even better: "just because, that's all"—a magical act ashamed of itself, which verbally makes the gesture of rationality, but immediately abandons the latter, and believes itself to be even with causality because it has uttered the word which introduces it. Tautology testifies to a profound distrust of language, which is rejected because it has failed. Now, any refusal of language is a death. Tautology creates a dead, a motionless world.

5. *Neither/Norism*. By this I mean this mythological figure which consists in stating two opposites and balancing the one by the other so as to reject them both. (I want *neither* this *nor* that.) It is on the whole a bourgeois figure, for it relates to a modern form of liberalism. We find again here the figure of the scales: reality is first reduced to analogues; then it is weighed; finally, equality having been ascertained, it is got rid of. Here also there is magical behavior: both parties are dismissed because it is

embarrassing to choose between them; one flees from an intolerable reality, reducing it to two opposites which balance each other only inasmuch as they are purely formal, relieved of all their specific weight. Neither/Norism can have degraded forms: in astrology, for example, ill luck is always followed by equal good luck; they are always predicted in a prudently compensatory perspective: a final equilibrium immobilizes values, life, destiny, etc.: one no longer needs to choose, but only to endorse.

6. *The quantification of quality*. This is a figure which is latent in all the preceding ones. By reducing any quality to quantity, myth economizes intelligence: it understands reality more cheaply. I have given several examples of this mechanism which bourgeois—and especially petit bourgeois—mythology does not hesitate to apply to aesthetic realities which it deems, on the other hand, to partake of an immaterial essence. Bourgeois theater is a good example of this contradiction: on the one hand, theater is presented as an essence which cannot be reduced to any language and reveals itself only to the heart, to intuition. From this quality it receives an irritable dignity (it is forbidden as a crime of *lèse-essence* to speak about the theater *scientifically*: or rather, any intellectual way of viewing the theater is discredited as scientism or pedantic language). On the other hand, bourgeois dramatic art rests on a pure quantification of effects: a whole circuit of computable appearances establishes a quantitative equality between the cost of the ticket and the tears of an actor or the luxuriousness of a set: what is currently meant by the "naturalness" of an actor, for instance, is above all a conspicuous quantity of effects.

7. *The statement of fact.* Myths tend toward proverbs. Bourgeois ideology invests in this figure interests which are bound to its very essence: universalism, the refusal of any explanation, an unalterable hierarchy of the world. But we must again distinguish the language object from the metalanguage. Popular, ancestral proverbs still partake of an instrumental grasp of the world as object. A rural statement of fact such as "the weather is fine" keeps a real link with the usefulness of fine weather. It is an implicitly technological statement; the word, here, in spite of its general, abstract form, paves the way for actions, it inserts itself into a fabricating order: the farmer does not speak *about* the weather, he "acts it" he draws it into his labor. All our popular proverbs thus represent active speech which has gradually solidified into reflexive speech, but where reflection is curtailed, reduced to a statement of the fact, and, so to speak, a timid, prudent, and closely hugging experience. Popular proverbs foresee more than they assert, they remain the speech of a humanity which is making itself, not one which is.

Bourgeois aphorisms, on the other hand, belong to metalanguage; they are a second-order language which bears on objects already prepared. Their classical form is the maxim. Here the statement is no longer directed toward a world to be made; it must overlay one which is already made, bury the traces of this production under a self-evident appearance of eternity: it is a counterexplanation, the decorous equivalent of a tautology, of this peremptory *because* which parents in need of knowledge hang above the heads of their children.

> The foundation of the bourgeois statement of fact
> is *common sense*—that is, truth when it stops on the
> arbitrary order of him who speaks it.

I have listed these rhetorical figures without any special order, and there may well be many others: some can become worn out, others can come into being. But it is obvious that those given here, such as they are, fall into two great categories, which are like the Zodiacal signs of the bourgeois universe: the Essences and the Scales. Bourgeois ideology continuously transforms the products of history into essential types. Just as the cuttlefish squirts its ink in order to protect itself, so it cannot rest until it has obscured the ceaseless making of the world, fixed this world into an object which can be forever possessed, cataloged its riches, embalmed it, and injected into reality some purifying essence which will stop its transformation, its flight toward other forms of existence. And these riches, thus fixated and frozen, will at least become computable: bourgeois morality will essentially be a weighing operation, the essences will be placed in scales of which bourgeois man will remain the motionless beam. For the very end of myths is to immobilize the world: they must suggest and mimic a universal order which has fixated once and for all the hierarchy of possessions. Thus, every day and everywhere, man is stopped by myths, referred by them to this motionless prototype which lives in his place, stifles him in the manner of a huge internal parasite, and assigns to his activity the narrow limits within which he is allowed to suffer without upsetting the world: bourgeois pseudophysis is in the fullest sense a prohibition for man against inventing himself. Myths are nothing but this ceaseless, untiring solicitation, this insidious and inflexible demand that all men recognize themselves in this image, eternal yet bearing a date, which was built of them one day as if for all time. For Nature, in which they are locked up under the pretext of being eternalized, is nothing but a Usage. And it is this Usage, however lofty, that they must take in hand and transform.

NECESSITY AND LIMITS OF MYTHOLOGY

I must, as a conclusion, say a few words about the mythologist himself. This term is rather grand and self-assured. Yet one can predict for the mythologist, if there ever is one, a few difficulties, in feeling if not in method. True, he will have no trouble in feeling justified: whatever its mistakes, mythology is certain to participate in the making of the world. Holding as a principle that man in a bourgeois society is at every turn plunged into a false Nature, it attempts to find again, under the assumed innocence of the most unsophisticated relationships, the profound alienation which this innocence is meant to make one accept. The unveiling which it carries out is therefore a political act: founded on a responsible idea of language, mythology thereby postulates the freedom of the latter. It is certain that in this sense mythology *harmonizes* with the world, not as it is, but as it wants to create itself (Brecht had for this an efficiently ambiguous word: *Einverstandnis*, at once an understanding of reality and a complicity with it).

This harmony justifies the mythologist but does not fulfill him: his status still remains basically one of being excluded. Justified by the political dimension, the mythologist is still at a distance from it. His speech is a metalanguage, it "acts" nothing; at most, it unveils—or does it? To whom? His task always remains ambiguous, hampered by its ethical origin. He can live revolutionary action only vicariously: hence the self-conscious character of his function, this something a little stiff and painstaking, muddled and excessively simplified which brands any intellectual behavior with an openly political foundation ("uncommitted" types of literature are infinitely more "elegant"; they are in their place in metalanguage).

Also the mythologist cuts himself off from all the myth consumers, and this is no small matter. If this applied to a particular section of the collectivity, well and good.* But when a myth reaches the entire community, it is from the latter that the mythologist must become estranged if he wants to liberate the myth. Any myth with some degree of generality is in fact ambiguous, because it represents the very humanity of those who, having nothing, have borrowed it. To decipher the Tour de France and the "good French Wine" is to cut oneself off from those who are entertained or warmed up by them. The mythologist is condemned to live in a theoretical sociality; for him, to be in society is, at best, to be truthful: his utmost sociality dwells in his utmost morality. His connection with the world is of the order of sarcasm.

One must even go further: in a sense, the mythologist is excluded from this history in the name of which he professes to act. The havoc which he wreaks in the language of the community is absolute for him, it fills his assignment to the brim: he must live this assignment without any hope of going back or any assumption of payment. It is forbidden for him to imagine what the rest of the world will concretely be like when the immediate object of his criticism has disappeared. Utopia is an impossible luxury for him: he greatly doubts that tomorrow's truths will be the exact reverse of today's lies. History never ensures the triumph pure and simple of something over its opposite: it unveils, while making itself, unimag-

---

*It is not only from the public that one becomes estranged; it is sometimes also from the very object of myth. In order to demystify Poetic Childhood, for instance, I have had, so to speak, to lack confidence in Minou Drouet the child. I have had to ignore, in her, under the enormous myth with which she is cumbered, something like a tender, open possibility. It is never a good thing to speak against a little girl.

inable solutions, unforeseeable syntheses. The mythologist is not even in a Moses-like situation: he cannot see the Promised Land. For him, tomorrow's positivity is entirely hidden by today's negativity. All the values of his undertaking appear to him as acts of destruction: the latter accurately cover the former, nothing protrudes. This subjective grasp of history in which the potent seed of the future *is nothing but* the most profound apocalypse of the present has been expressed by Saint-Just in a strange saying: "What constitutes the Republic is the total destruction of what is opposed to it." This must not, I think, be understood in the trivial sense of: "One has to clear the way before reconstructing." The copula has an exhaustive meaning: there is for some men a subjective dark night of history when the future becomes an essence, the essential destruction of the past.

One last exclusion threatens the mythologist: he constantly runs the risk of causing to disappear the reality which he purports to protect,. Quite apart from all speech, the DS 19 is a technologically defined object: it is capable of a certain speed, it meets the wind in a certain way, etc. And this type of reality cannot be spoken of by the mythologist. The mechanic, the engineer, even the user "*speak* the object"; but the mythologist is condemned to metalanguage. This exclusion already has a name: it is what is called ideologism. Zhdanovism has roundly condemned it (without proving, incidentally, that it was, *for the time being*, avoidable) in the early Lukács, in Marr's linguistics, in works like those of Bénichou or Goldmann, opposing to it the reticence of a reality inaccessible to ideology, such as that of language according to Stalin. It is true that ideologism resolves the contradiction of alienated reality by an amputation, not a synthesis (but as for Zhdanovism, it does not even resolve it): wine is objectively good, and *at the same time*, the goodness of wine is a myth: here is the aporia. The mythologist gets out of this as best he can: he deals with the goodness of wine, not with the wine itself, just as the historian deals with Pascal's ideology, not with the *Pensées* in themselves.*

It seems that this is a difficulty pertaining to our times: there is as yet only one possible choice, and this choice can bear only on two equally extreme methods: either to posit a reality which is entirely permeable to history, and ideologize; or, conversely, to posit a reality which is *ultimately* impenetrable, irreducible, and, in this case, poetize. In a word, I do not yet see a synthesis between ideology and poetry (by poetry I understand, in a very general way, the search for the inalienable meaning of things).

The fact that we cannot manage to achieve more than an unstable grasp of reality doubtless gives the measure of our present alienation: we constantly drift between the object and its demystification, powerless to render its wholeness. For if we penetrate the object, we liberate it but we destroy it; and if we acknowledge its full weight, we respect it, but we restore it to a state which is still mystified. It would seem that we are condemned for some time yet always to speak *excessively* about reality. This is probably because ideologism and its opposite are types of behavior which are still magical, terrorized, blinded, and fascinated by the split in the social world. And yet, this is what we must seek: a reconciliation between reality and men, between description and explanation, between object and knowledge.

---

*Even here, in these mythologies, I have used trickery: finding it painful constantly to work on the evaporation of reality, I have started to make it excessively dense, and to discover surprising compactness in it, which I have savored, and I have given a few examples of "substantial psychoanalysis" about some mythical objects.